# Retail Security and Loss Prevention

# Retail Security and Loss Prevention

by
## Read Hayes

**Butterworth-Heinemann**
Boston London Oxford Singapore Sydney Toronto Wellington

Recognizing the importance of preserving what has been written, it is the policy of Butterworth-Heinemann to have the books it publishes printed on acid-free paper, and we exert our best efforts to that end.

---

**Library of Congress Cataloging-in-Publication Data**

Hayes, Read.
  Retail security and loss prevention / by Read Hayes.
    p.   cm.
  Includes bibliographical references (p.  ) and index.
  ISBN 0-7506-9038-0 (case bound)
  1. Retail trade—United States—Security measures.
2. Inventory shortages—Prevention. 3. Shoplifting.
I. Title.
HF5429.27.H39    1991
658.4′73  dc20                   91-16865
                                    CIP

---

**British Library Cataloguing in Publication Data**

Hayes, Read
  Retail security and loss prevention.
  I. Title
  658.47

ISBN 0-7506-9038-0

---

Butterworth-Heinemann
80 Montvale Avenue
Stoneham, MA 02180

10 9 8 7 6 5 4 3 2 1

Printed in the United States of America

Dedication

To Cindy for all things.
Also, to Carrie and Bryan
who keep my priorities in order.

# Contents

# List of Figures

# Foreword

At a Horizons meeting in Chicago dealing with the future of electronic article surveillance (EAS), Ted Wolfe, CEO of Checkpoint Systems, Inc., and the keynote speaker had this to say:

> On the way to this meeting, I was at a loss to adequately describe both the Horizons concept and the persons being asked to address it. My answer came while browsing through a flight magazine. In it, I came across a horoscope for this month. It read:
>
> > **Capricorn:** You'll find yourself amid some magnetic, obsessive, creative, and self-destructive people who make you scream with breathless (and vicarious) delight over their trips to the outer limits of the galaxy. Since Saturn entered Capricorn last year, you've been squeezed by your commitments, and you've been getting more conservative. But now you need to prove that you're still free, open-minded, human, and democratic. So let November be a moment of departure from normalcy. Consort with a few oddballs.

A resolution was offered and passed that we refer to each other and the group as "Oddballs" when corresponding, which we still do to this day. I offer this story to describe the book you are about to read and the nature of the author as well. My long association with Read Hayes allows me to state that he is a true "oddball" meant in the finest sense of the word. He has explored the outer limits of our loss prevention universe and placed it in understandable language form in his book, *Retail Security and Loss Prevention*. You will find the book easy to read, understand and on the cutting edge of what is happening in our industry today.

The future of business per se, will be dictated largely by how well loss prevention has been implemented into the mainstream of the business community. Faced with rising crime rates due largely to the drug scene, overcrowded court calendars and jails, along with shrinking budgets, it falls to the "oddballs" of our industry, like yourself, to seek and find solutions to the complex problem of ensuring retail security. This book is very beneficial in accomplishing that end.

David Whitney
Vice President of Loss Prevention
ROSS STORES, INC.

# Preface

Retail theft is as old as retail. Historical records indicate that theft incidents were reported as early as 627 A.D. One of the earliest documented accounts of shoplifting activity was recorded in 1597.

A 1698 Act of Parliament defined shoplifting as "the crime of stealing goods privately out of shops" and it dictated death for violators. There are several accounts of shoplifters who were hanged for their crimes. Despite this harsh punishment, by 1726 shoplifting was so prevalent in London that merchants asked the government for help in apprehending the thieves and a reward system was established for those citizens who turned shoplifters over to the authorities.

A significant event in the history of shoplifting occurred in 1879 when Frank W. Woolworth opened his first 5-and-10-¢ store in Utica, New York, and changed the way merchandise was displayed. Woolworth took items for sale out of glass cabinets and put them on open display where customers could touch them. He also put price tags on individuals items. By tagging each item individually, Woolworth could lower his prices, as fewer employees were needed to provide service to customers. The result of these changes was two-fold—increased sales and a dramatic increase in shoplifting.

Through the years, retail and retail theft have experienced tremendous growth in terms of size and complexity. Due to the details involved with managing a successful retail operation, there is an urgent need for businesspeople to not only understand business and economics, but also understand how retail loss occurs and how to prevent and control it.

Retail theft is most often given national attention during the winter holidays largely because shoplifting provides the media with ready-made, interesting stories. However, even with this increased exposure, the problem of shoplifting goes unnoticed as a primary cause of loss in revenue. Due to the size of the retail industry, billions of dollars are lost annually to dishonest employees, vendors, and customers. Most retailers are aware of some of the loss threats that are faced daily and many retailers are familiar with effective methods and systems available for controlling those threats. However, a comprehensive guidebook has not existed, until now, that helps retailers step through the process of determining and prioritizing risks, and helps you design and implement a cost-effective shrinkage control plan.

To be effective in controlling losses, retail security activities should be proactive, rather than reactive. This book provides retailers with state-of-the-art information to assist them in establishing and managing an effective loss prevention operation.

This book also identifies loss threats, indicates how to best determine and prioritize those threats, and recommends specific programs and technologies that have proven to reduce vulnerability to theft.

The appendixes will also assist the retailer in quickly finding further sources of information and locating distributors of quality services and equipment.

# Acknowledgments

No single person can write a quality book without the help and support of many others. Therefore, I'd like to thank Fred Shenkman and Burt Weitz of the University of Florida, Bill Hunt and Rhett Pierce of Valencia Community College, and Alan Treadgold of the Oxford Institute of Retail Management. These individuals have provided me with the knowledge and discipline that formal education brings.

I'd also like to thank Greg Colvin, Jim Palmer, and Jim Cleary for their legal assistance, and Greg Franklin, Kevin Kopp, Andrea Seward, Laurel DeWolf, and Sharon Sillaman for their creative and industrious input into this manuscript.

Many of my peers in the industry have shared their wisdom and experiences with me. They include, but certainly aren't limited to, Mike Chuck, Rick Clarke, Jack Isaacson, Rich Martinez, Marty Gruenke, Libby Libhart, Randy Webb, Randy Eubanks, Sharon and Jim Simpson, Gary Johnson, Bill Clausen, Barbara Feasel, George Duke, Carl Schwenk, Ron Raymond, Mickey Carter, Bill Lieurance, Rich Laucks, King Rogers, Tom Yake, Dan Doyle, Lance Incitti, Randy Kerr, Greg Stephens, Bob Smith, Leon Caffie, Kirby Jordan, Gene Newman, and my professional mentor, Dave Whitney.

I'd also like to thank Ross Stores and the Loss Prevention Specialists' staff, especially Joe Langford, Tom Keel, Teresa Lyons, Karen Johnson, and Larrie Lacaillade for their critical roles in the development of this book.

Lastly, I'd like to thank my family for their patience and support, and Bill Zalud and Tony Slinn, two very talented security editors who provided valuable guidance and encouragement. *Retail Security and Loss Prevention* was a true team effort and I am grateful to every one of you.

# Introduction

During this time of decreased budgets and increased retail competition, retailers are looking for ways to boost profits by increasing revenues and cutting costs. Shrinkage (or retail inventory loss) is a tremendous deficit that few business people are willing to overlook. Many merchants have either ignored serious loss control efforts or "played games" with price markups and inventory procedures to cover up shrinkage problems. Currently, successful retailers are identifying the most prevalent and costly loss areas, and implementing cost-effective programs to reduce their loss. When well-researched shortage control programs are properly applied and implemented, they show a positive return on investment within 3 to 5 years.

All too often retailers make impulsive decisions to rectify business problems without fully examining them to determine the cause of the problem. When faced with a shrinkage problem, retailers should determine where they are experiencing their greatest financial loss and then install good, sound countermeasures to prevent loss.

I recommend a four-phase, integrated loss control program to control and prevent loss. During Phase I, the retailer, or a qualified consultant, conducts a comprehensive security survey. During Phase II, the retailer analyzes the data collected during the survey to determine risks and trends, and then prioritizes these risks to focus countermeasures. During Phase III, a loss control program is designed and implemented. During Phase IV, the program is continuously tested and adjusted as needed. Figure I–1 depicts the primary tasks associated with defining, designing, implementing, and maintaining an effective loss control program.

No retailer should take the problem of retail shrinkage lightly. Lack of a good, sound, consistent loss control program often leads to staggering financial losses. A commitment to loss prevention must be made at the top of the organization and must be positively reinforced throughout the organization every day. In this way, your business will experience an increase in profits due to an effective loss prevention program.

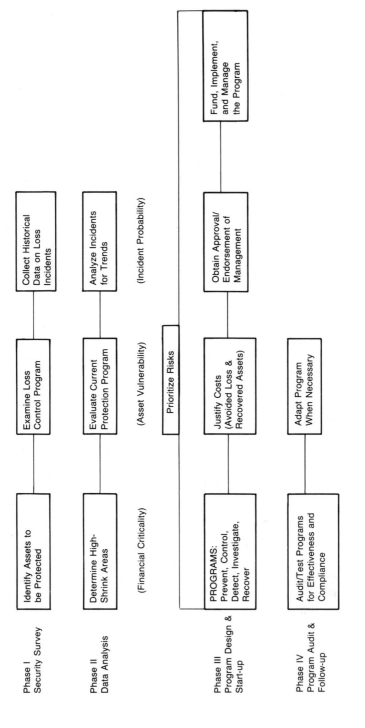

**FIGURE I-1**  *An integrated loss control program.*

# Retail Security and Loss Prevention

# PART I

# Retail Risks: Problems and Solutions

# Chapter 1

# Employee Theft

Most studies conducted on retail shortage indicate employee theft and error account for the majority of financial loss retail businesses experience on an annual basis. A recent survey conducted of varied types of retailers by Ernst and Young showed that the average theft per dishonest employee amounted to $890.[1] This figure is extemely high when compared to the average loss of $57 per shoplifting incident. While this survey, and others like it, indicate that shoplifting occurs more frequently than employee theft, the financial loss from dishonest employees is 15 times greater than the loss caused by shoplifters.[2] Employees steal in a variety of ways and all have the same result—loss of profits and low morale. Employee theft can even lead to the loss of the entire business.

Each type of retail operation has its own unique risk areas. Drug stores carry controlled substances (prescription drugs) and these products must be carefully guarded using guidelines established by the Drug Enforcement Administration. Grocers experience both employee and customer "grazing" (or eating of merchandise) on a regular basis. Fraudulent bottle returns occur frequently in grocery operations. Also, grocery "baggers" are in an excellent position to carry merchandise to their vehicles or to those of accomplices. Cosmetics, clothes, tools, auto parts, etc. are all easily worn or concealed and removed unlawfully by company employees. Employees have also been known to damage merchandise intentionally and mark it "out-of-stock."

The methods used by employees to steal company profits have been broken down into three categories—merchandise theft, cash theft, and miscellaneous business abuse. Retailers should realize that many types of internal theft, such as underringing sales or giving away free merchandise, don't generally show up as cash shortages, rather they impact the physical inventory. This loss is often times attributed to shoplifting.

Retailers should document all reported theft incidents. The data within the report will allow them to conduct a study to determine the most common methods of theft. Once this is determined, detection and prevention efforts can be focused to eliminate or control incidents of theft.

## EMPLOYEE ERROR AND WASTE

Before discussing types of employee theft, employee error and waste should be mentioned. When employees are poorly trained or motivated, costly errors can occur. However, many policies can be enforced that reduce loss due to employee error and waste. At the vendor delivery point, ensure that piece counts are carefully made to verify the quantity of incoming merchandise. Ensure that merchandise is properly priced and distributed. Also, ensure that cash register clerks remain alert to avoid misringing items. The best defense against "paperwork" shrink due to employee error and waste is thorough effective training, supervision, and discipline. Retail management should not tolerate an ill-conceived or poorly executed training program.

## MERCHANDISE THEFT

There are many types of merchandise theft—store and distribution employees may conceal and take, or wear company merchandise home on a regular basis. They may also hand off merchandise to friends or family members. This practice is called *sweethearting*. In malls or shopping centers, employees are known to allow clerks from an adjacent store or warehouse to take company merchandise in exchange for the same privilege in their store. A discussion of every method of merchandise theft is beyond the scope of this book. However, the primary methods of merchandise theft are discussed in the following paragraphs.

### Underringing

Similar to handing off merchandise is the practice of underringing a purchase or allowing an accomplice to purchase something for a reduced price. For example, $10 items are rung up as 10¢. Managers should be alert to any clerk who acts too familiar with a customer, while quickly glancing around. A computer-generated or hand-written report on price variances is an excellent tool for detecting this problem. This report should indicate the current price of the purchased item versus the price paid for the item. If a pattern of this type of transaction is evident, it may indicate system error, poor training, or theft. Managers and loss prevention specialists should also note if registers equipped with price "wands" or bar code readers are being bypassed and items are being hand-keyed into the register, as this may also indicate underringing of merchandise.

### Removal of Trash

Another common method used by employees to steal merchandise is to place items in plastic garbage bags that are being removed from the store. Clear trash bags will reveal their contents, but all trash removal should be supervised by management. Ensure that the employee tears open the bag and allows the contents to fall into the dumpster. Many store managers have been surprised by the sight of jogging suits, athletic shoes, etc. falling from trash bags. Also, never give employees store keys to remove trash or boxes.

### Controlling Merchandise Theft

Place disposable or one-way Electronic Article Surveillance (EAS) tags in certain items to deter theft. EAS tags work well, particularly if the tags are hidden in pockets or under the removable soles of shoes, for example. Hidden EAS tags work very well in warehouse situations, also.

Never allow employees to bring their purses or packages onto the selling floor. Only clear plastic purses should be allowed in work areas.

Store high-priced items in separate security cages for better protection and maintain an access log to document access to the area.

Use closed-circuit television (CCTV) and roaming security agents in both store and distribution facilities to assist in detection and deterrence of employee theft.

Offer employee discounts on store purchases to better facilitate legitimate purchasing of goods by employees and their relatives.

Control allocation of price guns and check prices when employees make purchases to avoid intentional marking down of items by employees and customers. Check employee purchases. This procedure is simple and requires that all purchases made by an employee be kept in a central location. These checks should be done on a random basis. Record each purchase made by an employee or family member.

Authorize and verify all shipments by an employee who is not responsible for controlling inventories.

Require all employees to enter and leave the work place through a designated employee entrance that is monitored by a security guard or management personnel.

Provide a coat room for overcoats and unusually large packages. Post a sign at this entrance warning employees that pilferage is a crime and those caught will be prosecuted.

Lock roll-up receiving doors at the bottom, not at their pull chains, since many employees use dollies to hoist the doors open and then slide merchandise out through the gap.

Secure all doors not used for regular customer traffic per local fire regulations and install panic alarms.

Ensure that a manager observes and documents all freight deliveries made at either the distribution facility or the store.

Restrict access to supply areas and ensure that these areas are monitored by a security guard.

Ensure that employees who enter the supply area are accompanied by a warehouse employee and ensure that they complete a sign-in sheet recording name, time of entrance and departure, and merchandise removed.

Keep customer returns and damaged items in a secure area.

Keep stockroom merchandise in neat stacks, rather than disorderly piles, so that it is easy to spot missing items. Bad housekeeping is a quick tip-off to possible employee theft.

Restrict employee use of photocopying machines, company gas pumps, telephones, postage meters, and other facilities designed for company use.

Escort guests and employees of other companies to their appointments.

Rotate employees of one department to a different department to take inventory and ensure that inventory-taking is supervised by a member of management.

Keep merchandise in neat, orderly displays and never stack items near doors or windows that can be opened.

Clearly mark company equipment with the company's name.

Ensure that tools are inventoried and locked up by a supervisor at the end of each workday.

Be suspicious of company equipment or merchandise that appears out of place. Encourage employees to report out-of-place items to management.

Ensure that security or management personnel periodically inspect rubbish piles and garbage containers for concealed items.

Inventory high-priced merchandise on processing lines in distribution facilities and keep it in secured areas.

Assure employees that the identity of anyone who reports dishonesty on the part of other employees will be held in confidence.

Install telephone hotlines or offer rewards for theft information.

Establish a toll-free, 24-hour hotline to better facilitate company employees reporting theft, fraud, substance abuse, or sexual harassment in the workplace. Companies may use an outside service or set up an in-house hotline operation. Management should be aware, however, that many honest employees may be unwilling to "snitch."

## CASH THEFT

Theft of cash by dishonest employees is a problem that is increasing in frequency. Retail firms are particularly vulnerable to cash theft, since many employees have access to cash registers and counting rooms, and routinely make cash deposits.

When customers purchase items with cash, that money goes into a cash register. Therefore, the first place to look for cash theft is at the point of sale. Some employees void legitimate sales transactions (and pocket the cash) to ensure that the register's money isn't "short" at the end of the day. Clerks will also take cash from a customer and fail to ring up the sale. In many cases, the dishonest employee keeps a written record of the amount of cash they have accumulated and sets that money off to one side in the cash drawer. If the employee is "spooked" or unable to retrieve this cash from the register, an overage occurs. This also occurs when an employee fails to take out the sales tax or odd change collected.

## Refund Fraud

In today's hassle-free customer service environment, the retailer is vulnerable to refund fraud. Customers should be able to exchange or return merchandise to retailers with relative ease. Retailers can implement refund policies and procedures that provide a happy medium between "no refunds" and "anything goes." When employees decide they need cash immediately and don't want to "till-tap" or void a transaction, the next easiest thing to do is pull out a phone book and a refund slip, pick a name from the phone book, write that person's name and address on the slip, record the amount of cash they desire as the refund amount, and sign and date the refund slip. The slip is then substituted for the cash.

Some refund fraud countermeasures include numbering refund slips and logging them out as needed. Refunds greater than $100 should be authorized by a member of management. Customers should sign the refund slip, along with the issuing clerk and the employee who takes the returned merchandise back to the sales floor. Management personnel should randomly call customers who returned merchandise and inquire if the transaction was handled to their satisfaction. This is not only a positive customer service move, but if a customer claims to have never been in the store, this action may expose a dishonest employee case. Positive comments from customers should be passed on to store employees in a meeting. This serves to recognize the courteous employee, while at the same time indicates that refunds are checked.

## Layaway Fraud

Many stores have layaway plans and employees can use these to steal cash from the till. The three most common methods to steal via layaways involve voiding a layaway payment, canceling a layaway transaction, and forfeiting a layaway deposit. To prevent employees from fraudulently forfeiting a layaway deposit, all deposit transactions should be authorized by management. To prevent fraudulent layaway cancellations or payment voids, a manager's authorization should also be required.

## Embezzlement and Employee Fraud

Embezzlement in retail companies can occur at any level of the organization. The term embezzle refers to the stealing of money from an employer by someone in a position of trust. Cash theft from cash registers is a form of embezzlement. Other common forms of embezzlement found in retail operations include bank deposit rolling, check kiting, lapping, payroll fraud, travel and expense account fraud, and vendor kickbacks and collusion, which is discussed in Chapter 4.

### Bank Deposit Rolling

Rolled bank deposits usually occur in stores where employees make up the daily sales receipts for deposit. The employee steals all or part of the day's deposit and makes up for the stolen cash with monies from future deposits. This type of crime is not very common and can be prevented by having two separate employees verify each day's deposit on a rotating basis.

### Check Kiting

Employees authorized to write checks or make deposits in two or more bank accounts may attempt to "kite" (or float) funds between a legitimate account and one set up by the employee or an accomplice. Once a check from the company is deposited into the employee account, the employee makes a withdrawal of cash in that amount from their account. Before the original check clears the company account, the employee deposits a check from their account into the company's to cover the original account. This cycle continues until the kite "breaks" when either the company or one of the banks refuses to honor the checks.

### Lapping

In lapping schemes, dishonest employees keep part of the payments made on accounts received. This method is similar to deposit rolling, because parts of other payments are skimmed to cover the loss. Account records and statements are altered by the employee. This type of crime can go undetected for years. To avoid this type of theft, all bank deposits should be verified and approved by a member of management.

### Payroll Fraud

Payroll fraud usually occurs when an employee with the access and the authority to add employees to payroll rosters, adds fictitious names to the rosters. Paychecks are then issued to the dishonest employee or an accomplice. Payroll functions should be divided between at least three people who prepare, verify, and distribute the payroll.

*Travel and Expense Account Fraud*

As more employees travel and fill out expense reports, more travel and expense accounts are targeted for fraud. Personal expenses such as meals and telephone calls are traditionally listed on reports filed for reimbursement, but firm policies should be established and publicized regarding legitimate expenses. Appropriate supervisors should verify and authorize all submitted expense reports.

## Controlling Cash Theft

There are other recommended measures that retailers can use to control theft of cash by employees.

Ensure that names on payroll rosters are authorized, in writing, by a designated company official.

If nonregistered sales are suspected, retail establishments may effectively enlist the customer's assistance. Signs posted by each cash register announcing that, "Any customer who does not receive a sales receipt with every purchase is entitled to a cash bonus" may help to put an end to the problem.

Hire "outside shoppers" through private shopping services and local women's clubs or auxiliaries. These shoppers are provided with funds to make purchases in the store and they then provide valuable information on whether sales are being recorded properly, and the proficiency and courtesy of the salespeople.

Designate a responsible company official, who is not on the accounting department's staff, to receive and investigate customer complaints.

Bond key employees for theft.

Establish a good audit program. An employer should establish and maintain a working climate of accountability in which accurate records are kept and regularly audited. (Audit programs are discussed in greater detail later in the book.)

The Small Business Association (SBA) also recommends the following procedures.

Carefully check the background of prospective employees, particularly those to be given fiduciary responsibilities. This check should include oral and written contacts with previous employers, credit bureaus, and personal references. Make sure that an employee who will handle funds is adequately bonded.

Ensure that a member of senior management supervises the accounting employee who opens and records receipt of checks, cash payments, and money orders.

Ensure that a manager prepares bank deposits daily. Return duplicate deposit slips, stamped "RECEIVED" by the bank, to the accounting department.

Ensure all payments are approved by senior management as well as by the person who draws or signs the checks.

Ensure senior management examines all invoices and supporting data before signing checks. Verify that merchandise was received and that prices seem reasonable. In many false purchase schemes, the embezzler will neglect to complete receiving forms or other records purporting to show receipt of merchandise.

Mark all paid invoices as "CANCELED" and file them in a secure area to prevent double payment. Dishonest accounting department employees have been known to make out and receive approval on duplicate checks for the same invoice. The second check may be embezzled by the employee or by an accomplice at the company issuing the invoice.

Periodically inspect prenumbered checkbooks and other prenumbered forms to ensure that checks or forms from the back or middle of the books have not been removed for use in a fraudulent scheme. Place authorized spending limits on employees.

Do not permit employees responsible for making sales or assigning projects to outside suppliers to process transactions affecting their own accounts.

Ensure that an employee who does not draw or sign checks reconciles bank statements and canceled checks. Ensure management examines canceled checks and endorsements for unusual features (see Chapter 7).

Payroll should be prepared by one person, verified by another, and distributed by others not involved with payroll preparation or time slip approval.

## MISCELLANEOUS BUSINESS ABUSE

The third major category of internal theft risks is *miscellaneous*. Abuses such as unethical conduct, time theft, and drug abuse are discussed in this section.

In the U.S., business ethics are coming under more scrutiny as more well-known government and private enterprise individuals face criminal indictment. In a retail business, most key employees are in a position to accept a bribe or kickback from a product or service vendor. Merchandise buyers, purchasing agents, traffic managers, in-house agents, new store and distribution center real estate locators, and in-house construction supervisors are just some of the individuals in a position to recommend or authorize agreements with outside vendors. Retailers can reduce their vulnerability to this type of crime by taking some of the following actions:

Require competitive bidding for business.

Separate receiving operations from purchasing operations so buyers cannot accept short deliveries in return for kickbacks.

Ensure that all key employees read and sign a Conflict of Interest Policy Form. This type of agreement defines unethical behavior and serves as documented proof that the employee understood unethical conduct, should an incident occur. Appendix 1 contains a sample conflict of interest policy.

Ensure that an executive from outside the purchasing department reviews bids and inspects incoming goods.

Require that employees, particularly those in purchasing, file monthly reports on received gifts and gratuities. Set a limit on the value of gifts that may be accepted.

Insist that gifts be sent to the office, not to employees' homes.

Inform vendors of acceptable gift-giving practices.

When a supplier other than the low bidder is selected, insist that the reason be documented and sent to top management for review and approval.

Rotate the assignment of purchasing agents and suppliers.

Instruct employees to report any demands for payoffs made by customers or vendors.

Make estimates of reasonable costs for products and services, so that possible kickback costs can be identified.

Develop policies that ensure maintenance of a professional distance between management and union officials.

Institute procedures that alert management when payments of commissions by vendors to employees are not documented by the usual paperwork. Commissions not in line with recognized trade practices or made through banks not usually used, may indicate unethical behavior.

An employee or official of a company or government organization involved in a bribery, kickback, or payoff scheme may have violated any of a number of local, state, or federal laws. If you suspect that one of your employees is either receiving or giving bribes or kickbacks in dealings with another non-government firm, do not confront the suspect immediately. Instead, discuss your suspicions with your company attorneys to determine what action should be undertaken. It is essential that your business stay within the law. Therefore, do not attempt an investigation on your own. Remember, it is not necessary that a bribe, kickback, or payoff actually be received in order for a crime to have been committed. Under most existing legislation, the mere offering, conferring, or agreeing to confer a benefit is considered an offense.

Another form of miscellaneous abuse is time theft. Time theft occurs when an employee clocks in for another employee who is late or absent, calls in sick for a paid day off, leaves early, takes long breaks, or uses the company's time to conduct an outside business. Positive leadership practices by supervisors, including good discipline, two-way communication, and good morale all help control time abuse.

In an effort to make company employees or associates feel like they are a part of their company, many retailers offer employee discounts on store merchandise—an average of 10% on low-margin items and an average of 20% on all other items. Employee discount programs are a boost to employee morale. The company's discount policy should be in written form and monitored by store managers. Unfortunately, discount policy violations are now the most common form of internal theft. Abuse of this privilege involves allowing individuals who are not authorized to receive discounts to obtain them. Some employees purchase items with their discount and have an accomplice return the items for the higher regular price.

Stores that have discount programs report that they average between .25% and 1.10% of gross annual sales in employee purchases. This percentage varies with the size of the company and the type of merchandise sold. If a chain has a store that greatly exceeds or doesn't meet the established, average percentage of gross sales in employee purchases, employees may be abusing the privilege or just outright stealing the merchandise.

A brief mention should be made at this point about employee pilferage of supplies and equipment from a company. Tools, office equipment, and supplies disappear from businesses at an alarming rate. This type of theft may occur sporadically or in an organized manner. All employees should be made aware of the company policy regarding "using" company assets for personal endeavors. Valuable items should be inventoried and permanently marked, and sensitive areas should be secured to help control this type of loss.

Another significant method of employee theft is the practice of filing false workers' compensation claims. This practice may be replacing unemployment claims as a desirable source of income. All workman's compensation claims should be investigated to determine if abuse is occurring.

Unsupervised work crews, laid-off employees, and others such as disgruntled union members may inflict damage on the retailer in the form of vandalism or sabotage. Distribution of company assets, and work stoppage are examples of this type of risk. Supervisors should keep the lines of communication open in an effort to determine if morale problems exist. Also, terminated or laid-off employees should be debriefed prior to departure and denied access to sensitive areas.

Every business is vulnerable to theft by cleaning crews. Supervision of in-house or contract cleaning personnel is essential. Random checks of tool boxes, cans of wax, vacuum cleaner bags, and, of course, trash is a must. Contract crews should be licensed and bonded for the company's protection.

In today's society, the use and abuse of illegal drugs and alcohol is still on the rise. Alcohol and drug abuse constitute tremendous threats to the safety and security of any organization. Accidents and increased theft activity are generally the result of drug-addicted or alcoholic employees attempting to function within the company. Employers should attempt to screen applicants to keep individuals with untreated addictive or criminal tendencies from entering the work place. Train supervisors to detect and refer problem employees to Employee Assistance Programs (EAPs). Retailers face liability if dependent employees go untreated and severe losses, injuries, or even death occur. Consultation with government or private experts regarding an effective EAP is recommended. Some retail businesses are placing undercover agents in their operation to discover the source of suspected theft or substance abuse activity.

## PROPRIETARY INFORMATION

All retail operations possess information that is considered proprietary (or sensitive) in nature. Confidential information may include future corporate expansion goals or locations, sales figures, and customer mailing lists. All proprietary information may be confidential, but all confidential information may not be proprietary. Personnel and training files are confidential, but are not considered proprietary. Information regarded as confidential should be carefully guarded. There is a difference in the civil and criminal rights afforded to retailers depending on the type of information being protected. Trade secrets may be subject to greater protection under federal law if it can be established that the sensitive information gives the company economic benefit and that the company makes reasonable efforts to maintain its secrecy. Employees can seriously damage their company if they intentionally or inadvertently give away trade secrets. A minimal proprietary information security plan should include the following:

1. Restrict nonemployee access to places containing secret information.
2. Place warning signs and instructions to alert employees to the sensitivity of certain things and places.
3. Inform employees and visitors that information obtained or things seen in certain locations within a facility are secret.
4. Store sensitive documents separately in containers for which special security precautions are taken.
5. Impose area controls within a facility among different classes of employees with respect to certain information or operations.
6. Instruct employees and suppliers not to disclose information entrusted to

---

# RESTITUTION AGREEMENT
# AND
# PROMISSORY NOTE

Non-Interest Bearing

To Whom It May Concern:

I, _____ , do hereby promise to repay the amount of: _____
($ _____ ).
This amount of money is the amount which I am responsible for taking from my employer
_____ from _____ to _____ .
I, _____ , agree to repay the above amount ($ _____ ) as follows:
  1.  Equal monthly payment of $ _____ for _____ months.
  2.  Lump sum repayment of $ _____ on or before _____ .
  3.  Final payment of $ _____ due on or before _____ .
The above agreement is voluntarily signed by:

NAME  (PRINT)  _____

ADDRESS  _____

CITY  _____  STATE_____

DATE  SIGNED  _____

D.O.B.  _____  PHONE (       )  _____

SIGNED  _____  DATE  _____

WITNESS  SIGNATURE  _____  DATE  _____

FIGURE 1–1  *Sample restitution agreement and promissory note.*

them to other employees unless such employees exhibit a legitimate "need to know."

## INVESTIGATING EMPLOYEE THEFT

Employee pilferage or embezzlement is uncovered in a variety of ways, but the following are the most common: when an accomplice or witness tips off management intentionally or unintentionally, through spot audits, and through follow-up investigations based on inventory shortages, gross margin problems, price variances, etc.

All accusations and indications of theft activity should be vigorously investigated by in-house loss prevention personnel or trained consultants. The goals of any investigation are to substantiate the accusation or clear the suspect, discover the extent of the damage or loss and employee involvement, recover lost assets, (see Figure 1–1 for a sample restitution agreement), and determine the circumstances that allowed the incident to take place. A retail investigator should be a neutral, third party and enter the investigation with an open mind. The normal investigative routine is to first gather evidence of wrongdoing through review of documentation and/or surveillance activities. Next, a list of suspects should be narrowed down and preliminary interviews may follow. When the thief has been discovered, the investigator should then determine whether enough evidence is present to take action (such as termination, criminal prosecution, or civil action) or whether the investigation should be dropped due to lack of evidence. Investigators should work closely with Human Resource or Personnel representatives and store operations throughout any investigation. Cooperation and sharing of expertise among these individuals enhances any investigation. Tremendous liability exists if investigations are not handled in a professional and confidential manner. All implicated employees are considered innocent until proven otherwise. Thorough investigations should be conducted in an environment that stresses employee rights. Investigators should keep in mind that union activity is not to be investigated by the retailer. Only acts that are violations of the law or company policy are to be investigated.

## NOTES

1. Ernst and Young. *An Ounce of Prevention Security Survey* (New York: Chain Store, 1990), 17.
2. Ibid., 17.

# Chapter 2

# Managing Employee Honesty

It is helpful to have some insight into the reasons why employees steal from their employers. First of all, there is no typical, dishonest employee. Anyone that has access to company assets may decide to steal them. However, certain traits may indicate potential problems. In determining which social psychological theories best explain an employee's theft activity, numerous studies have been conducted. The majority of these studies have been conducted since 1980 and the results are similar. Terris and Jones reviewed 24 studies that include psychological predictors and identified 11 significant ones. Employee theft is more common among those who

1. hold a variety of theft-tolerant attitudes
2. are more tolerant of violence and aggression
3. are more accepting of illicit drug use
4. experience higher levels of stress or burnout
5. are more dissatisfied at work
6. believe their crimes are less likely to be detected by management
7. believe management would be more lenient with punishment
8. are aware of more co-worker theft
9. have less impulse control
10. are more tolerant of crimes by insiders
11. are more likely to endorse certain altruistic values[1]

Overall, Jones concludes that the best, single psychological predictor is employees' attitudes toward theft. He summarizes the literature researched by stating that the "typical" employee thieft

1. is more tempted to steal
2. engages in many of the common rationalizations for theft
3. would punish thieves less
4. often thinks about theft-related activities
5. attributes more theft to others
6. shows more interthief loyalty

7. feels more vulnerable to peer pressure to steal compared to an honest employee

In 1979, Clark et al.[2] conducted a study on sociological cases of employee theft. As part of a larger study, questionnaires were administered to more than 1400 employees from nine retail companies. The relationship was explored between self-reported employee theft and four sets of predictor variables. The first set of variables consisted of personal characteristics of the employee. When these variables were cross-tabulated with employee theft, some notable relationships were found. Employee theft was significantly higher among employees who were

- young
- male
- caucasian
- never married
- living in high-income households, but contributing less than 20% of the total income
- concerned about their financial and educational/career situation

The second set of variables concerned occupational characteristics—especially wages, tenure, and job status. Employee theft was significantly higher among employees with

- lower-paying jobs
- lower-status jobs
- jobs providing easiest access to merchandise and money (i.e., sales clerks, cashiers, and managers)
- more numerous and frequent social interactions with co-employees

The third group of variables focused on job satisfaction. Employee theft was significantly higher among employees who were

- dissatisfied with their immediate supervisors
- dissatisfied with the organization for which they work
- dissatisfied with opportunities for promotion
- dissatisfied with the day-to-day workload

The fourth set of predictor variables concerned the deterrent effect created by formal and informal social contacts. Employee theft was significantly higher among employees who believed that

- they would not get caught if they stole something
- their employers were unaware of employee theft
- no one would care if certain things were stolen

- management and co-workers would not react to theft as a very serious problem

Based on the data collected during these two (and other) studies, a combination of the following three factors tend to result in employee theft:

I. Rationalization
   A. Employees convince themselves that dishonesty is a form of compensation
   B. Anger (e.g., supervisor, co-workers, company)
   C. Big company (cash/merchandise won't be missed)
II. Need/Desire
   A. Specific needs (e.g., low salary/high bills)
   B. Outside pressure (e.g., desire for prestige)
   C. Overwhelming desire for money or specific merchandise
III. Opportunity
   A. Presented with situation in which employee perceives little chance of being caught
      1. Exact change left by customer
      2. Receiving doors unlocked/unsupervised
      3. Poor loss prevention practices by management
   B. Internal/external help

A three-tiered prevention program, designed to control losses caused by dishonest employees, is recommended to retailers. The retail executive may choose to use all or part of this plan—Pre-employment Screening, Access/Procedural Controls and Audits, and Store/Company Atmosphere.

## PRE-EMPLOYMENT SCREENING

To prevent losses due to employee theft, the logical place to start theft prevention is during potential employee interviews. Screen individuals before they enter the organization and identify those who are likely to steal. There are seven common methods, used by today's businesses to screen employee applicants.

1. *Application Screening*—The employment application, which conforms with current legal standards, should be completely filled out. Follow-up on any gaps in employment or questionable responses.
2. *Personal and Professional Reference Checks*—Individuals listed by the applicant as references should be contacted and questioned about the subject in a positive manner. The reference should be asked to give the name and phone number of other acquaintances for further reference.
3. *Employment and Education Verification*—Jobs and education listed by the

prospective employee should be checked. A rule of thumb in checking past employment history is to go back 3 to 5 years. If the job for which the individual is applying requires a certain level of education, the applicant must sign an authorization form allowing colleges and schools to release transcripts.

4.  *Integrity Interviews/Scenarios*—There appears to be some merit in the practice of giving each applicant at least two interviews, preferably by two different interviewers. The interviewer should ask open-ended questions to allow the subjects to display their thoughts and ideas. There are courses and books available that demonstrate techniques to determine if a subject is being truthful or deceptive. Some retailers, after gaining legal validation, put applicants in a simulated work or decision-making situation and observe how they perform. This practice also gives applicants a feeling for the job for which they are applying.

5.  *Written Honesty/Aptitude Tests/Surveys*—With the loss of the polygraph as a screening tool, many states allow the use of "pencil-and-paper" tests/surveys to determine honesty. Some tests exist that rely on a great deal of empirical research data to predict future behavior, based on past behavior or tolerance of deviance.

6.  *Handwriting or Graphoanalysis*—Empirical data for handwriting analyses do exist and are used to confirm personality traits based on handwriting samples. The use of handwriting analysis as a screening tool is widespread in Europe and is being used more frequently by U.S. firms.

7.  *Background Checks*—Many retailers use in-house personnel or outside companies to check the criminal conviction and credit history of applicants for positions that require this type of information. Workers' compensation claims and driving records are also frequently checked. Books and software programs are available to assist retailers in these types of checks.

## ACCESS/PROCEDURAL CONTROLS AND AUDITS

The next part of the plan to control employee theft is to establish workable controls and, once implemented, to follow-up on the relevance and effectiveness of the controls. When designing control procedures, operational (or "real world") employee activities and customer service must be considered so as to not unnecessarily impede the normal flow of business. Cumbersome procedures may not only drive off good customers, but are also quickly abandoned by company employees.

### Merchandise Control

Merchandise control can be effectively maintained by adhering to the following seven suggestions:

1. *Electronic Article Surveillance (EAS)*—Electronic and dye tags attached to or concealed inside high-loss merchandise not only deters shoplifting by customers, but also by some employees.
2. *Spot Audits/Counts*—Unannounced store audits or selected merchandise piece counts help detect and deter employee pilferage by putting employees on notice that management closely tracks their assets.
3. *Purse/Package Checks*—A policy allowing management or security to check employee purses or packages when exiting the store or distribution center can be implemented. If used, this policy must be made clear to all employees and must be applied consistently.
4. *Trash Removal/Cleaning Crew*—Ensure that all removal of trash and containers by in-house, contract, and vendor employees is observed.
5. *Receiving/Pick-up Policy*—Keep receiving doors secured when not in use and monitor all receiving and customer pick-up activity.
6. *Damaged and Return-to-Vendor Merchandise*—Log all merchandise slated for destruction, return-to-vendor, or donation to charity and secure it in a wire enclosure until it is disposed of to avoid employee pilferage or fraudulent refund schemes.
7. *Employee Discount and Purchase Control*—Log and sign all employee purchases. In order to receive a discount, employees and their immediate family members should present a valid company identification card.

## Cash Controls

Cash control can be effectively maintained by adhering to the following seven suggestions:

1. *Register Accountability*—Don't assign too many employees to one register, simultaneously, if at all possible. Have all employees log their employee number into each transaction. These two policies reduce cash overages and shortages, and help to quickly determine who may be responsible for missing cash.
2. *Journal Tape Review*—Randomly check journal tapes and ledger sheets from point-of-sale terminals and cash registers to check for errors or questionable practices. Training deficiencies and skill or integrity problems may be detected as well.
3. *Post-Void Authorization and Follow-Up*—When clerks void transactions, or parts of transactions, verify this activity as soon as possible. Check to see whether the purchases were rung in, again, correctly. If a customer decided not to purchase the items, find out where the clerk put them. Also, track post-voids for trends, such as reasons for the void and clerk employee number.
4. *Cash Refund Authorization and Follow-up*—Have customers supply their name, address, and phone number, as well as sign a refund slip, for a cash refund. Use three-part forms that are numerically issued and logged. Give

one copy to the customer, attach one copy to the returned merchandise, and send one copy to the cash office. When the merchandise is returned to the sales floor, have the clerk returning the item sign under the issuing clerk's signature. Depending on the average store price-point, if the transaction is over $100 for example, have management personally authorize the transaction.

5. *Tracking Cash Variances*—Post all cash overages and shortages so that trends can be determined. If there are no patterns, a "shotgun" shortage exists, and somebody, such as management or head clerks with access to all registers, may be responsible.

6. *Tracking Price Variances*—An automated price look-up system enhances any operation. In any case, a manual or automated system that tracks transactions that were rung up for less than the purchase price is recommended. A clear pattern of low or high price ring-ups may indicate intentional underringing or manipulation.

7. *Deposit Verification*—Teach cash office personnel the proper way to count money. Using a calculator with a non-add key, count the deposit once and total by denominations. Put this information on the adding machine tape, along with the date. Have the clerk recount the deposit in the same manner and compare the total with the previous total documented on the tape. If the totals are the same, have the clerk initial and date the tapes. Ensure that management repeats this process then staple the tapes to a copy of the deposit receipt and save them for record-keeping purposes.

## Audits

Conduct audits of cash and merchandise-handling procedures randomly to determine if proper controls are in place and being followed, and to determine if and where problems exist. Audits are discussed in detail in Chapter 17.

## STORE/COMPANY ATMOSPHERE

Corporate executives and supervisors at all levels should display a knowledgeable, concerned attitude toward protecting the company's assets, including the well-being of all employees. Employees need to know that their supervisors care about them. However, the "country-club" atmosphere that exists in some operations needs to be integrated with a sense of discipline. Employees must know that theft will not be tolerated and all incidents will be vigorously investigated.

## Across the Board Policy—
## Termination/Prosecution/Civil Action

All company employees should know the corporate standards of behavior and should be aware of recognition they will receive for upholding those standards. Employees must also know that if any employee, at any level, steals or violates company policy, that employee will receive a fair hearing; swift, consistent, and serious sanctions will be imposed; and termination from employment, criminal prosecution, and civil action may result.

### Employee Awareness—Training and Reinforcement

All employees, from the CEO down through the organization, should be made aware of the security risks that exist within the company, and the simple actions they can take to reduce and/or report loss incidents, and their reward for taking this action. Chapter 12 discusses loss prevention awareness training programs designed to accomplish these goals.

### Communication

Morale plunges, union activity increases, and theft and error increase when employees do not feel they can communicate their concerns, ideas, and problems to upper management. Supervisors at all levels must be taught to communicate effectively and be rewarded for doing so. The CEO should have an open line of communication to all employees. This can be effected by a written-suggestion format.

Some retailers are installing subliminal messaging systems in their stores and distribution facilities to pass on messages emphasizing courtesy, safety, and honesty. The effectiveness and legality of these systems should be verified with legal counsel and retail companies currently employing this technology.

### NOTES

1. W. Terris and J.W. Jones, "Attitudinal and Personality Correlates of Theft Among Supermarket Employees" *Journal of Security Administration* 2(1980):65–78.
2. J.P. Clark, R.C. Hollinger, C.F. Smith, P.W. Cooperi, P.F. Parilla, and P. Smith-Cunnien, Theft by Employees in the Work Organization—A Preliminary Final Report (Minneapolis: University of Minnesota, 1987).

# Chapter 3

# Vendor Theft and Error

Merchandise vendor theft and error can amount to hundreds of thousands of dollars in lost revenues by the retailer. Retailers generally purchase their merchandise from specific vendors. Vendors then ship merchandise directly (or through a distributor) to the retailer. In the case of grocery operations, a large quantity of products are delivered to the store by a vendor delivery person. In many cases, the vendor representative stocks and displays these items. Vendors, like all businesses, are prone to error and, in some instances, dishonesty. This chapter describes some of the risks of vendor theft and error that currently exist and recommends preventive measures for these risks.

## RISKS

Theft and error by vendors, is a risk that is commonly overlooked. Many retailers never consider vendor fraud and error when designing total loss control programs. However, it is a real problem. The first step in preventing and controlling this is to ensure that receiving supervisors inform Accounts Payable of any discrepancies in shipping, such as damaged goods or detected shortages.

Vendor employees, from the CEO down to the packing clerks, may intentionally short a retailer or third-party distributor on the number of items or the quality of the items ordered. Therefore, ensure that receiving personnel open merchandise and verify proper quality and piece counts. Depending on the volume of the shipments, check all merchandise containers. If the shipment is large, perform random spot checks.

Freight charges are frequently overpaid in many operations. Before authorizing the payment of an invoice, verify the shipment. Freight rates, weights, and classifications may be overstated. Therefore, weigh all incoming shipments. To eliminate duplication of payment of freight invoices, attach the bill or vendor invoice to the receiving document, and stamp the document as "PAID." If applicable, have the receiver run a computer check for duplicate freight invoice numbers. Ensure that the receiver checks for shipping terms that have been altered, merchandise that has been shipped by a more expensive route or mode, requests for payment of back orders when merchandise should have been shipped in one delivery, and merchandise that has been shipped by the wrong carrier. When merchandise returns to the vendor are due to vendor error, be aware that all incoming and outgoing freight charges should be paid by the vendor.

After all paperwork has been delivered to the Accounts Payable Department, there are certain actions that Accounts Payable personnel can take to detect vendor error or fraud. Check all invoices and compare them to the appropriate purchase orders. The invoice could contain unauthorized charges, such as insurance or packing costs, that should not be paid. Check for invoices with prices that exceed the purchase order amount. Also, be aware that vendor-issued credit memos can exceed charge-backs. Therefore, adjustments need to be made to open credit memos on vendor statements.

When charge-backs and returns-to-vendor are required, proper credit is given. The credited charge-back cost (or percentage of cost) must be the same as the original invoice cost; the vendor should pay the outgoing freight. Also, ensure that a vendor is not accidentally paid, instead of deducted, for returns and charge-backs.

Another risk in dealing with vendors involves delivery personnel. Delivery persons, whether employed in-house or by the vendor, are in a position to commit various types of fraud and theft.

These route drivers may either commit outright theft by shoplifting, eating (grazing), wearing store merchandise, or making "honest" mistakes. These mistakes are, in reality, fraud schemes that may, if discovered, appear to be an unintentional error made by the delivery man or may be blamed on the manufacturer. Examples of the more than 50 ways route drivers steal include

- walking the same cases of merchandise by the store receiver more than once for delivery credit
- invoice math errors that charge billed customers more than cash customers and keeping the cash receipts
- delivering damaged items mixed in with first-quality goods
- substituting less expensive, lesser quality, or counterfeit merchandise for ordered items
- delivering partially filled or empty sealed cartons along with full cases
- giving less credit for returned merchandise than should be given
- multiplication errors when charging the retailer for items delivered

For example, the driver may charge a six-pack price for beer or soft drinks and multiply this price by 24, for the 24 individual cans in the case, rather than the four six-packs in the case.

In many cases, buyers negotiate cash discounts, volume rebates, or an advertising allowance when placing a purchase order. They may also be eligible for new store discounts or early-buy discounts. All deliveries must be verified by the designated merchandise receiver to ensure all agreed discounts have been taken and credited. Communication between the buying staff, accounts payable, and receiving and marking personnel is critical. Buyers must ensure the purchase order is written correctly and that discounts, delivery and cancellation dates, and shipping requirements are clearly indicated.

Another prevention technique for vendor fraud and error includes appointing a designated receiver. Periodically "test" this person to detect evidence of collusion. Schedule all deliveries so that the receiver is not overwhelmed by simultaneous shipments. Computerized receiving systems are helpful in eliminating some of the risks previously mentioned (such as detecting invoice discrepancies) but should not be considered the ultimate prevention technique. Receivers should not allow friendships or embarrassment to interfere with their thorough scrutiny of incoming merchandise. *All* merchandise should be received through the receiver.

Other delivery control procedures include

scheduling receiving. By limiting direct store deliveries to certain days and/or hours, confusion is minimized and retailers can ensure that experienced receiving personnel are scheduled during this time.

training receivers. While merchandise receiving is not considered the most desirable job in the company, it is imperative that competent employees be identified and trained to properly count and secure deliveries.

avoiding front door deliveries. If possible, deny delivery personnel access to other store merchandise. This practice also eliminates the possibility of injury to customers entering by the same entrance.

receiving merchandise away from trash-disposal areas and customer or employee parking areas. This practice discourages easy pilferage and concealment of store goods.

comparing piece counts with the invoice, not with the packing slip. It is common for receivers to refer to a vendor-generated packing slip, instead of the company's invoice, for an accurate piece count.

separating buying functions from receiving functions. Merchandise buyers should not be responsible for verifying shipments or handling the receiving copy of the purchase order. This practice helps to avoid fraudulent collusion between vendor and buyers.

auditing purchase orders. Periodically audit purchase orders to verify delivery addresses. This practice detects whether or not employees are having merchandise delivered to their residence or another warehouse.

As with all good prevention programs, vendor fraud and error control should include tests of controls. Store management should pick vendors, on a rotating basis, and check on their delivery and billing procedures. A count of on-hand merchandise in the vendor's display area should be done and the purchase order pulled for the upcoming delivery. Allow the delivery person and receiver to go through their regular routine. However, as the driver is leaving, ask her to accompany the manager to ensure that returns are properly credited and delivered items are the quality and quantity ordered. These types of checks indicate to employees and vendors that the store is serious about shortage control.

# Chapter 4

# Controlling Cargo Theft

When merchandise is shipped or received, it is very vulnerable to pilferage by employees and drivers. According to American Trucking Association estimates, dishonest employees account for as much as 70% of all cargo losses. Between $1 billion and $3 billion are lost annually in the transport phase.[1] Thieves may be customers working in collusion with employees or they may be highway robbers, workers employed by the shipping company, or truck drivers. Most theft occurs not in transit, but in freight handling areas.

## SHIPPING

The first method of controlling cargo theft is to ensure that shipping and receiving take place in different areas. This helps to eliminate confusion as to whether merchandise is coming or going. Confusion can lead to mistakes or can be used to conceal intentional theft.

The shipping process normally begins when an authorized manager signs orders approving the shipment of merchandise either from the vendor to the retailer or from the distribution center to individual stores. An unauthorized shipment begins in the same way, however in this case, no legitimate order has been placed and the merchandise may be shipped to a drop-off point selected by the dishonest employee. Illegal activity is covered up by destroying or altering invoices or shipping instructions. In fraudulent over-shipments, excess goods are shipped and subsequently sold by an accomplice at the receiving end.

Problems are generally more prevalent in companies that do not investigate or require the return of overshipped merchandise. A strictly controlled ordering and invoicing system is critical to reducing the risk of unauthorized shipments. Ensure that vendor invoices are numbered and access to the secured copies is limited to authorized accounting personnel. Also, number products, either individually or in crates, and ensure that the numbers correspond to the products recorded on the sales ticket, the shipping instructions, and the invoice. These numbers can then be checked against inventory records by the auditing and accounting departments.

## STAGING

Merchandise is then assembled and packaged for transit—commonly called the staging process. Crime-ridden assembly areas are usually those in which employee and customer access are not controlled, products are not arranged in an organized manner, and sound inventory control procedures are not followed. Dishonest employees and customers may take advantage of the lack of order by walking off with merchandise or concealing it for later removal.

Planning and organization virtually eliminate theft during the staging process. The assembly and packaging of goods for shipment should always take place in an area specifically set aside for that purpose, such as a warehouse or packaging plant—never at a loading dock or any other location where merchandise is readily visible and accessible to employees and customers. Limit access to the staging area to assigned employees and ensure that the area is guarded by a manager or security officer. Require inventory control throughout the staging process. An effective inventory control system might operate in the following manner:

1. Give sales or "picking" tickets to an employee who is solely responsible for pulling the merchandise from stock.
2. Ensure that the employee writes the product registration or inventory number on the sales ticket. Some warehouses attach a removable inventory control number to every item.
3. When the item is pulled from stock, ensure that the number is removed from the item and attached to the sales ticket.
4. When the order has been filled, have the employee initial the sales ticket and pass it on to another employee who checks the merchandise against the sales ticket, initials the sales ticket, and packages the merchandise.
5. Have that employee pass the sales ticket to the accounting department, which records the inventory control numbers in an inventory register.

Employees involved in the assembly and packaging processes should have their assignments regularly rotated. Also, randomly check all shipments to verify that orders are being filled properly.

## LOADING

Merchandise is then loaded onto trucks for transit. The loading process provides dishonest employees and customers with many theft opportunities. In poorly controlled operations, where customers and employees are permitted to congregate in the loading area, cargo can be easily carried off and concealed in waiting trucks or cars. Another common loading dock crime is short-packaging. Employees divert a truck driver's attention long enough to slip packages away from the driver's shipment. The driver then signs the delivery receipt, acknowledging that he has verified the count of the shipment. Usually drivers do not realize that they have been shortchanged until after their deliveries. At that stage, drivers are held responsible for any shortages.

Similar precautions to those used to limit access and control activities in the staging area are also effective in preventing theft in the cargo loading area. Limit access to the loading area to authorized personnel and vehicles. Ensure that one employee is made responsible for overseeing each transaction or shipment. Have the employee initial the delivery receipt, thereby verifying that the proper merchandise has left the loading dock. If possible, have one employee handle the physical transfer of the merchandise and have another employee, preferably a member of management, oversee the accuracy of the transaction. Employee assignments should be rotated periodically. Also, ensure that the drivers, or whoever picks up the merchandise, examine the shipment and sign the delivery receipt.

## TRANSPORTING

Merchandise is then transported by truck or tractor-trailer to the point of delivery. Theft directly from delivery vehicles may involve the removal of small, costly items from a shipment by a driver or may involve a pre-planned robbery of the entire contents of the truck.

Before the shipment leaves the store or warehouse, ensure that all contents are listed on a manifest and provide copies to the dispatcher, the delivery company (if different), the receiving store, and the driver. When the items are loaded and in transit, observe the following precautions:

Keep merchandise locked and sealed with a high-quality, numbered seal at all times.

Avoid the use of flatbed trucks, which make merchandise visible and easily accessible.

Lock loaded vehicles that are parked overnight so that the delivery doors cannot be opened and attach a fifth-wheel lock to the trailer hook-up to prevent unauthorized trucks from hauling the trailer.

Ensure that parking areas are well-lit and, where possible, guarded. Some large truck stops provide protected areas for a reasonable fee.

Avoid parking loaded delivery vehicles in high-risk areas, such as inner cities.

Install alarms in delivery vehicles, particularly in those that must often park overnight when full of merchandise.

Arrange schedules so that, whenever possible, shipments can be made without overnight stops.

Have trucks travel in a convoy when a shipment requires the use of more than one vehicle or when several vehicles are heading in the same direction.

Have security agents follow shipments of particularly high value or risk.

Ensure that information on shipment contents, such as departure and arrival times and route plans, is kept confidential.

Place radio and telephone communication devices in delivery vehicles to facilitate emergency calls for assistance.

Mark the company's name and address on all sides of the delivery vehicle so that police can quickly identify stolen vehicles.

## RECEIVING

When merchandise reaches the store, ensure that a piece count is taken and documented. Some retailers have manifests that list all items and some manifests only list cartons that are numbered. In either situation, reconcile the shipment and report overages or shortages. Periodically, have central distribution center-based security officers overstock shipments to stores on a random basis to determine if reconciliation is occurring or if personnel are failing to report variances.

Interstore merchandise transfers also present problems in real and "paper" shortages. To avoid these shortages, ensure that the central accounting office matches copies of sending store paperwork with those of the destination store to be sure that all charged merchandise sent to the store is actually received. All discrepancies should be resolved within 48 hours.

## NOTE

1.  Virginia Shomp, *How to Protect Your Business* (Elmsford: The Benjamin Co., 1985), 136.

# Chapter 5

# Shoplifting

All businesses are vulnerable to theft from their own employees and, to some extent, vendors, but only retailers experience the theft of their merchandise on a routine basis by their customers in the form of shoplifting. According to the 1989–90 edition of the IMRA, Ernst and Young security survey, shoplifting costs retailers approximately 3% of their gross annual sales.[1] This cost is generally absorbed by consumers in the form of higher retail prices. In an effort to prevent these losses, this chapter familiarizes retailers with the different types of shoplifters, some current theft methods, and various shoplifting prevention techniques.

## TYPES OF SHOPLIFTERS

Retailers frequently ask experts to determine the typical shoplifter particular to their stores. The retailers need to know the types of merchandise that are taken most frequently and how the merchandise is stolen. In most cases, the store manager can provide this information.

Experts on the subject of shoplifting agree that there are different types of shoplifters and each type is based on motive. The most common type of shoplifter is the *opportunist* or *amateur*. A subset of this type of shoplifter includes juveniles and other impulse shoplifters. The opportunist is often a customer who frequents the store and who is suddenly placed in a situation in which the opportunity to steal presents itself. Examples of this type of situation include an unattended fitting room or an unwatched merchandise aisle. Generally, the type of merchandise taken is the merchandise that is sold in the greatest quantity and is highly desirable and easily resold. In grocery stores, tobacco, beer, health and beauty aids, and deli meats are targeted the most. In drug stores, health and beauty aids, and over-the-counter drugs are most frequently taken. In clothing stores, athletic shoes, women's apparel, and jogging suits are frequent targets. In hardware and specialty stores, impulse items are stolen most frequently. Small quantities of these items are usually taken by amateurs and rarely does a first-time thief take more than one item. The most common places in which merchandise is concealed include a pocket, purse, or shopping bag.

The type of shoplifter that costs retailers the most may well be the *professional* shoplifter. Professional shoplifters operate at different levels of sophistication. At the bottom of the hierarchy are basic diversion groups or individual hard-core shoplifters who steal to make money to buy illegal drugs, such as "crack" or "crank." The next level of professional shoplifter includes diversion groups, which have complicated schemes to divert store employees' attention from the theft activity, and order-buy groups, members of which often wear beepers or use car phones to take "steal-orders" (i.e., orders to steal specific merchandise). This type of professional shoplifter may go through the store and mark targeted goods, such as steaks, cigarettes, and designer jeans, for an accomplice. At the top of the hierarchy of professional shoplifters is the *true professional* whose sole source of income is shoplifting. These individuals are very difficult to detect and, if stopped, are adept at getting released. When stopped they may either create a scene or appear so remorseful that they are not turned in to the police. True professionals steal high-ticket items, such as compact disks, high-quality meats, and expensive clothing. Very often, this merchandise is returned directly to the retailer for a refund. Sometime professionals have insurance quote printers that can precisely duplicate store receipts.

## SHOPLIFTING METHODS

The methods shoplifters use to steal are as varied as the human imagination and the list grows every day. Opportunists usually conceal merchandise in their socks, pockets, purses, or packages. They may also simply wear or carry the item out of the store (known in some regions of the U.S. as hit-n-git or hit-and-run); conceal it in a woman's elastic girdle, put it in elastic pantyhose, socks, spaghetti strainers attached to a bra (which make them appear pregnant), or in a "booster box" or "booster coat" with hooks. Often times, professionals will place the stolen items in a purse or box that is lined with foil, in an attempt to defeat electronic security devices. Many shoplifters switch price tickets on items rather than attempt to steal the goods. Bar coding and price checks help defeat this practice.

Several shoplifting schools and how-to manuals have been discovered by private security and law enforcement authorities in Florida, Texas, and California in recent years. These schools operate out of prisons and hotels, for example, and concentrate on teaching basic theft techniques and ways to spot store security and management. See Appendix 1 for an unedited how-to manual for shoplifters.

## DETECTION OF SHOPLIFTERS

Shoplifters can be detected via physical and behavioral characteristics. By picking up on different types of cue, the trained manager or loss prevention specialist can spot most shoplifters. Physical characteristics of shoplifters include inappropriate dress for the season (including not wearing any shoes), carrying a large open purse while shopping, carrying cash in-hand while shopping to distract attention from their theft activities, and carrying backpacks, plastic garbage bags, large worn shopping bags, and very worn shoes or other clothing that may be switched for new items without paying for them.

Shoplifters tend to give off behavioral clues that indicate their intentions. This is primarily due to the anxiety that builds up and the subsequent release of adrenalin when the decision to steal is made or when suspects feel they may be discovered. Examples of this behavior include quick glances or *scoping* (during which subjects are looking for witnesses to their activity; holding the hands down low to conceal items (rather than holding the hands up like most customers who are studying price, quality and style), moving quickly about the store, holding quick conversations with other suspicious individuals, and shopping quietly right after store opening or right before closing.

## SHOPLIFTING PREVENTION

Every retailer needs a shoplifting prevention program. The best programs are those that are basic and uncomplicated. Physical design, systems (which will be discussed in more detail in Chapter 13—Security Systems), and store personnel are the primary elements of any effective prevention plan. Environmental design and layout of the store and its merchandise is the first place to start in reducing loss. Most stores display their merchandise in ways that are designed to induce customers to buy something. Many times, this practice runs contrary to good security. However, a happy medium between effective merchandise display and good store security can often be reached. Store merchandise can be physically protected by restricting access to it or by restricting its mobility. Display cases, display models, and cable tie-downs are examples of restricting the movement of merchandise. Visibility of merchandise is also very important in deterring theft activity. High-ticket or high-loss items should be easily visible by trained employees. Another effective physical shoplifting prevention method involves the use of electronic (or dye) article tags. The placement of a notification sign, the detection antenna, and the actual EAS tag on merchandise serves as a deterrent to theft. Many shoplifters avoid stores that have EAS systems, security agents, cable tie-downs, or display alarms. Would-be shoplifters often head to other stores that do not employ these theft prevention techniques.

Examples of prevention methods that involve employees include awareness programs, plainclothes agents, and fitting/dressing room control.

### Employee Awareness and Training

Employee awareness is probably the most important method of theft prevention. Ensure that senior management, district management, store management, and store employees are aware of how shoplifters work and know how to stop them. Hold meetings during which employees can learn about current theft and prevention techniques. These meetings should be relatively short in duration (between 45 minutes to an hour) and should highlight basic actions that employees can take to prevent theft. Meetings should be not only informative, but entertaining as well. Upbeat video training kits are available to retailers for this purpose. Examples of appropriate employee participation include providing good customer service, taking time to make price checks, making security announcements over public address systems, and using effective incident-reporting procedures.

### Plainclothes Agents

Retail operations that gross more than $50 million in annual sales may employ some type of in-house loss control specialist. Plainclothes agents are very effective at curbing losses from shoplifters. It is very important that individuals chosen for plainclothes agent positions be thoroughly trained. Figure 5–1 is a sample of the curriculum used to train loss prevention specialists.

Each retail operation should have a complete training course set up for all personnel who are authorized or expected to detect and detain shoplifting suspects. A qualified consultant should be able to recommend the specifics for creating such a training workshop. Another available option is to hire graduates of a high-quality retail/security training course. Also, be aware that there is an interactive computer training simulator on the market that is used to train store detectives. These simulators, when used in conjunction with a comprehensive security curriculum of approximately 100 hours, teach trainees with the complexities of detecting, surveilling, and apprehending shoplifters. The simulators provide the trainers with reports that indicate the trainee's discretionary judgment skills and aggressiveness. Different retail organizations have different titles for these detectives—retail protection specialist, agent, operative, and detective are the most common. It is important to provide quality, documented training; competitive salary and benefits; a suitable title; and senior management support of loss control personnel. This allows the retailer to attract and retain the high-quality personnel needed to implement and run an effective loss prevention program.

In many communities, it is beneficial to the retailer to install and promote a consistent prosecution and civil action plan. When "the word" gets out to neighborhoods and schools that a store has security systems and well-trained

| Day 1 | Day 2 | Day 3 | Day 4 |
|---|---|---|---|
| Intro, to the Retail Industry | Laws that Affect: Our Company, Our Jobs and Our Customers | Shoplifting Detection | Shoplifting Surveillance |
| Intro. to Retail Loss Prevention | Our Policies on External Theft: | Physical Security | Report Writing |
| | | Shoplifting Surveillance | |
| Problems Retailers Face Today | Shoplifting, Refund Fraud, Electronic Article Surveillance | | Review for Quiz 1 |
| Day 5 | Day 6 | Day 7 | Day 8 |
| Shoplifting —apprehension | Processing | Civil Liabilities Bad Stops | EAS Systems |
| —escorting | Report Writing | Case Studies | Employee Theft |
| Employee Awareness | | Decision Making | |
| | | | Courtroom |
| Quiz 1 | | Privileged for Counsel Reports | Testimony |
| Individual Evaluations (PM) | | Final Exam Review | Professionalism Final Exam |
| Day 9 | | Day 10 | |
| Computer Testing | Computer Testing Make-up | | |
| Oral Board | | | |
| Awareness Presentations | Awareness Presenta- tion Make-up | | |
| Emergency Procedures | Oral Board Graduation | | |

**FIGURE 5–1** *Sample training course curriculum*

loss prevention specialists that prosecute and sue shoplifters, if you're caught stealing, the result is usually a drop in shoplifting activity.

Closed-circuit television (CCTV) combines a physical surveillance system with human, loss prevention specialists. CCTV offers an exciting array of possibilities to retailers. These systems can be used to simultaneously detect and deter shoplifters and dishonest employees, deter and record an armed robbery, track customer buying and shopping patterns, activate burglar alarms, and much more. Many departments within a retail chain can benefit from CCTV. Time-lapse recorders and "dummy" systems are also available to retailers, including a new mount that has a visible false lens that can be quickly replaced with a "live" lens. One drawback to using CCTV on shoplifters is the need for two loss prevention specialists—one to observe the subject on CCTV and one to follow and apprehend the suspect. This additional manpower requirement incurs a greater cost than other theft prevention methods.

## Fitting/Dressing Room Control

Many apparel retail stores have fitting/dressing rooms in their stores. These areas provide shoplifters with ideal locations to steal unless some type of control is established. Dressing room control procedures provide retailers with a tremendous opportunity to prevent thefts. A good dressing room control program should ensure that either an employee is assigned to the dressing room area on a full-time basis or that salespeople escort customers to the dressing rooms. Limit the amount of items permitted in a dressing room to eight per person. Provide the customer with a pre-numbered tag that corresponds to the number of items taken into the dressing room. The retailer may also use plastic tags that have a specific number of notches on them that correspond to the number of hangers being taken into the room. Control of these tags is very important. Keep a logbook or post a display board out of the customer's reach to track merchandise flow to and from specific dressing rooms. Be aware that shoplifters may steal #0, #1, or #2 tags for later use. A typical shoplifting scenario at a dressing room may be one in which the subject takes eight garments and a #8 tag into the room. Once inside the room, the subject conceals the #8 tag, hides seven items, and exits with one item and a #1 tag that was previously stolen.

Clerks assigned to the dressing room area can prevent losses while increasing sales. While checking customers into the dressing room, the clerk can make positive comments about the customer's taste in garments and can suggest additional sales. Smart managers put their best sales people in the dressing room area. Clerks in this area are often the first employee the public sees and this is the retailer's chance to make a good impression.

## FIVE STEPS TO FOLLOW PRIOR TO DETAINING A SUSPECT

Many retailers take action against shoplifters in the form of deterring a theft in progress (a "burn") by letting suspected shoplifters know they are being observed or by choosing to apprehend the offender. In either case, retailers need to be familiar with the criminal laws in their state. Two factors tend to create the most problems (in terms of costly law suits) for merchants— unlawful detention and unreasonable detention. Detaining individuals without good reason is a major cause for concern. Although some states have provisions within their specific statutes that allow for shoplifter detentions based on concealment or probable cause, managers or security specialists should follow five simple steps before detaining anyone.

1. Watch the subject approach the merchandise, to eliminate any question about where the merchandise came from.

2. Watch the subject take the merchandise.
3. Watch the subject conceal the merchandise (if he does).
4. Observe the suspect at all times, watching carefully for any signs that the merchandise will be "dumped" or "ditched."
5. Watch the subject pass the last point of sale without paying for the merchandise.

If there is a group of suspects or a potentially violent subject and the decision is made to apprehend, for safety purposes the security specialist may wish to detain the subjects prior to their leaving the premises.

Once you have detained the suspect, obtain statements from witnesses and ring a "no-sale" on area cash registers. This precludes subjects from later claiming that they did, in fact, buy the merchandise.

## WHEN SHOPLIFTING IS SUSPECTED

Most retailers are advised to attempt to get suspects to drop the goods before they leave the premises, rather than attempt an apprehension. There are several ways to recover merchandise, but remember that customers should never be accused of stealing. Retailers should attempt to intimidate subjects enough so that they will ditch the merchandise. Shoplifters avoid eye contact and don't like salespeople waiting on them or working around them. By looking directly and frequently at the subject, while "working" in close proximity, the subject may go and dump the shoplifted items if they're given a little room. Another method to get the suspects to drop the merchandise is to directly confront them without making accusations. Ask "helpful" questions such as, "Can I help you find a shirt to go with those pants?" This confrontation may make the shoplifter nervous. Continue making eye contact and stay close, but give the subjects enough room to ditch their merchandise.

If the shoplifter attempts to leave the store before the first two "bluff" techniques can be employed, a manager should walk quickly and loudly behind the subjects as they approach the exit. Many shoplifters will detour back into the store and dump the merchandise. If you wish to apprehend the suspects at this point, "spook" the suspects before they are so close to the exit, that they are psychologically committed to exiting the store. Many shoplifters would rather risk apprehension than be too obvious in returning to the store. If a shoplifter confronts a store employee, the employee is best advised not to escalate the situation by arguing with a suspect. If all five steps have been followed, an apprehension may be attempted. If these steps have not been followed, the subject should be allowed to move on.

The point of these different techniques is to signal to suspects that a store employee is aware of their activity and is ready to take action. The retailer's ultimate goal is to recover merchandise without accusing a customer of theft.

Retailers should realize that while burns or bluffs often work, they are temporary measures, since many shoplifters return to a store to steal again. This is especially true in the case of true professionals who often steal merchandise in order to obtain cash for illegal drugs.

## APPREHENDING THE SHOPLIFTER

If the decision is made to apprehend a shoplifter (and all five steps have been followed), the manager or security specialist may wish to use some of the following suggestions.

Wait until the suspect passes the last point of sale with the stolen merchandise. While not a requirement in many jurisdictions, this action helps to prove the suspect's intent to steal the merchandise in question. When possible, a second person should accompany the security specialist making the stop and act as a witness and back-up.

Move quickly behind suspects, then step in front of them to impede their direction of travel. *Do not touch the suspect.* If a suspect attempts to strike you or attempts to escape, use *reasonable* force to either defend yourself or detain the suspect.

Identify yourself by saying, "I am a [manager/security specialist] for [company name]. I'd like to talk to you inside the store. Please come with me." At times, suspects may ask why you want them to return to the store. Without making an accusation, simply say, "I want to talk to you about some merchandise that *may* not have been paid for." Never suggest that the suspect "forgot" to pay for the items; this can be used as a defense in court. Don't get into an argument or discussion with suspects at this time. Encourage them to return to the store by saying that you'll discuss everything in the office. This is a good method to recover stolen merchandise in a low-key manner.

Remember the first words of the suspect, especially if they resemble a "confession." Often, a suspect will say, "Can I just pay for it?" This is your assurance that the suspect has the item and may cooperate.

Escort suspects back into the store to a back room or office—some place that provides some privacy. Observe their hands at all times to be certain that they do not dump the items prior to entering the office or pull some kind of weapon. Have suspects carry packages. This will impede their actions and leave you free to deal with any situations that are created.

## DETAINING THE SHOPLIFTER

After the subject has been apprehended, the security specialist must handle the situation in a professional manner. Many states have statutes or laws that allow merchants to detain shoplifting suspects based on probable cause (without making a formal arrest) in order to conduct an investigation to determine if the suspect either took store merchandise without permission or had the intent to steal. Detention and investigation must be conducted in a reasonable manner, for a reasonable length of time, without using excessive force or threats of prosecution to coerce a civil release or confession. If the security specialists determine that a theft took place, they may decide to take criminal and civil action.

Retailers may choose to follow some of the following guidelines when detaining a suspect:

> Once inside the private office, ask the suspects if they know why they have been asked to return to the store. This opens the door for a confession and keeps you from making any accusations.
>
> If the suspects deny knowing why they were asked to return, ask if there is an item that has not been purchased. If the suspects still deny everything, be more specific. Name the exact item and the location of concealment, and ask for the item.
>
> Once the merchandise has been recovered, analyze the suspect. Remove anything that could be used as a weapon (e.g., scissors, a pencil, etc.) from within reach of the suspect. For your protection, you generally have the right to search for weapons (females search females). If the suspect is uncooperative call the police immediately and have them take over the situation. Local police or sheriff's departments can be contacted to demonstrate proper search techniques.
>
> If the suspect is cooperative and you feel safe, begin filling out the incident paperwork. Figures 5–2 and 5–3 are examples of security incident reports. Note that most police agencies prefer to have all paperwork completed prior to their arrival. Any security/safety incident that takes place on company property should be documented and saved for at least 3 years. Incident reports serve as valuable evidence at subsequent criminal or civil trials. They are also very useful for incident projection. By tracking incidents by type, time, and location, trends may become apparent—thereby allowing for better allocation of loss control resources.
>
> It is not required that a security agent read any "rights" to the suspect. Never leave any detainee alone.
>
> Question the shoplifter to recover all merchandise and determine identities of all suspects.
>
> Obtain a confession and pick up any valuable intelligence or information the suspect may have about shoplifting activity in the local area. The practice of interviewing subjects that have been apprehended for shoplifting provides retailers with valuable information when planning loss prevention efforts. Note that many shoplifting suspects will refuse to talk, but those that do often provide information regarding the perception, "on the street," of security at various retailers in the surrounding area. Any

STORE NAME: _____ STORE NUMBER: _____

MANAGER/EMPLOYEE  NAME:  _____

DATE: _____ TIME OF INCIDENT OCCURRENCE: am/pm

OFFENSE (Check One)
Shoplift _____ Employee _____ Other (explain) _____

SUBJECT  NAME: _____

SUBJECT ADDRESS (STREET, CITY, STATE, ZIP):

_____

_____

SUBJECT  PHONE: _____-_____-_____ DRIVERS  LICENSE  #: _____

DATE  OF  BIRTH:  _____/_____/_____  RACE  _____  SEX  _____  AGE  _____

HGT     WGT        HAIR      EYES          SS#

_____  _____  _____  _____  _____

PARENT/GUARDIAN  NAME(S):  _____

PARENT/GUARDIAN  ADDRESS(ES):  _____

EXPLAIN INCIDENT IN DETAIL (WHO, WHAT, WHERE, WHEN) (*include if merchandise was recovered, damaged, saleable, lost, etc.)

_____

_____

_____

_____ (con't on back if necessary)

JUVENILE _____ ADULT _____ ARRESTED _____ NOTICE FORM ISSUED _____

EVIDENCE: TAKEN BY POLICE _____ HELD AT STORE _____ OTHER_____

QTY      ARTICLE NAME/DESCRIPTION          $

_____  _____  _____

_____  _____  _____

_____  _____  _____

THE LISTED ARTICLES HAVE A TOTAL VALUE OF: $ _____

**FIGURE 5–2**  *Sample incident report.*

information gained by the interviewer should be verified, if possible, by another source before being considered absolutely credible.

Ask suspects for a form of identification. Then ask suspects to state their full name, date of birth, and current mailing address. Compare the verbal information with the information printed on the subjects' driver's license or other valid identification.

When the paperwork is nearly finished, call the police (from another room, whenever possible).

Don't make any threats or promises to the suspect, at any time.

If the subject is to be prosecuted, give the responding police officer the original report. Send a copy to the corporate offices, if applicable, and

Confidential

## Subject Information

| Last Name | First Name | Middle Name | Social Security Number | Case File Number |
|---|---|---|---|---|
| | | | | |

| Home Address (City/State/Zip) | Height | Weight | Phone Number |
|---|---|---|---|
| | | | |

| Date of Birth | Age | Gender | Race | I.D. Number (type) | Eye Color | Hair Color | Build | Date of Incident | Employee Date of Hire |
|---|---|---|---|---|---|---|---|---|---|
| | | ☐ Male ☐ Female | | | ☐ Brown ☐ Blue ☐ Other ☐ Green ☐ Hazel | ☐ Brown ☐ Black ☐ Red ☐ Blond ☐ Grey | ☐ Small ☐ Med ☐ Lg | | |

| Last Name | First Name | Middle Name | Social Security Number | Case File Number |
|---|---|---|---|---|
| | | | | |

| Home Address (City/State/Zip) | Height | Weight | Phone Number |
|---|---|---|---|
| | | | |

| Date of Birth | Age | Gender | Race | I.D. Number (type) | Eye Color | Hair Color | Build | Date of Incident | Employee Date of Hire |
|---|---|---|---|---|---|---|---|---|---|
| | | ☐ Male ☐ Female | | | ☐ Brown ☐ Blue ☐ Other ☐ Green ☐ Hazel | ☐ Brown ☐ Black ☐ Red ☐ Blond ☐ Grey | ☐ Small ☐ Med ☐ Lg | | |

## Incident Information

Day of week ____
Location of Incident ____

Cash on Person
1. ____
2. ____

Disposition
☐ Released ☐ Referred ☐ Other

Verify Address
Subject 1 ☐ Yes ☐ No
Subject 2 ☐ Yes ☐ No

Store Location (Address)

Store Number

Release To (If Parent - Juvenile Form Attached)
☐ Police Department ☐ Store ☐ Self ☐ Other

☐ / If Police Dept. Officer's Name and I.D. Number Below

Type of Incident
☐ Shoplifter ☐ Employee ☐ Known Theft
☐ Burglary ☐ Robbery ☐ Violation of Policy
☐ Other ____

Location/Time Subject First

Evidence Held By:
☐ Police Department ☐ Parent ☐ Returned to Stock ☐ Photograph

Police Dept. Case Number

Time Subject Brought to LP Office | Time Police Dept. Was Notified | Time Police Arrived at LP Office | Time Subject Out of Office | Place/Time Detained

## Court Information

| Court Date | Representative | Disposition | Court Date | Representative | Disposition | Court Date |
|---|---|---|---|---|---|---|
| | | | | | | |

Observed by (LP Person Handling Case

Witness to Incident
1. ____ 2. ____

**Subject Brief**

1. Theft method used? ____
2. Other methods known? ____
3. Why choose this store? ____
4. Other suspects known? ____
5. Word about this store? ____
6. Word about other stores? ____
7. What would deter? ____
8. What wouldn't deter? ____
9. Willing to become C.I.? ☐ yes ☐ no
10. Additional Info: ____

## Acknowledgement Information

I ____________, residing at ____________, do voluntarily and without threats, force, fear or promises of any kind, admit and declare that on the ______ day of ____________ 19____, I took from ____________ at ____________ without making payment for the merchandise and with the intent to use the merchandise for my own purpose. I know or had cause to know that the merchandise was the personal property of ____________ and can be described in the evidence section below.

Witness ____ Signature ____

Witness ____ Date ____

## Evidence Information

Photographer ____ Officer ____

| Dept # | Sku Number | Description | Units | Unit Price | Total |
|---|---|---|---|---|---|
| | | | | | |
| | | | | | |
| | | | | | |
| | | | | | |
| | | | | | |
| | | | | | |
| | | | | | |
| | | | | | |
| | | | | | |
| | | | | | |
| | | | | | |
| | | | | | |

Notary Seal

State of ____
County of ____
The forgoing instrument was acknowledged before me this ______ day of ______, 19____, by ____

Notary Public state of ____
at large.
My commision expires____.

| Dollar Amount | Cash | Merchandise | Total |
|---|---|---|---|
| Recovery at Incident | | | |
| Admission Over Above | | | |
| Total Loss | | | |
| Recovery at Incident | | | |
| Other Recovery | | | |
| Total Recovery | | | |

**FIGURE 5–3** *Loss prevention report.*

keep a copy in a *locked* file cabinet at the store. Record the case number, the name of the company employee who made the apprehension, and the police officer's name on the incident report.

Only detain the suspect for a reasonable length of time (1 hour is the average).

Grant any *reasonable* requests such as certain medications, bathroom privileges, or a drink of water. Use caution when granting requests for medication and trips to the bathroom.

If suspects say they are ill or need assistance of any kind, provide it immediately. Don't assume that it's a phony complaint.

After the police officer arrives, mark the evidence and seal it in a bag. Staple a copy of the incident report to the outside of the bag. Place the evidence in a locker (access to this locker must be limited to management and security) and do not disturb it until it is requested in court. Some states, or jurisdictions within states, allow retailers to photograph merchandise and require only a photograph during trial, thereby allowing the merchandise to be sold. A check with local prosecuting attorneys will provide the proper procedure to follow.

## CIVIL ACTION

If it is decided to pursue civil action under the more than 40 state civil demand statutes, the following guidelines are suggested.

Fill out a report to take civil action against the person who was detained and only when the security specialist can prove that the subject did take cash or merchandise without proper permission and that the subject intended to deprive the company of the full value of the cash or merchandise.

Avoid civil action against individuals who may be unable to form criminal intent, such as juveniles under the age of 10, indigent and aged /elderly persons or those under the care of a physician for emotional disorders.

Make every attempt to properly identify the subjects that committed the theft. Ask for two forms of identification. If the suspect is a juvenile, get both parents' names.

Obtain a current mailing address, including city and zip code, and a current phone number.

Avoid the appearance of extortion by not accepting payments at the point of apprehension or by threatening subjects with criminal prosecution if they fail to satisfy your demands.

Ensure that the incident report includes full name, driver's license number or state-issued identification number, current and complete mailing address, and a short narrative describing the incident.

Send a legible copy of the incident report to the civil recovery firm or to other appropriate individuals or groups.

What if a customer is detained in error? Not only is this an awkward and embarrassing situation, but it could lead to legal action by the angry customer. Security specialists and other store employees can take the following steps to avoid liability claims.

Make an apologetic statement such as "Thank you for your time; we apologize for any inconvenience you've experienced."

Be sincere. Stay calm. Be friendly, helpful, and courteous.

If a customer appears hostile, antagonistic, or outraged, politely excuse yourself and withdraw from the scene immediately. Indicate to the customer that you will summon the store manager.

Make absolutely no commitment to the customer, and above all, *never* admit liability.

Discuss the incident with no one except the Director of the Loss Prevention Department, the Director of the store, the Risk Management Department, representatives of the company's insurance brokers, and the company's insurance carriers and law firm.

If an immediate response is needed by the customer, get the store manager and have her inform the detainee that someone from the central office will contact him as soon as possible.

If possible, politely obtain the name and address of the customer. *Do not insist.* Obtain reports from employee witnesses and forward all documentation to the Risk Management Department as soon as possible.

## NOTE

1.  Ernst and Young, *An Ounce of Prevention* (New York: Chain Store, 1990), 5.

# Chapter 6

# Point-of-Sale Risks

There is no other place that a retailer is more vulnerable to theft than at the point of sale. Whenever a minimum wage, poorly trained, and unmotivated register clerk goes head-to-head with a determined and experienced thief, the odds are good that the store will incur a loss of some type. Bad checks, credit card fraud, currency switches, counterfeit bill-passing, quick-change scams, price tag switches, container switches, and refund and exchange fraud afflict all retailers to some degree.

## BAD CHECKS

Bad checks cost retailers billions of dollars in lost revenues annually and the problem does not appear to be diminishing. Offenders range from "good" customers to professionals that move from region to region across the United States passing hundreds of thousands of dollars in "bad paper."

The most frequent type of check fraud is NSF or insufficient funds. This occurs when customers issue checks, either intentionally or unintentionally, without the funds in their account to cover the checks. Writing checks on an account known to be closed is another bad-check scheme. In many states, this ation is *prima facie* evidence of the intent to defraud the merchant. If the account is not closed, the bank's written reason for not honoring the check may constitute *prima facie* evidence of knowledge of insufficient funds and, therefore, intent to defraud.

Checks that have been completely falsified or fabricated are another method of passing bad checks. In many cases, individuals may steal unused checks and fill them out to benefit themselves. Another variation of this type of crime involves stealing issued checks and altering the payee name and, often, the payment amount. The following actions can control check losses:

> Track bad check incidents by store and authorize clerks to determine significant trends. Often times, a small percentage of stores and a small percentage of a store's cashiers will accept the majority of a company's bad checks.

Be wary of checks for more than $100 being cashed or used prior to a holiday or weekend. *Paper hangers,* as bad-check passers are commonly known, realize that it will take several days for banks to notify the retailer of a problem.

Insist on proper identification. Checks should be imprinted with the customer's name and address, and the customer should have a valid driver's license or state identification signed and with a recent photograph. Merchants should be aware that if stolen checks are being used, credit cards, Social Security cards, and other forms of identification may also be stolen property.

Examine all checks. Insist that checks be written and signed in front of the clerk. Signs of worthless checks include: check that contain oddly shaped, possibly altered, numerals; variations in ink color or thickness of lines or letters; erasures and obscured sections; unusual spacing; ink that appears to have been traced over pencil; and endorsement signatures that differ from the signature on a valid ID.

Watch for signatures that appear "out of character" for the individual cashing the check. This is very subjective, but when in doubt, the subjects should be asked to sign their name again in front of the clerk.

Use on-line check-clearing services, if possible. They are valuable for screening checks, particularly in large operations. One service that is currently available will take responsibility for bad checks that were accepted, provided their screening procedures were precisely followed. Other services allow for quick screening by comparing the check's account number and checkholders name against an updated list of overdrawn accounts or known, worthless-check passers.

Beware of individuals who take extreme caution and a lot of time to sign their names, and who attempt to distract the clerk while they sign the check or when the clerk is examining the check.

Verify certified checks. Checks that indicate that their validity has been certified by the bank can be forged.

Examine traveler's checks. Check fraud artists know that merchants believe that even stolen traveler's checks will be redeemed by the issuing companies. Major traveler's check companies will honor stolen traveler's checks that have been unknowingly accepted by a merchant. However, if the endorsement of the stolen check does not closely resemble the authorized signature, the check issuer may refuse to redeem the check.

Do not accept traveler's checks that have been endorsed in advance. Ask customers to sign their name again.

Request that checks be made out with the proper date of purchase.

Do not accept second-party checks.

Set reasonable dollar limits on checks, based on the average purchase price for the business.

Don't accept post-dated checks.

Consider charging customers $1 for each check cashed. Generated funds help cover losses incurred from bad checks.

If a check is accepted that has been written against insufficient funds, send the issuer a notice by registered mail. Ensure that the notice contains a copy of the bad check, along with a notice from the state authorities. If the notice brings no response, follow up with a phone call. The retailers may file for prosecution with the local police or prosecuting attorney. However, unless the check is felony-level or part of a suspected bad check-passing ring, the authorities may be reluctant to pursue the issue. Note that it is possible to take civil action in the form of a written demand or small claims court. Another option is to use a collection agency.

Bad checks can be controlled by alert cashiers and store management. By at least eliminating the obvious bad checks, a significant part of the problem disappears.

## CREDIT CARD FRAUD

With the more than 600,000,000 credit cards in circulation throughout the United States, it is easy to see the opportunity for credit card fraud. The committee on Bank and Finance of the U.S. Congress reported that 73,000,000 credit cards are lost or stolen annually.[1]

Some common forms of credit card fraud include

- retail employees using a card left by a customer or using a customer's card number to make unauthorized purchases
- a dishonest merchant working with a counterfeiter who imprints phony sales receipts using plain cards embossed with real account numbers and submits them, along with legitimate receipts, to card companies for payment
- ironing card numbers flat and restamping new numbers
- using stolen credit cards to make purchases

Cashiers should be trained to look for the following signs that indicate a credit card fraud in progress.

- altered, expired, or not-yet-valid credit cards
- signatures that do not match the card or the sales slip
- cards that do not register imprints on carbon copies
- customers who make numerous, small credit card purchases under the amount for which an authorization call must be placed to the card issuer
- impatient applicants for department store credit cards who use impressive names or titles to try to hasten the approval process.

Credit card companies are using new technology to foil most counterfeiters, such as holographs, ultraviolet inks, bank identification numbers that are micro-imprinted in magnetic strips, and fine-line printing. Also, with new (POS) systems, retailers can instantly identify customers and determine available credit balances. Retailers who don't have these systems, should call the issuing bank for verbal verification.

The following actions may prevent credit card fraud:

Use electronic authorization terminals, call credit card issuers for authorization on all card purchases, or conduct random authorization checks on small purchases.

Require a valid photo ID for acceptance of credit card purchases.

Copy the name, address, and phone number of the credit card customer from the photo ID and then ask the authorization center to verify that information.

Keep a list of local bank telephone numbers near each cash register and check local card bank identification numbers (BINs) with the issuing bank to verify credit availability. After banking hours, call telephone directory assistance. Although they will not *provide* addresses, they will *verify* addresses given by questionable credit card users.

Check carbon copies to be certain that clear imprints have been made. The carbon paper, which also contains the imprint of the credit card number, should be destroyed, or merchants should use carbonless receipts or perforated carbons that split after use.

Guard proprietary credit cards from theft.

Credit cards are the property of the issuing companies. Those individuals who legally carry and use credit cards do so with the permission and authorization of the issuer. A credit card company will instruct a merchant who is presented with a card that is being used in an unauthorized manner to refuse to allow the purchase and, often, will further authorize the merchant to confiscate the card. Most issuing institutions emphasize the importance of attempting to retain the card and thus prevent its further illegal use. However, they also caution that an effort should be made to confiscate a card only if it seems reasonably safe to do so. If not, try to discreetly copy the card's account, BINs, and any other pertinent information (e.g., the suspect's name, address, driver's license number) before returning the card.

Police authorities recommend that a merchant stall an individual suspected of using a stolen or counterfeit card for as long as possible without resorting to physical detention. While the suspect is "waiting for verification of the card," inconspicuously telephone the police. If the suspect insists on leaving before the police arrive, try to get a license number and description of the suspect's vehicle. A detailed description of the suspect and any companions, and an indication of the direction taken by the suspects are helpful to police.

While credit card fraud is a federal crime and violators can and should be prosecuted, merchants who suffer losses by not following verification procedures may have difficulty recovering lost funds. Some credit card issuers may agree to reimburse some initial losses, but businesses that frequently bypass the transaction verification procedure may be forced to cover their own loss. Like bad check incidents, credit card frauds should be documented. Trends may develop that will focus theft awareness campaigns.

## COUNTERFEIT CURRENCY

Counterfeiting of currency is one of the oldest crimes in history. It was a serious problem in the early history of the United States, when banks issued their own currency. At that time, there were approximately 1600 state banks that were designing and printing their own notes. Each note carried a different design, making it difficult to distinguish the 4000 varieties of counterfeits from the 7000 varieties of genuine notes. It was hoped that the adoption of national currency in 1863 would solve the counterfeiting problem. However, the national currency was soon counterfeited so extensively it became necessary for the government to take enforcement measures. Therefore, on July 5, 1865, the United States Secret Service was established to suppress counterfeiting.

There are three types or classes of U.S. paper currency in circulation. The name of each class appears on the upper face of the bill. The different classes of bills are further identified by the color of their treasury seal and their serial numbers.

| CLASS | COLOR OF TREASURY SEAL AND SERIAL NUMBER | DENOMINATION |
|---|---|---|
| Federal Reserve Notes | Green | $1, $2, $5, $10 $20, $50, and $100 |
| United States Notes | Red | $2, $5, and $100 |
| Silver Certificates | Blue | $1, $5, and $10 |

The best method of detecting a counterfeit bill is to compare the suspect note with a genuine bill of the same denomination and series. Pay particular attention to the quality of the printing and the paper's characteristics. Look for differences, not similarities.

Examine the tiny red and blue fibers imbedded in the paper of a genuine note. It is illegal to reproduce this distinctive paper. Often, counterfeiters try to simulate these fibers by printing tiny red and blue lines on their paper. Close inspection reveals, however, that on a counterfeit bill the lines are printed on the surface, not imbedded in the paper.

Notice the workmanship of the note's design. Genuine money is made by the government's master craftsmen using expensive steel engraving and printing equipment designed for that purpose. Most counterfeiters use a photomechanical, or "offset," method to make a printing plate from a photograph of a genuine note. The resulting product looks flat and lacks fine detail.

Also, look closely at the lines in the portrait background—they form squares. On counterfeit bills, some of these squares may be filled in and many of the delicate lines in the portrait may be broken or missing.

The belief that a bill must be counterfeit if the ink rubs off is not accurate. Genuine currency, when rubbed on paper, can leave ink smears.

## CURRENCY SWITCH

Another form of counterfeiting is called the currency switch. Subjects will usually attempt to pay for a purchase with a bill that has been altered to appear to be a higher denomination. In a typical scenario, subjects will hand over a $20 bill that is actually a $1 bill. The subject takes a number of $20 bills and clips the numerical value from one corner of each bill. (Mutilated bills with three corners are still negotiable.) The clipped corners are then pasted over the corners of the $1 bill and the edges are sanded to blend color and texture. In some locales, this currency is known as *raised currency*.

Train cashiers to examine bills quickly for counterfeits. A quick look at the appearance and feel of the corners or presidential portraits of high-denomination bills should be sufficient to quickly detect a counterfeit bill.

## CONTAINER SWITCH

In a container switch, the subject removes the contents from a ticketed container and refills the container with a similar but higher priced, item. Designer underwear, for example, may be removed from its plastic tube and placed in a tube that originally contained a less expensive pair. The subject may also add more items to the container.

Grocery stores that allow customers to bag their own groceries experience customers concealing expensive produce in bags of less costly items.

Retailers should ensure that product containers are tightly sealed. Containers with broken seals, that are presented for purchase, should be opened and their contents examined in an inoffensive manner. In grocery stores, make cashiers aware of the container switch and ensure that they can identify different types of produce. Retailers should use transparent plastic bags to expose high-loss items. Instruct cashiers to shake and check bags to be certain that other tiems haven't been mixed in with less costly merchandise.


## PRICE SWITCH

Adhesive-backed price tags came into widespread use in the 1950s and price tag switches became a very common crime. Subjects peel price tags off merchandise and replace them with lower priced tags. In grocery stores, subjects switch the ticketed lids of containers of similar products. For example, the plastic top of an expensive can of coffee may be exchanged for the top from a less expensive can before the item is brought to the cashier.

The increasing use of UPC bar codes stamped directly on product packages is the most effective deterrent to price tag switching. In stores where price tags are still used, managers should ensure that the tags are affixed so that only the cashier can remove them or so that the tags are destroyed upon removal. On clothing, for example, garment tags affixed with plastic loops can be removed only by breaking the loop, and once the loop is broken the tags cannot be reattached easily. Adhesive-backed labels are available that rip when they are removed and consequently cannot be reused for merchandise labeling.

The use of electronic cash terminals hooked up to a central computer that contains current price information filed under stock numbers, called *price look-up,* is very effective if mark-downs are recorded properly. Provide cashiers with current lists of sale items and ensure they become familiar with item prices and call for price checks when in doubt.


## REFUND FRAUD

The following are examples of customer refund and exchange fraud.

Merchandise is shoplifted and then returned for a refund or exchange. The subject may or may not leave the store.

A shoplifter collects discarded sales receipts, "lifts" items priced at the amounts shown on the salvaged receipts, and then returns the items, with receipts, for refund.

An article is purchased by check; the customer stops payment on the check and, before the check bounces, returns the article for a refund.

Merchandise that was broken or damaged by a customer is repackaged and returned for exchange, refund, or credit.

An item purchased at one store is returned for credit to another store that sells the same item at a higher price.

Most stores offer three basic options—refund, exchange, and credit—as an important part of their customer service policy. Every retailer should establish a return policy that finds a balance between a no-return policy and an anything-goes policy. Policies should be simple, understandable, consistent, and posted in a prominent location, such as over the cash register area. Sales receipts should carry a printed explanation of the store's refund/exchange policy. In some states and localities, consumer protection laws specify the acceptable manner of posting the merchants' refund and exchange policies.

Return policies should stipulate that the customer must have a cash register or credit card receipt as proof of purchase to return merchandise.

Many stores mandate that the refund of high-priced merchandise be credited to the customer's charge account or sent via a refund check to the customer's home address.

There have been numerous cases of criminals purchasing bulk shipments of damaged or defective goods at a fraction of retail costs and then returning the items for credit or exchanging them for non-defective products. Exchange policies should cover only merchandise that is in a condition to be resold or that contains defects for which the customer cannot be held responsible, and should require, at minimum, a sales receipt, cash register receipt, canceled check, or other proof of purchase.

Returns for credit should require that merchandise be returned within a specified time period. Subjects may purchase bulk quantities of out-of-date or no longer stylish items at greatly reduced prices and return them for credit or refund.

## QUICK-CHANGE SCHEMES

Quick-change artists are well versed in the art of fast talking. Con artists will bring a small purchase to the cashier and offer to pay for it with a high-denomination bill. As the cashier hands over the proper change, subjects "discover" that they have a smaller denomination bill and withdraw the large bill. With their hands already on the change, the customer attempts, through a rapid exchange of money, to confuse the cashier into believing that the correct amount of money has changed hands. Con artists usually end up walking away with all of the change from the small bill plus all or part of the change issued for the larger bill. An alert cashier, who understands the importance of taking time and not becoming rattled when money is being transacted, is the best defense against quick change artists.

Place the cash register out of the reach of customers so that subjects cannot "assist" the cashier in making change. When cashiers ring up a sale, they should take bills from customers and place them on a safe, but open, spot away from the open cash drawer. The customer's money should not be immediately placed in the cash drawer.

The cashier should count the change at least twice, once to herself and a second time to the customer. If a customer attempts to exchange a smaller bill for the original large bill, the cashier should retrieve the change she was about to give the customer, return it to the cash register, and start over by making change for the new bill. Do not mix the customer's and cash register's money until the sale has been completed.

If cashiers become confused, they should close the cash drawer immediately and call for the store manager to assist in the transaction. Speed and confusion are quick-change artists' allies—when complications develop, they will usually abandon the scam.

## NOTE

1. Virginia Shomp, *How To Protect Your Business* (Elmsford: The Benjamin Co., 1985), 110.

# Chapter 7

# Miscellaneous Risks

Employee theft and error, shoplifting, and vendor theft account for the majority of losses retailers experience annually. However, there are other damaging miscellaneous risks for which a company should prepare.

## ROBBERY

Crimes against retail businesses are increasing annually. Violent crimes, such as robbery, can cost the merchant not only financial loss, but also loss of life. By definition, robbery is a violent crime—that uses force or threatens the use of force while committing the crime. Stores are known (by potential robbers) to have cash on hand and have inadequate security. These factors make the stores very vulnerable to theft, especially isolated stores like convenience stores and small stores at gas stations. Retail robbery targets include cash registers, cash rooms, and cash deposit runs. Loss of life or serious injury can result from any robbery and retailers should keep this in mind whenever confronted with a robbery situation. Criminals may use scissors, knives, or guns during robberies and it is rare for a store employee to be able to determine if threats are real or bluffs. Robbers are unpredictable and almost anything can happen.

The three primary types of robbers are professionals, semi-professionals, and amateurs. Retail stores are rarely "hit" by true professionals, since the volume of ready cash is not as high as in many banks. Professionals are often given assignments by organized crime groups and will frequently flee rather than use force. Semi-professionals plan their own crimes, to a certain extent, but the sophistication and timing doesn't compare with professional "jobs." The chance of violence is greater with semi-professionals and this possibility is enhanced by the fact that robberies seldom go as planned. Incidents such as a robbery taking longer to accomplish than planned, victims not complying with robbers' requests, and little or no money on hand can cause the robbers to lose their composure and act unpredictably.

Amateur robbers, such as local juveniles or addicts, are prone to rob area stores even if the stores are not known to carry a lot of cash. Amateurs are very dangerous, since their crimes are poorly planned and are often based on crimes enacted on television. A weapon is generally used by the amateur robber. If amateurs feel that they are losing control at any time, they can become violent. Be aware that most amateurs are not proficient in the use of weapons or in defeating security measures.

Each of these types of robbers may have differing skill levels, but all of them use the same basic method to commit a robbery. Robbers will survey the store and wait until all customers leave before attempting the robbery. They then quickly enter the premises, make the confrontation, grab the money, and flee.

Retailers should determine their vulnerability to robbery and train store employees in proper reaction techniques. Before attempting the crime, robbers normally conceal their weapons and survey the location for police or security. Both of these actions are tip-offs to observant employees that a robbery may be about to take place. By contacting the local police or sheriff's department for uniform crime statitistcs and current robbery trends, and by reading the local paper, any merchant can keep up with robbery trends and methods being used to commit robberies.

Robbery prevention involves a combination of training and security hardware. By determining local trends and the stores' high-risk areas, an effective prevention plan can be designed and implemented. Systems that have proven effective in reducing the number of robberies that occur in a given store include CCTV, cash storage or cache devices, and metal detectors. CCTV may help deter some robberies and may be used as evidence to convict arrested robbers. However, as "dummy" cameras become common place, robbers pay less attention to this type of deterrent system. The most effective robbery deterrents are to reduce the amount of cash on hand and increase the visibility of clerk areas. A new CCTV system supports live, two-way video and audio between the store and a central monitoring location. This type of system may have a deterrent effect on robbery, shoplifting, and employee theft. The following are some suggested robbery prevention methods:

Be totally unpredictable in regard to taking cash to the bank for deposit. Routes, times, methods of money concealment, and deposit personnel should be changed constantly.

Train and retrain all employees in robbery reaction procedures. Keeping clerks alive is the priority issue when faced with a robbery.

Keep safes and money boxes locked (not on "day lock"), except when in use.

Keep the amount of cash in cash registers and safes to a minimum— under $75 is recommended.

Never handle or display cash in public view.

Keep all access doors to cash areas locked and unmarked, and include a peephole for identification purposes.

Use "bait" money, or numbered bills, to assist in robber apprehension.

Advise employees not to wear expensive jewelry to work.

Never reopen the store for anyone after closing, regardless of their innocent appearance.

Test all alarms monthly.

If you are working alone, keep a TV or radio playing in the back room to give the impression that others are present.

If a robbery does take place, there are certain actions that an employee can take.

*Remain as calm as possible.*
Try not to stare at the robbers or their weapons.

*Obey any commands given to you.*
Move smoothly and keep your hands in plain sight. Talk in a slow, polite manner.

*Never argue or play games* with the robbers.

*When it is safe, activate your burglary alarm.* Do not attempt to activate any alarms while the robber is present.

Inform the robber of any problems or surprises. If someone may enter the area, let the robber know this may happen.

*Give the robber time to leave the area.*

*In the event* that shooting starts, drop to the floor and seek cover. If a hostage situation occurs, do as you are told and try to observe and listen. Be calm and cooperative.

After a robbery takes place, the following procedures are suggested:

Check for any injuries and call for medical assistance if needed.

Ask all witnesses to stay in the area until the police arrive.

Determine the robbers method of operation, habits, speech, any robbery techniques.

Identify property that was taken.

Prepare a physical description of the robbers, such as height, weight, age, race, sex, hair and eye color, scars or facial hair, speech problems, etc.

Describe any get-away vehicles by their color, year, make, model, damage, and license plate number.

Don't allow others into the area until the police arrive.

Do not discuss the robbery with other witnesses until the police question them.

Do not touch areas the robbers may have touched.

Cooperate fully with the police investigation.

Do not exaggerate or estimate anything; give factual information.

Evaluate the crime and take preventive measures against future similar incidents.


## BURGLARY

Every retailer is vulnerable to some form of burglary. The most common types of burglaries include stay-behinds, smash-and-grabs, drive-offs, and break-ins.

There are a variety of measures that retailers can take to prevent burglaries. Check offices, store rooms, rest rooms, closets, dressing rooms, and display fixtures for individuals who are attempting to remain in the store after it closes. Due to fire regulations, most stores have fire doors that have "panic alarm" locks on the inside. These doors are used for an easy escape after selected merchandise and cash are bagged for removal. Some states allow these doors to be locked after closing. Equip the store burglary alarm with motion-detection sensors, such as passive infrared, which detects movement in and out of its sensor field, and ultrasonic sensors, which sense movement by the contraction or disruption of the microwaves emitted by the sensor.

In smash-and-grab burglaries, robbers either smash display windows and glass doors with bricks or other objects, or drive their vehicles through glass windows and doors. The thieves then grab the merchandise and rush to their get-away vehicle. Very strong glass film or glazing and metallic coverings for windows can prevent this type of crime.

No retailer that sells gasoline can escape the inevitable drive-off. Many convenience chains report multi-million dollar losses for this type of burglary. Requiring patrons to pay prior to pumping their gas and providing for good visibility of the pump area are means of deterring this type of crime.

A break-in burglary occurs when robbers enter either by force or with keys. In the case of a forced entry, doors, windows, and vents or hatches in roofs are favored as entry points. To prevent burglars from using company keys to gain entry, all keys should be carefully controlled and locks changed when employees with access to keys leave the company. If the retailer's alarm system requires the employee to enter a personal code in order to enter the premises, it is recommended that a district manager or loss control manager track store openings and closings, and follow up on irregularities.

Burglars can be categorized in general terms. Professionals carefully select their targets, case the building, study store routines, and plan the burglary. Professional burglars often create diversions to tie up police patrols and monitor police scanners to listen for police calls. This type of burglar seldom attacks retailers unless the retailer is carrying a large quantity of cash or valuable merchandise.

Semi-professional burglars are, generally, criminals that float between robbery, burglary, shoplifting, and drug-dealing. Unfortunately, when police agencies close down on the individuals who sell stolen goods ("fences"), semi-professional burglars turn to more violent crimes, such as robbery.

Semi-professional and amateur burglars may be local thieves that have conducted some surveillance and planning before burglarizing the retail location. Store employees may see these individuals loitering in the area prior to the burglary taking place.

Good burglary prevention starts with installing security equipment outside the store, then focuses prevention techniques on high-risk areas.

Ensure that the front doors are clear and made of break-resistant glass or polymer that has been coated with a window-glazing film.

Use high-quality door locks that are "pick-resistant" and have interchangeable cores.

If fire regulations permit, use double cylinder locks that require keys to open the lock from two sides.

Locate pin hinges on the inside of the door and anchor them so the doors cannot be lifted out or forced in.

Wire the doors to the perimeter burglar alarm system.

The following burglary prevention techniques are also recommended:

Remove attractive merchandise from display windows after the store is closed.

Install windows that are of the same break-resistant quality as the doors and wire them to the alarm system. Glass-breakage sensors can be used, but may be defeated if the burglar tapes the glass before breaking it.

Ensure that the interior of the store is visible from the parking lot, so that police or passersby can detect unauthorized individuals moving about the store. Keep signs or displays that block this visibility to a minimum.

Ensure that the store address is displayed prominently to allow police to quickly locate the business in an emergency.

Ensure that parking areas and the perimeter of the building is well-lighted to discourage individuals from loitering in the area.

Equip each location with a burglar alarm system. The perimeter alarm should cover all doors, windows, and roof hatches. The interior alarm network should contain motion-detection sensors in likely movement and high-risk areas. The safe should also be equipped with a proximity sensor.

Check the alarm system monthly.

Ensure that the alarm system is monitored either by an outside firm or by the retailer.

Place high-grade bars on all vents and skylights to prevent surreptitious removal and entry.

Keep some lights on after closing to highlight movement inside the store.

Secure high-risk merchandise, such as jewelry, cigarettes, steaks, liquor, and furs, in cases and safes for additional protection.

Remove all cash from registers at night and leave the drawers open to prevent the burglar from damaging them.

Mark all office equipment and computers with identification numbers. Secure all high-cost items.

If computer data or sensitive files are kept at a retail location, secure original copies of the data, make back-up copies, and store them off-site.

If a burglary occurs, the following actions are recommended:

Evaluate the situation before entering the premises. If you know or suspect that there are burglars still in the building wait in a safe place until the police arrive. Let them search the building.

Do not touch or alter anything that could be valuable evidence.

After the initial police report is made, provide the police with a list of missing merchandise and money that is as complete as possible.

Report any suspicious incidents or persons that could be linked to the crime.

Do not immediately release the suspected dollar amount or loss until a follow-up report is given, so that the media doesn't release this information.

Notify company management of the situation as soon as possible and report the current status of the store in regard to whether or not it can open for business.

Get competitive bids on repair work and take photos of any damage for insurance purposes.

Critique the reasons for the crime and make prevention recommendations.

Burglaries create a serious drain on company profits and disrupt morale and the flow of business. Prevention and quick response are the keys to reducing adverse impact from this type of crime.

## BOMB THREATS

While the probability of receiving a legitimate bomb threat is relatively low, the retailer should still plan for this type of incident. There are two objectives to reporting to company employees or authorities that a bomb is going to detonate in a place of business.

1. The caller has reason to believe an explosive device will detonate and wants to minimize injury and damage.
2. The caller wants to disrupt normal activities by creating an atmosphere of anxiety and panic.

Prior to receiving a bomb threat, the retailer must ensure that clear-cut levels of authority are established and notification phone numbers are distributed with simple instructions to all facilities (see Figure 7–1).

The most important of all decisions to be made by management in the event of a bomb threat is whether or not to evacuate the building. Management policy may be to either immediately evacuate or to evaluate the threat to avoid costly shut-downs and possible panic situations. Management's first concern must be the safety of its customers and employees.

---

### SAMPLE BOMB THREAT INSTRUCTIONS*

Notify the Store Manager immediately of any bomb threat. In his absence, notify the Assistant Manager. Upon receiving a call, the person answering the phone must attempt to complete the Bomb Threat Checklist.

I.   Have the designated employee make the following calls:
    A.   Call the local law enforcement agency. Advise police that a bomb threat has been made and ask for their recommendation. Have the Bomb Threat Checklist with you to help answer any questions they may ask.

    FOLLOW THE INSTRUCTIONS GIVEN BY THE LAW ENFORCEMENT AGENCY!!!

    If it is necessary to evacuate the building, refer to the Evacuation Instructions.

    B.   Notify central office personnel:    OFFICE #      HOME #
       1.   District Manager         _____   _____

       2.   Vice President of Operations   _____   _____
    C.   Send a written report to the Vice President of Operations and to the District Manager after the condition is controlled. Include a copy of the bomb threat checklist.
II.  Let the responding officers or other experts supervise the inspection and removal of any suspicious packages or materials.

---

*Check with local authorities before implementing a program.

---

**FIGURE 7–1.** *Sample bomb threat instructions.*

The following are some guidelines to follow when preparing for and when facing a bomb threat.

Contact police agencies for further information on preparing a bomb threat reaction plan.

Establish strict procedures for control and inspection of suspicious packages.

Identify and control access of personnel entering critical areas.

Have local authorities point out vulnerable areas.

Ensure all employees are alert to unfamiliar or suspicious persons or objects.

Instruct personnel answering company telephones in the procedures for handling bomb threat calls. Provide a bomb threat checklist at each telephone answering area (see Figure 7–2).

Ask the caller where the device is located and when the bomb will detonate. Tell the caller the building is occupied and that death or serious injury could result from detonation.

Keep the caller on the line as long as possible.

If possible, have a second person listen to the call.

Note peculiar background noises such as music, aircraft, etc.

Listen carefully to the caller's voice for clues such as sex, age, accents, etc.

Remember, when searching for bombs, the rule of thumb is "move people away from a bomb," not "move the bomb away from people." For further information on this topic, contact local authorities.

## COUPON FRAUD

Increasingly, retailers are issuing discounts or special coupons for promotions. This is in addition to an increase in the use of vendor coupons, particularly in grocery stores. As a result of this increase in coupon usage, the incidents of fraud and theft are also on the increase. Coupons are usually redeemed for cash or cash equivalency. If blocks of coupons are credited against purchases that never occur (misredemption) or are counterfeited, the result to the retailer can be thousands of dollars in lost revenue. Additionally, the promotion doesn't stimulate the intended buying activity of targeted customers.

Generally, a coupon is a written offer of a discounted or free product. Legitimate coupons contain the terms of the offer and inform retailers that the issuer of the coupon will reimburse them for its face value. The issued coupon may be redeemed by the consumer from the retailer selling that prod-

## BOMB THREAT CHECKLIST FOR
## TELEPHONE OPERATORS

Instructions:

Pretend you are having difficulty hearing the caller. Keep the caller talking. Inform the caller that the building is occupied and that detonation could cause injury or even death. *Be calm and courteous. Listen. Do not interrupt the caller except to ask the following questions:*

1. WHEN WILL THE BOMB GO OFF? _____
2. AT WHAT HOUR? _____
3. HOW MUCH TIME IS REMAINING? _____
4. WHERE IS THE BOMB PLANTED? BUILDING _____ AREA _____ FLOOR _____
5. WHAT DOES THE BOMB LOOK LIKE? _____
6. WHAT KIND OF BOMB? HOMEMADE _____ CHEMICAL _____ FIREBOMB _____
   EXPLOSIVE _____ OTHER _____
7. HOW DO YOU KNOW SO MUCH ABOUT THE BOMB? _____
8. WHY US? _____
9. WHERE ARE YOU NOW? _____
10. WHAT IS YOUR NAME AND ADDRESS? _____

Leave the phone off the hook even if caller hangs up.

DID THE CALLER APPEAR FAMILIAR WITH THE BUILDING BY HIS DESCRIPTION OF THE BOMB LOCATION?

OPERATOR NAME _____ EXACT TIME OF CALL _____ DATE _____

CALLER'S IDENTITY:
MALE _____ FEMALE _____ ADULT _____ JUVENILE _____ APPROX. AGE _____

ORIGIN OF CALL:
LOCAL _____ LONG-DISTANCE _____ BOOTH _____ INTERNAL (from within building) _____

| VOICE CHARACTERISTICS | | SPEECH | |
|---|---|---|---|
| ___ Loud | ___ Soft | ___ Fast | ___ Slow |
| ___ High Pitch | ___ Deep | ___ Distinct | ___ Distorted |
| ___ Raspy | ___ Pleasant | ___ Stutter | ___ Nasal |
| ___ Intoxicated | ___ (Other) | ___ Slurred | ___ Lisp |
| | | ___ Precise | ___ (Other) |

| LANGUAGE | | ACCENT | |
|---|---|---|---|
| ___ Excellent | ___ Good | ___ Local | ___ Not Local |
| ___ Fair | ___ Poor | ___ Foreign | ___ Regional |
| ___ Foul | ___ (Other) | ___ Race | ___ (Other) |
| ___ Use of certain words or phrases | | | |

| MANNER | | BACKGROUND NOISES | |
|---|---|---|---|
| ___ Calm | ___ Angry | ___ Office | ___ Street Traffic |
| ___ Rational | ___ Irrational | ___ Machinery | ___ Airplanes |
| ___ Coherent | ___ Incoherent | ___ Factory | ___ Trains |
| ___ Deliberate | ___ Emotional | ___ Machinery | ___ Voices |
| ___ Righteous | ___ Laughing | ___ Bedlam | ___ Music |
| | | ___ Animals | ___ Mixed |
| | | ___ Quiet | |
| | | ___ Party Atmosphere | |

**FIGURE 7-2**  *Bomb threat checklist for telephone operators.*

**ACTION TO TAKE IMMEDIATELY AFTER CALL**

POLICE DEPT. TEL. # _____ FIRE DEPT. TEL. # _____

1. Notify the store manager of the bombthreat (or the person in charge), if you were unable to contact the manager, while the caller was on the line. Talk to no one other than those individuals the store manager or person in charge instructed you to speak to.
2. Notify local authorities that a bomb threat has been received and that a search is underway.
3. Write out the exact threat in its entirety, as it was received from the informant.

_____

_____

_____

_____

_____

_____

**FIGURE 7–2** (cont'd) *Bomb threat checklist for telephone operators.*

uct or service. Most coupons are sent by the retailer to the clearinghouse, rather than directly to the manufacturer. These clearinghouses sort the different coupons, count them, and tabulate their value. Retailers are then reimbursed for the total value of coupons received. The clearinghouse ships the canceled coupons to the various manufacturers, which in turn pay the clearinghouse the face value of the coupons plus a handling charge for its services.

There are numerous opportunities for coupon fraud throughout this system. Common abuses include

- theft of coupons by printing employees
- sale of newspaper coupon inserts by newspaper employees
- theft of coupons (by dishonest retail employees) to be used for later purchases or to substitute for cash from a register
- interception and sale of direct-mail coupons by postal workers
- redemption by retailers of coupons for purchases of merchandise other than that specified by the manufacturers and the subsequent submission of those coupons to the manufacturers for reimbursement
- submission of illegally obtained coupons by clearinghouses to manufacturers
- production of counterfeit coupons and their submission—in single amounts to local retailers or in bulk amounts to clearinghouses

The following security features should be checked in the printer's office, newspaper office, and company facilities:

- little or no apparent security in the storage of coupons or inserts

- a poorly supervised or undocumented distribution and/or mailing system
- lack of a clear-cut procedure for recovering or accounting for undistributed coupons or inserts
- no periodic checking system to determine whether coupons or inserts are distributed and disposed of properly

The only transfers of money in coupon redemption take place between the consumer and the retailer, and between the retailer and the advertiser or its clearinghouse.

Businesses are not required to accept coupons that are suspected to be counterfeit. Usually, counterfeit coupons are poorly printed copies of the originals and the printing is in one color and on one side, only. Legitimate coupons should give the name and address of the manufacturer, an expiration date or indication that there is no expiration date, and a description of redemption guidelines. Businesses that use coupons in their promotions can make the counterfeiter's job more difficult by issuing coupons that contain all of these elements and that are printed on both sides and in at least two colors.

When inserts are provided by the business, the newspaper should verify that

- the number of inserts received matches the number shipped
- inserts are placed in a secure area until removed by authorized personnel
- inserts are placed in the newspaper for distribution according to the agreement
- leftover inserts are disposed of in a manner that makes them unusable for redemption

When the newspaper prints the inserts, its circulation department should verify that

- press room reports or statements list the number of sections run for each issue
- spoiled coupon sections and sections remaining after printing and insertion are disposed of in a manner that makes them unusable for redemption
- coupon sections printed prior to the date of insertion are placed in a secure area until removed by authorized personnel for insertion in the newspaper
- printing plates or other material used to print coupon sections are disposed of properly

Newspapers should provide the retailer with

- auditable records or statements to confirm the disposition of returns, leftovers, and unsold copies from employees, distributors, carriers, drivers, and others responsible for the recovery and destruction of newspapers containing coupons

- statements from wastepaper companies (or other firms that purchase newspaper copies containing advertising coupons) that coupons are disposed of in a manner that makes them unusable for redemption

Coupon fraud and theft can be controlled by setting standards of security in the printing, inserting, distributing, and storing phases.

## COMPUTER CRIME AND DATA LOSS

Too few retail security directors or other executives consider their computer management systems to be significant loss risks. Part of this feeling stems from a lack of knowledge about the capabilities, procedures, and vulnerabilities of computer systems. A number of computer security books are published annually and the retail loss control coordinator should read them to acquire a working knowledge of the basic functions of their management information systems in order to protect sensitive corporate information.

Massive amounts of data can be concentrated on relatively small, easily concealed storage units, such as floppy disks, magnetic tapes, and cassette tapes. This portability creates a tremendous loss threat. Valuable data can be easily stolen or easily destroyed.

Some common computer crimes include

- issuing fictitious payroll checks
- stealing expensive computer time
- stealing highly confidential company data
- placing incorrect data in system files
- placing code viruses in a computer system
- writing a code that causes software to periodically malfunction so that programmers are required to make "maintenance" visits
- destroying lists of inventory to cover theft activities
- adding fictitious vendors or supplies to accounts payable lists
- intercepting the transmittal of sensitive data
- loss of data files due to power surges or loss of power

A computer loss control program requires the following actions:

Screen all consultants or employees who have access to computers.

Restrict access to data-processing areas by using identification systems.

Secure computer areas using sound physical security procedures.

Separate computer functions from other administrative functions and assign work to different individuals. Periodically audit the work of these employees and place them on other assignments.

Use passwords, security codes, and code-scrambling devices to provide some means of access control. Passwords should be a combination of six or more numbers, letters, and symbols that are picked at random and have no particular significant meaning. Do not note these codes in the computer area or discuss them on the telephone. Change the codes periodically; the frequency of change depends on the level of access or sensitivity of stored data.

Program the computers to track unauthorized attempts to gain access.

Do not consider facsimile machines and cellular phones as secure means of communication unless they have sophisticated scramblers.

Protect against loss of data files from power surges or outages by using surge protectors, shutting down systems during lightning storms, and not having computers on the same electrical circuit as other office machines.

Back up all computer files daily and store a copy off-site in a secure facility.

Audit company records and computer security and procedures annually. Recommendations on the effectiveness of the operation should be acted on immediately.

## NATURAL AND CIVIL DISASTERS

All retail businesses are subject to the adverse affects that disasters can bring. Loss of life, serious injury, loss of cash flow, and even loss of reputation may all result from incidents that cannot be controlled by the business. Floods, fires, explosions, hurricanes, tornadoes, earthquakes, product-tampering, and violent strikes must be planned for to minimize potential injury and damage, and to assist in resuming business as quickly as possible. The disaster plan should include emergency evacuation procedures, identification procedures, emergency team appointments and training, communication capabilities, and coordination with other companies and outside agencies.

A comprehensive plan should be drawn up by retailers after they research and consult with authorities and experts. Document the plan and make copies for all personnel. Elements of the plan should include the following points:

- potential risks and the degree of vulnerability for each risk
- descriptions of the corporate offices, distribution facilities, and stores, including square footage, construction, specific location, entry/exit points, roster of personnel and schedules, and communication and power line locations
- the chain of command and quorum list
- primary and secondary command center locations

- emergency supplies locations
- primary and secondary evacuation rosters
- list of mutual aid agreements
- emergency phone numbers
- location and telephone numbers of personnel with cellular phones and satellite beepers for emergeny communication capabilities
- shut-down and evacuation procedures
- specific information for each retail operation
- plans for protection and storage of vital records
- media-relations procedures

This is a partial listing of some of the preparations that must be made before a disaster strikes. In 1989, Hurricane Hugo and the San Francisco Earthquake were pointed reminders that a disaster can strike anywhere, at anytime. Some businesses were devastated and some were up and running within 24 hours of the disaster. In most cases, thorough planning, training, and testing made the critical difference.

## CIVIL LIABILITY AND LITIGATION

Retailers are increasingly vulnerable to civil claims, such as employee and customer accidents, false arrest, wrongful discharge, inadequate security, slander/libel, and negligent hiring. The United States, in particular, is becoming known as a litigious society. An abundance of personal injury lawyers and "victims" are cause to put the retailer on alert. Every effort should be made to determine risk areas within the company and to promote technology and training to reduce vulnerability to these hazards.

### Customer and Employee Accidents

When employees are injured on the job, the company suffers losses due to decreased productivity, workers' compensation claims, and civil claims of negligence. Retailers are beginning to experience employee injury claims on an almost routine basis. This is an expense that can be partially controlled by gaining an understanding of the problem. Many times, an increase in employee accidents stems from one-way (down) communication between supervisor and employee. This type of communication can cause a passive resistance, on the part of the subordinates, in which they either ignore directives or deliberately disobey them. The result is increased accident rates and tremendous costs. As accident frequency escalates, so does insurance premiums. Some recommended techniques to overcome resistance and error include the following:

Investigate and document all accidents.

Hold monthly or bi-monthly safety meetings and ensure they are chaired by first-line or middle managers. These meetings should be relatively short (1 hour) and to the point.

Give each supervisor a copy of the accident report at the safety meeting. Read the reports out loud and discuss the incident so that the group can decide whether or not the accident was preventable. Design and implement preventive measures. Examples of preventive measures are:

- on-the-job training in safe operating procedures
- using a safety checklist to identify and correct safety hazards
- improving guarding of hazardous equipment or supplies
- altering methods of operation
- ensuring better employee matching of skill to duty
- ensuring that supervisors are aware that feedback and recommendations from their employees is important and not a threat to their authority
- holding quarterly safety-awareness workshops for store or distribution employees

Safety awareness meetings should be less than 1 hour in length and should allow for two-way interaction. Fast-paced, humorous videos are available to retailers for teaching purposes. Reinforce all safety instructions using paycheck inserts, posters, and a reward system for individuals who report or correct safety hazards.

Be aware that customers make legitimate and contrived civil claims against retailers daily. Some retailers have stores in their chain that experience so many "slip-and-fall" lawsuits that they have a difficult time making a profit. All store employees must be instructed of the importance of identifying and removing unsafe conditions. Wet floors, children in shopping carts, sharp merchandise display fixtures, and pins in fitting rooms are all examples of hazards that can be eliminated. If a customer does report an accident, store management should

- summon medical assistance if needed
- *not* admit liability at any time
- apologize for the incident
- document the incident fully and contact their risk management department or superior

### False Arrest and Imprisonment

Retailers are plagued by employee theft and shoplifting and, when this activity is detected, these individuals are generally detained so that follow-up action can be taken. Whether the individual is released, criminally prosecuted, or civilly remanded, the processes leading up to the apprehension and the circumstances of the detention must conform to accepted standards. A single, poor decision by a store manager or loss prevention specialist can wipe out that store's annual profit. The store employee can generally detain a theft suspect based on reasonable cause, but, as we discussed in Chapter 5, once the reasonable cause is in doubt, the detaining employee must make a quick decision to minimize possible problems. Any detention should be made in a reasonable manner and last for a reasonable length of time. How the suspect is approached, the use of force, and the accusations made all have an impact on the outcome of possible subsequent civil proceedings.

The key to preventing false arrest claims is thorough training programs for employees who have the authority to detain theft suspects. The training course should stress methods of detection, apprehension, processing, and case follow-up. How to react in a situation in which something goes wrong should also be taught. Any training program should be documented and geared toward protecting the suspect's rights, not geared to protecting just the retailer.

### Wrongful Discharge Suits

Retailers employ large numbers of employees and are increasingly vulnerable to civil claims charging wrongful discharge and unfulfilled job promises. In the past, employers could hire and fire their associates at will, but specific statutes, collective bargaining agreements, and employment contracts can eliminate this traditional business right.

The reasons for terminating an employee may now be closely scrutinized by federal, state, and local authorities. These authorities apply legal tests to determine what constitutes legitimate reasons for personnel decisions, especially if personnel actions are retaliatory, arbitrary, discriminatory, or pretextual.

Some recommendations to avoid wrongful discharge claims include the following:

Be aware that a court will hold any promises or statements of job security against the employers.

All statements or promises made to recruits or employees should be carefully weighed.

Retailers should never assume that they are immune to wrongful discharge suits because it appears that no federal, state, or local discrimination acts are in effect.

Terminated employees are likely to consult with the Equal Employment Opportunities Commission or an attorney. Therefore, carefully document all personnel policies and specific actions dealing with the terminated employee.

Ensure that each employee receives a well-written personnel policy handbook and signs a receipt statement when they are hired.

Ensure that all employee policies reflect the employee's right to due process and adhere to these policies.

Handle all personnel matters in a fair and consistent manner and keep them confidential.

## Inadequate Security Lawsuits

Most businesspeople are aware that their business is, in some way, vulnerable to burglaries, robberies, internal theft, and many other potential loss hazards. However, very few retailers are aware of and prepared for lawsuits against them or their company alleging inadequate security. Currently, the number of inadequate security suits is growing. Florida, New York, and California lead the pack.

Any business that opens its doors to the public and invites them in is expected to provide a reasonably safe environment for employees and customers. Owners of retail stores and shopping centers are examples of those most vulnerable to inadequate security claims. While they are not required to guarantee the complete physical safety of all who enter their premises, they do have a duty to provide reasonable care in regard to safety and security.

Reasonable care is not well defined in existing laws or literature, but it is usually decided by the court based on all evidence presented during a particular trial. Many courts are now ruling that if a criminal act took place on the retailer's premises and if that act was foreseeable, and, furthermore, if the retailer did nothing to prevent it, the retailer is civilly liable. Generally, a crime or safety hazard is foreseeable if, in the past, similar stranger-to-stranger acts occurred on or near your property, or on a similar type of property in the local area.

When these cases come before a court, all facts are weighed and a finding for either the plaintiff or defendant is rendered. Any finding for the plaintiff means that an award for compensatory damages will be set. Usually, these damages can be paid by either the business or its insurance company. However, if negligence on the part of the owner is proven, punitive damages are assessed and the insurance company may not pay these fines.

Every business should have forms to document every accident, crime, or suspicious incident. A good filing system for keeping these reports is also necessary. Most lawsuits aren't brought before the courts for months or even years. The retailer will need to access these files when the court date is set. Include copies of all company forms and procedures for handling security sitations in the company's operations manual. Adhere to and upgrade these policies. Make sure that all company procedures are easy to follow and that all employees are made aware of any changes.

Once the retailer has analyzed the possible causes that prompt these lawsuits, devise a plan of action and document both the causes and the plan. Periodically check the program to make sure it is relevant and works as planned. The plan may need to be modified to include better security measures, such as adding lighting to improve visibility, or increasing patrols. Review inhouse or contract security departments to determine whether adequate training and supervision is being given.

Every business owner or CEO should take immediate steps to avoid and defend against inadequate security lawsuits. A complete, well-documented security survey, plan of action, and audit process is the best prevention effort the retailer can make.

### Negligent Hiring

If an employee of a retail operation commits a crime against a fellow employee, customer, or other member of the public, the retailer may be held civilly liable, to some degree, for the employee's action. Therefore, employers should screen applicants for positions that have access to the public to determine if they have a history of convictions for violent crimes. This issue is very complex and the corporate attorney should be consulted before a policy is implemented.

### Slander and Libel

Retailers should be cautious when making spoken or written comments about theft suspects, vendors, or competitors since these actions could result in claims of slander or libel. This topic (as are all topics in this section) is best discussed and reviewed with the corporate legal counsel to avoid misunderstandings and to devise a comprehensive litigation avoidance program.

# PART II

## Identifying and Prioritizing Risks

# Chapter 8

# Security Surveys

Many businesses and public law enforcement agencies tend to throw money and limited resources at highly visible or perceived risk areas rather than determining, through survey and incident analysis, the risks that are the highest and where the resulting negative financial impact is greatest. The first step in designing a cost-effective loss control program for any retail operation is to conduct a complete security survey. A security survey is generally defined as an on-site examination of a business to determine risks, probability of each risk, vulnerability to those risks, security measures and policies currently in effect, and the status of those measures and policies. This information is collected through visual inspection, employee interviews, responses to employee questionnaires, and review of company documents and computer data.

To ensure accurate data collection, the individuals who conduct the survey must be experienced in determining risks and adequacy of security measures. The survey used should focus on risks to the organization in three areas—physical security, personnel security, and information security. In defending the company's physical, personnel, and information assets against the risks identified in the previous chapters of this book, retailers should use a two-fold protection strategy. This strategy includes *Defense in Depth* (layers of physical and psychological barriers that deter, delay, or stop perpetrators in their efforts) and *Accumulated Delay Time,* which is achieved by delaying perpetrators with layered defenses so that the probability of their becoming discouraged or being apprehended increases with time.

Any good survey will take these two factors into account and will help measure the probable effectiveness of current and recommended defense efforts in accomplishing the goals of defense in depth and delay. These defensive efforts must not hinder positive customer service efforts, but must fit well within the company's overall goal of increased profits.

Before starting the survey, it is important to step back and look at the retail operation as a whole. Normally, the process begins with the merchandise buyer agreeing to purchase a quantity of merchandise from a vendor. A purchase order is generated and the merchandise is delivered. At this point, the merchandise is processed, priced, and displayed or sent to individual stores. Once in the stores, items are stored or displayed for sale. As the items are sold, clerks accept cash, checks, or credit cards for payment. The sales receipts are then deposited in a bank. At every point of this oversimplified process, corporate assets are vulnerable to theft and waste. Therefore, the survey should include every aspect of this process.

## HISTORICAL DATA

A major aspect of any security survey is the collection of historical data from local retailers and law enforcement agencies on past incidents. The type of incidents taking place in the business or in similar businesses, as well as frequency and location information should be collected. When historical data are considered with other data types, keep two facts in mind.

1. Studies indicate only $3^1$–$10^2$% of shoplifting incidents are detected. If thieves and their activities aren't detected, they can't be apprehended and the incidents can't be documented.
2. Of those individuals actually apprehended, it is estimated only 35%[3] are referred to law enforcement agencies.

This information indicates that other local retailers, who keep detailed records, should have a more accurate picture of the major retail threat risks (e.g., employee theft, vendor fraud, and shoplifting) than federal, state, or local police agencies. Law enforcement agencies should, however, have relatively accurate data on robbery and burglary incidents in a given area, since these crimes are more frequently reported. Although retailers consider each other as competitors, this is generally not the case when it comes to the area of security. If informal contact is made with another retailer in the area, a discussion of security problems and a sharing of information is usually the result.

Document *all* loss incidents and store them for later study. The best predictor of the future is often the past and this axiom holds true for the retail business. Retailers forecast anticipated sales and merchandise needs based on past experience and so too should the security practitioner forecast security needs.

The system used to collect and analyze theft data does not have to be expensive or overly sophisticated—just consistent and usable. Incident reports should have information blocks, to be checked where appropriate, that indicate certain minimal information. Examples of required information include

- date of the incident
- time of the incident

- location of the incident
- type of incident
- method of operation (i.e., how the offense was committed)
- distinctive case number
- a short descriptive narrative

The surveyor needs to enter historical incident data. Any prevailing crime or incident patterns need to be identified, such as which loss threats impact the operation, who is likely to cause the threat, how these threats are likely to occur, and when these threats are likely to occur.

The way to understand the data collected is to express them as incident rate by opportunity. This form of data expression compares the number of incidents of a particular type to the number of potential targets of that particular incident over a specified period of time. For example, if there were 3000 reported shoplifting incidents in the company in the last year and there are 100 stores, the incident rate by opportunity for shoplifting was 30. If, for the same company, there were 24 armed robberies during the same period, the incident rate by opportunity factor would be .24. In this example, the probability of a shoplifting incident occurring is much greater than the probability of an armed robbery.

Other information that can be gleaned from historical data includes the dollar amount of loss per incident, the location of theft incidents, common theft methods used, the identity of the offenders, and how the incidents were detected.

## ASSETS TO BE PROTECTED

After probable risks are identified and historical data on incidents involving these risks are collected, the next step of the survey involves identifying the assets to be protected. Obvious examples include

- corporate offices/buying offices
- sensitive information
- employees
- computers
- office equipment
- integrity of merchandise buyers, purchasing agents, real estate site locaters
- company reputation
- physical facility security
- merchandise buying operations
- distribution centers, receiving/vendor delivery, merchandise movement and pricing, invoice processing, inventory control process, shipping to stores, physical facility security, safety of employees

- store safety of employees and customers, merchandise, cash on hand, physical facility security

The surveyor should list assets to be protected and the approximate average retail dollar value of these assets, if possible. Company reputation and loss of life are examples where the assignment of a numerical value is difficult or inappropriate.

## Flow Charting

Make a chart to illustrate the flow of cash, documents, and merchandise through the business (see Figure 8–1). This effort helps the loss control team to step back and view the *total* organization. This view of the company as a system, not a static entity, should be the mind-set of those involved in shortage control. This type of chart will also prove useful in the initial and periodic analysis of survey data.

## Review of Current Company Policies and Practices

An examination of the company's current protection program is the final part of the security survey. Every retailer should have some sort of security or prevention program. We can break the protection program down into the following three general categories:

1. *People*—All personnel involved, in some way, with the loss control effort (which should be all employees) are included in this category. Examples include selection, orientation, training, duties, and responsibilities of company employees in regard to safeguarding corporate assets.
2. *Programs*—This category includes all policies and procedures designed to control losses, such as policies and procedures that restrict access, require transaction verification by a supervisor, or require that all employees be trained to detect and prevent potential loss situations. Policies generally indicate what senior management wants specified personnel to do. Procedures are the directions needed to enact and enforce policies.
3. *Systems*—This category includes physical and psychological deterrents to theft and error. Alarms, lighting, locks, doors, EAS, CCTV, computer or manually-generated trend reports, and subliminal messaging machines are all examples of security systems.

### Company Policy and Document Review

Obtain and review copies of company goals, policy statements, delegations of authority, responsibilities, directives, and job descriptions to understand where the company is, where it wants to go, and how it plans to get there.

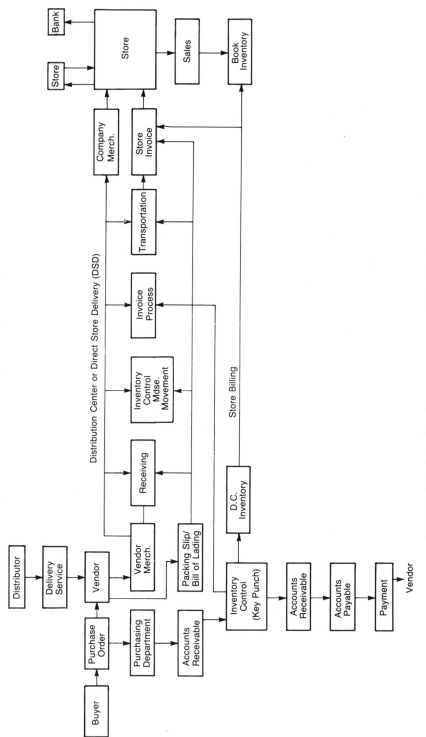

**FIGURE 8–1** *Merchandise processing cycle for distribution centers.*

Compare this information to the data collected in subsequent interviews and observations.

## Interview

Interview individuals involved in loss prevention, and groups of store and distribution facility employees to gain an understanding of what is actually taking place in the work environment. Find out how well control policies and procedures are understood and adhered to. Many times, a retailer will have well-planned and documented security policies, but the policies are not routinely followed. Company employees are usually aware of loss problems and may have even worked out solutions to perceived problems. It is important to gain company employees' cooperation by putting them at ease. Employees must know that they can speak candidly, without negative repercussions.

## Observation of Operations

Make a preliminary tour of the targeted facility noting areas for later closer study. Revisit the facility, observe and carefully note employee activity, and photograph protection equipment and vulnerable areas for later study.

Appendix 4 provides an abbreviated survey and Appendix 5 contains a sample completed store audit report to be used when collecting data for a loss control program. The data contained in these tools will be used during the analysis phase to determine key asset vulnerability.

## SUMMARY

A thorough, open-minded security survey is the first critical step in determining the type of loss control program for a given organization. Every retail operation should have an experienced consultant or in-house security personnel conduct the initial survey. The operation then should be fully surveyed on an annual basis, although high-risk or problem areas should be surveyed more frequently.

The retail risk survey, when properly conducted, will identify probable loss areas within the organization. Additionally, it should reveal the actual effectiveness of current prevention activities. By personal observation of routine activities, review of company documents and interview of company employees, the security specialist can determine the majority of the problem areas. The detail of the conducted survey is dependent on the objectives of the loss control director.

## NOTES

1. U.S. Department of Commerce, "1981 Revised Monthly Sales and Inventories: January 1971–December 1980," *Current Business Reports*, BR-13-805 (January 1981).

2. E. Blankenburg, "The Selectivity of Legal Sanctions: An Empirical Investigation of Shoplifting," *Law and Society Review* 11 (1976).
3. R. Griffin, *Shoplifting—A Twelve Year Review, 1966–1977* (Van Nuys, CA: Commercial Services Systems, 1978).

# Chapter 9

# Data Analysis

Phase II of designing a cost-effective protection program involves the breakdown and study of data collected during Phase I, The Security Survey. If the conducted survey was fairly comprehensive, there should be enough information available to determine loss trends and indicate future security needs.

This chapter describes a three-step approach to prioritizing risk threats. The study of loss targets, the current protection program, and past loss incidents allows the retailer to assign a priority value to each risk. By prioritizing risks, the retailer saves time and resources in the future by first focusing on major problems.

## POSSIBLE AND PROBABLE FINANCIAL LOSS

Each type of loss identified in the security survey must be ranked according to two factors—possible maximum loss and probable maximum loss. *Possible maximum loss* is the total loss sustained if a risk target or asset is lost and/or destroyed. *Probable maximum loss* is the loss the risk target is *likely* to sustain. Certain parts of a target are more susceptible or vulnerable than others. If the target under examination is the merchandise inventory of a particular store, certain items are more likely to be stolen (e.g., fine jewelry vs. men's ties) than others. These losses should be expressed in terms of dollars, since that is a measurement common to all retailers. The security specialist must show senior management the total ramification of their losses.

Every loss can be broken down into two types of costs to the company—direct and indirect.

I.   Direct Costs
    A.   Cash—operating capital needed to service debts and fund expansion
    B.   Merchandise—the cost of buying, shipping, processing, and advertising merchandise held for sale
    C.   Property—the replacement cost of nonsalable property (i.e., damaged or destroyed)

    D.  Information—sensitive information, such as customer addresses, future store sites, etc.

II.  Indirect Costs

    A.  Reputation with public or creditors—Retailers with shrinkage problems are suspected of suffering from bad management.

    B.  Loss of employees—Recruiting, hiring, and training costs are multiplied when employee turnover increases due to dishonesty or poor morale.

    C.  Employee morale—Honest employees are demoralized by the presence of dishonest employees and rampant shoplifting.

    D.  Goodwill—the loss of targeted customers due to public perception of an unsafe atmosphere or the absence of desired merchandise due to theft

These costs are measured in terms of loss of assets, replacement costs, or loss of income. If an asset such as merchandise or critical information is lost, the resulting costs may come from one or all of the following areas.

*Permanent Replacement Cost*—Permanent replacement cost includes the wholesale purchase price, shipping charges and costs, and the cost to prepare and display merchandise lost to theft, accident, or error.

*Insurance Cost*—The cost of applicable insurance premiums and deductibles should be subtracted from the coverage amount. The amount of coverage should then be subtracted from the maximum probable cost amount to accurately determine real costs.

*Temporary Replacement Cost*—If a part of a store location is damaged by fire, temporary costs may include rent or lease expenses and additional labor costs.

*Related Cost*—If a store is damaged by a natural disaster, an example of a related cost includes the salary cost of idle store employees.

*Lost Income Cost*—The loss of the use of a store or key merchandise can result in the operation having to divert cash, which could be earning interest elsewhere, to subsidize replacement and related costs. This is in addition to the loss of revenues. The following simple formula is used to determine lost income cost:

$$I = \frac{i}{365} \times P \times t$$

Where  I  = income earned

          i  = annual rate of return

        P  = principle amount available for investment

        t  = time, in days, during which P is available for investment.

## ASSIGNING FINANCIAL IMPACT RATES

By affixing a total cost to each projected loss target, a rate can be assigned to each target. This rate reflects the financial impact the loss or destruction of that target would have on the retail organization. There are five rates that can be assigned to projected loss targets.

A Rating—Grave—a loss of this magnitude could result in the abandonment or long-term shutdown of the company.

B Rating—Critical—a loss of this magnitude could have a major negative impact on company assets or could force a major change in the company's investment policy.

C Rating—Serious—a loss of this magnitude would have a noticeable impact on annual earnings.

D Rating—Moderate—a loss of this magnitude would be covered by normal contingency reserve funds.

E Rating—Unknown—this is a temporary rating that is assigned until all priorities are established and a specific financial impact rate is assigned.

Every retailer can use this rating system, since it is subjective in design. The level of a company's annual revenues and its contingency funds determine the rating assigned to a potential loss. A $10,000 loss for a small retailer may equate a $100,000 or even a $1,000,000 loss to a larger retailer. Therefore, a small one-store jewelry operation that grosses $100,000 a year might assign a "grave" rating to a potential loss of $50,000 worth of inventory.

## PROBABILITY OF INCIDENT OCCURRENCE

In order to more accurately rank loss threats from grave to moderate, the analyst needs to determine the probability or likelihood that a particular incident will occur. The study of data collected during the survey should focus on two areas—current security and protective measures, and review of past loss incidents that have affected the company.

A major factor to consider when determining probability and frequency of adverse incidents is the historical data collected in the survey. Every attempt must be made to acquire this type of information. If there are no records of this information, the analyst should obtain similar information from businesses in the area and from local law enforcement authorities. Interviews and written surveys from employees can reveal much of this information.

As past incidents are examined, trends should become apparent. Trends to look for include

- type of incident
- predominant time of occurrence, such as time of day, day of week, season, etc.
- type of merchandise taken, such as apparel, jewelry, health and beauty aids, etc.
- particular store, district, or region
- method of theft used, such as robbery, armed robbery, etc.
- profile of offenders, such as age, race, sex, employee, etc.
- average dollar amount of loss and/or recovery

One factor to consider when determining a target's vulnerability is the number of ways a particular loss event can happen. In the case of high-cost merchandise, the target may be damaged, lost, stolen by vendors, employees, and customers. Since the variety of ways to lose this target is so extensive, the probability of a financial loss is much higher than other lower cost merchandise.

Characteristics of the target must also be considered when determining vulnerability to loss. Examples include the mobility of the item, access to the item, the people who have access to the item, and the real or perceived value of the asset. Also, in the case of natural or man-made disasters, physical and political environments must be considered.

There are several tools that the security analyst can use to help determine probability and frequency of adverse incidents, such as incident calendars and plot maps. Incident calendars are large calendars on which incidents are entered by the date on which they occurred, to determine if patterns are taking place. Plot maps are geographical maps or schematic charts of a business that have been covered with plastic or acetate so that loss incidents can be plotted to indicate patterns of occurrence. Plot maps are also used to indicate whether prevention efforts are displacing incidents from one locale to another.

## EXAMINING SECURITY DATA

Once financial impact rates have been assigned and probability of incident occurrence has been determined for potential losses, the next step is to analyze the data collected during the survey regarding current security efforts. Starting with grave loss targets and working down to moderate loss targets, review stated policies and procedures for those loss targets and compare them to the actual practices taking place. In each case, barriers, control procedures, and employee training designed to detect and deter theft and error should be in place. If there are no controls, no adherence to control policies, or an inadequate training effort, this should be noted. This information indicates the vulnerability of that asset to loss and suggests that effective countermeasures should be implemented.

Individuals who analyze data from any survey must have a high level of expertise in order to correctly interpret collected data. It is also helpful to understand the day-to-day operation of the business. The probability of a particular crime or loss incident changes constantly. Employees may be more liable to steal cash from a register if their personal needs are strong, there is a large amount of cash available, or if a more lax member of store management is on duty.

There is no secret formula or mathematical equation that will ensure perfect analysis of loss threat data due to the number and complexity of social and environmental factors that affect loss incidents. However, the primary results of a thorough analysis include

- trends or patterns of similar type incidents
- suspect or crime links, that indicate a possible perpetrator
- target profiles that indicate merchandise or other assets that are frequently victims of losses
- forecasting of future incidents or shrinkage percentages

## ASSIGNING LOSS INCIDENT PROBABILITY RATE

After all available data have been collected and examined, a probability rating should be assigned similar to the rating used to rank impact of financial loss on a business. This rating is made before any new countermeasures are implemented. The assigned rating indicates the likelihood of an event occurring compared to all other significant adverse events. There are five loss incident probability rates.

1 Rating—Almost Certain—Barring major changes in circumstances, this event will occur or will occur frequently, compared to other events.

2 Rating—Very Probable—This type of incident is more likely to occur than to not occur.

3 Rating—Probable—This type of event should occur if circumstances remain stable.

4 Rating—Improbable—This event is less likely to occur.

5 Rating—Unknown—More data is required to assign a rate.

While this type of rating system is not exact, it does allow the security specialist to make educated guesses. When in doubt, assign a higher rating.

## PRIORITIZING RISKS

Now that risks have been assigned financial impact and probability rates, the security specialist must then prioritize risks, starting with listing the most serious risks. By prioritizing risks in descending order, attention can be focused on the most serious threats first. By following this method, risks would be listed as follows:

1.  A1, A2, A3, A4
2.  B1, B2, B3, B4
3.  C1, C2, C3, C4
4.  D1, D2, D3, D4

The analyst must make the determination if greater weight should be given to the financial impact or the vulnerability of the asset when prioritizing risks. Once all risks have been ranked, the formal security data analysis is complete. The security specialist has identified and prioritized risks, and can now design and implement cost-effective countermeasures to reduce overall corporate losses.

# PART III

# Designing and Implementing Prevention Programs

# Chapter 10

---

# Loss Prevention
# Program Design

The third phase of the integrated approach to controlling retail loss is the design of a comprehensive countermeasure program. Because the retailer has already prioritized identified risks, the loss control program can be very focused. The required level of sophistication of the program depends on the extent of loss problems and the available investment capital.

## BASIC PROGRAM FOCUS

Using a basic matrix (as shown in Figure 10–1), the loss control director decides which of five risk management methods to use to reduce losses. Depending on the rates assigned during the ranking process, one or more risk management techniques are recommended for a given counter measure program. The five generally accepted risk management techniques include

- risk avoidance
- risk reduction
- risk spreading
- risk transfer
- risk acceptance

One or all of these methods can be used to manage loss risks to some extent.

### Risk Avoidance

Risk avoidance involves removing the loss target so that risk is avoided. When a retailer deposits sales receipts in a bank, the risk of losing these funds on the retail premises no longer exists, at least temporarily. This technique is the most effective way of removing risk, but because it is so severe, it is impractical. A grocery store would not normally consider removing all health and beauty aid products from their stores, because they are considered high-

| Severity of Loss | Financial Probability or Frequency of Loss Incidents | | |
|---|---|---|---|
| | High | Medium | Low |
| High | Risk Avoidance | Risk Avoidance and Risk Reduction | Risk Transfer |
| Medium | Risk Avoidance and Risk Reduction | Risk Spreading and Risk Transfer | Risk Acceptance |
| Low | Risk Spreading | Risk Spreading and Risk Acceptance | Risk Acceptance |

**FIGURE 10–1**  *Sample risk management decision matrix.*

risk items. Very few significant risks can be completely avoided, but, where possible, the loss control director should at least consider this method.

### Risk Reduction

Since most risks cannot be avoided completely, risk reduction is the most preferred risk management method. A retailer can reduce the maximum probable loss of risks by reducing the amount or attractiveness of specific loss targets. Instead of removing all expensive jewelry from their inventory, store managers can keep only those items that are absolutely essential, in-stock or on display. Another example of risk reduction is to make periodic cash pick-ups from point-of-sale registers to reduce the amount of cash vulnerable to theft.

Risk reduction should be considered prior to considering the more expensive risk-spreading method, since the success of the risk reduction depends more on standard operating control policies and procedures, and not on costly hardware or services.

### Risk Spreading

After avoidance and reduction techniques have been applied or examined, risk spreading should be considered, particularly for high-risk targets. Risk spreading is perhaps the best known of the risk management methods and involves the application of security systems and procedures to accomplish the four Ds.

1. *Deter potential incidents* by discouraging perpetrators with control hardware and procedures, and by educating customers and employees about hazards and security techniques.

2. *Deny access to sensitive information,* unsafe areas, or high-risk assets.
3. *Delay offenders* with a series of physical and psychological barriers so that they might be identified and/or apprehended.
4. *Detect unsafe or dishonest situations* as part of an overall loss prevention program.

Examples of risk spreading include intrusion detection devices, access control barriers, surveillance systems, inventory control procedures, employee awareness training, and accounting control and verification procedures.

Many retailers pass on costs of theft and security to their customers in the form of higher prices. This is a form of risk spreading that is increasingly unpopular with retail operations and their customers. With the use of civil lawsuits dramatically increasing, and increasing competition, higher pricing tactics will continue to decrease.

Another form of risk spreading is sharing or passing on civil liability to merchandise and service vendors with contracts. Court rulings will determine, over time, the effectiveness of this practice. Currently, many companies view incorporation and partnership agreements as a form of risk spreading.

## Risk Transfer

The next option available to retailers is to transfer the risk to another entity. The primary method used to accomplish this is the purchase of a comprehensive insurance policy. Insurance should not be purchased until the first methods have been applied or the insurance will be so expensive that risk transfer may not be cost-effective.

Risk avoidance, reduction, and spreading methods should be well planned, documented, and presented to the insurance agent before a cost quote is requested, to keep unit cost to a minimum. Insurance is an excellent risk management tool and should be used, but thoroughly researched before premiums are budgeted.

## Risk Acceptance

The final method used by retailers is risk acceptance. This method is considered a last resort and is used only after all other methods have been tried or are found to be not cost-effective. In accepting risk, the retailer accepts the maximum probable loss of a particular risk as a cost of doing business. Risk acceptance is generally defined as the level of loss a retailer can sustain without financially impacting the business. This cost may be budgeted for specifically, covered by a general reserve fund, or simply absorbed. Examples of risk acceptance include replacement costs for small items that have been pilfered, insurance premiums, or insurance deductibles.

## RISK CONTROL COUNTERMEASURES

Retail organizations exist to make a profit. Therefore, when designing risk control countermeasures, the security specialist should keep several factors in mind.

### Cost-effectiveness

Any loss control program (or part of the program) should prove cost-effective over a period of time. The total cost of security must be kept to the minimal amount required to control losses. Most retailers express their cost to control shrinkage as a percentage of sales.

The cost of control can range from almost nothing (loss control procedures) to moderate cost (employee awareness training programs), to high cost (placing EAS systems in distribution centers and all stores). All of these programs may be cost-justified based on the threats that a retailer faces, but the security specialist should think in terms of least-cost techniques and sound management principles before recommending that sophisticated security hardware be used.

### Redundancy

The company employee responsible for loss control should keep in mind that systems designed to protect very high-risk assets should have back-up security systems in case of primary system failure. For example, perimeter and internal alarm systems should be separated in case one system fails.

### Teamwork

While planning the loss control program, security specialists should take into account the fact that there may be policies, personnel, and equipment inside and outside of their control that must be altered or eliminated. When possible, these factors must be identified and made a part of the action plan and budgeting process. Senior management must be made aware of the situation and a teamwork approach should be taken to resolve these issues, so that working relationships among the loss control department and other departments are not hindered.

Both security and management executives should be sensitive to each other's goals. Total access to items enhances the tendency to buy them. However, this practice also guarantees tremendous shrinkage. Many retailers start off with a few control procedures and practices, and move toward more control as losses continue to mount. It is possible to work together to accomplish the ultimate goal of increased profitability.

## Customer Convenience and Perception

Store planners use store layout and fixturing schemes to induce customers to buy more of their merchandise. Also, the smart retailer strives to make their customers' shopping experience a convenient and pleasant one. As the loss prevention program is designed, the security specialist should work with store operations and merchandise display personnel to reach a happy medium between displaying all merchandise on the sidewalk and locking everything up.

The appearance of security practices and equipment should also be considered during the loss prevention program planning phase. Some customers or employees may consider a practice or piece of equipment offensive, many won't notice it at all, and still others will be deterred from committing theft *because* of the practice or equipment. Again, negative perceptions of a program or system should be weighed against the economic need or personal safety.

Bar coding is an example of a system that decreases the time a customer spends at the cash register, while enhancing inventory control.

## Labor Requirements

Loss control procedures or programs may require an increase in the labor force or may divert employees' attention from primary work functions to loss prevention. These factors must be considered and planned for. Many security systems actually reduce labor intensity by simplifying procedures or by assuming functions formally handled by employees or outside contract agencies. Card access, EAS, and CCTV systems all take over functions that may have been previously provided by security personnel.

## Time Sensitivity of Countermeasures

Many procedures or security systems become obsolete annually or even monthly because of new technology, sociological changes, or new court rulings. Therefore, retailers should consider countermeasure timeliness as a part of their program design. A retailer should not, however, wait indefinitely before implementing needed policies and equipment.

## Program Manageability

Another factor to be considered during the design phase, is the ability of executives in charge of the security function and their staffs to effectively manage the loss prevention program. Before attempting to implement a costly, sophisticated program, the personnel involved should be carefully selected and trained. Individuals in supervisory roles must have demonstrated technical proficiency and leadership qualities, or the best-designed program in the world is doomed to minimal effectiveness.

## No Guarantees

Retailers at all levels should realize that there is no such thing as an infallible security system. Incidents will occur and losses will take place. The key is to prepare for and attempt to reduce adverse incidents, and reduce the negative effects of previously uncontrolled losses.

## Threat Analysis

Each risk requires certain actions or inactions to take place in order for the loss to occur. For example, if the asset to be protected is high-loss merchandise, such as fragrances in the distribution center awaiting shipment to stores, threats to that asset may include employee pilferage. In analyzing the threat, a link chart may be drawn up indicating the events that must take place in order for the loss to occur (see Figure 10–2). In this case, an employee must gain access to the items, surreptitiously take possession of the items, and exit the premises. By identifying the actions that must take place for the loss to occur, the security specialist can design countermeasures to eliminate these actions or inactions.

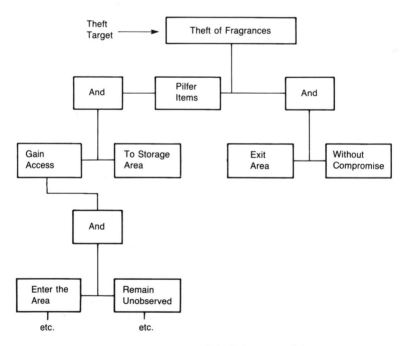

**FIGURE 10–2** *Simplified threat model.*

In this example, certain countermeasures are indicated that would disrupt the chain of events that must take place for the theft to occur. Access to the merchandise can be controlled or limited by identification and barrier systems. The high-risk goods can also be secured in an enclosed area to make entry more difficult. High-risk goods might have EAS tags installed when they are received or implanted by the vendor. The CCTV system might have a camera trained on the storage area to discourage or identify perpetrators. An employee package check policy might detect items being carried out of the store. Finally, a well-motivated employee who has been made aware of the company's ability and intent to detect and prosecute offenders might prevent the situation in the first place.

Threat analyses should be performed on priority risks in order to design comprehensive countermeasures. Countermeasures should

- eliminate or reduce probability of loss events
- prevent "and" connections within the threat model
- disrupt or interrupt required event sequences
- include the ability, if possible, to neutralize more than one link or "and" point in the event chain
- give the required reliability, which can often be illustrated as a 1 in 10 (or 1 in 100, etc.) chance of failure or defeat
- compound the impact of countermeasures by selecting those that reduce more than one risk
- involve the fewest countermeasures, at the lowest cost, while reducing risks to the necessary level of reliability

## PROTECTION PROGRAM DESIGNS

One step of the integrated loss prevention program is to define an appropriate protection program based on a variety of security-related factors.

### Types of Security

There are three basic types of security protection in any organization:

1. *Physical*—the protection of assets by implementing physical equipment and services to deter, delay, and detect loss events.
2. *Personnel*—the protection of assets by screening employees, implementing procedural controls, training employees to perform their jobs (including loss control procedures), and implementing fair and consistent disciplinary procedures.
3. *Information*—identifying sensitive information, controlling access to that data, and informing employees, vendors, and customers of their roles in the protection of confidential information.

## Levels of Security

It is helpful to categorize the level of security desired or required for any organization. The following security levels serve as a guide.

- Level 1—Minimum Security
- Level 2—Moderate Security
- Level 3—Medium Security
- Level 4—Maximum Security

The level of assigned security should be looked at as a system approach and should not be based on its individual parts or components. Any system that is designed is as much psychological in nature as it is physical.

### Level 1-Minimum Security

Minimum security policies and systems are designed to impede some unauthorized activity by employees or non-employees. Examples of minimum security include the use of standard door locks and the requirement that all merchandise transactions be rung up at a cash register.

### Level 2-Moderate Security

Moderate security policies and procedures are designed to impede, detect, and, in some cases, assess most unauthorized activity by internal and external sources. This level is applied in addition to the basic procedures and barriers used at Level 1. Basic or advanced alarm systems; window glazing or bars; high-security locks; trained, unarmed guards; better lighting systems; employee awareness training; and more elaborate procedural controls are examples of moderate security.

### Level 3-Medium Security

Distribution centers, computer facilities, and store safe rooms are examples of areas requiring medium security. This level of security is designed to impede, detect, and assess most unauthorized internal and external activity. Examples of medium security measures include CCTV systems; advanced perimeter, fire, internal motion detection, and safe "teleproach" alarm systems; high-security lighting; trained guards and plainclothes agents; card access systems; and coordination with local law enforcement agencies.

### Level 4-Maximum Security

Security at this level is rare for retailers and is described as a total, diversified, redundant system designed to allow the strength of one component to offset the weakness of another. Distribution or storage facilities for very high-risk merchandise, such as expensive jewelry, fuel, or controlled pharmaceuticals may require this level of protection. Examples of maximum security include layered fencing and wire cages, sophisticated alarm systems with layered "dummy" and "live" sensors, and highly trained and armed response forces.

### Defense in Depth or Layering

Regardless of the level of protection required, the concept of defense in depth remains a must. By designing countermeasures from the threat target outward, the perpetrator must bypass or defeat more than one barrier to cause the loss of a valuable asset. Figures 10–3 and 10–4 illustrate two simplified layering charts.

By layering defenses in this manner, perpetrators may be displaced to another area, discouraged from the attempt, or delayed so long that they are detected.

### THE PROTECTION PLAN

All retailers use two types of plans to guide their businesses. The business plan and the budget are the result of careful study and reflect forecasted sales and expenses. The point in having a plan is, first of all, to promote thorough planning; secondly, to have a reference guide for day-to-day operations (in addition to operating procedures); and, thirdly, to use in assessing the results of efforts and accuracy of previous assumptions.

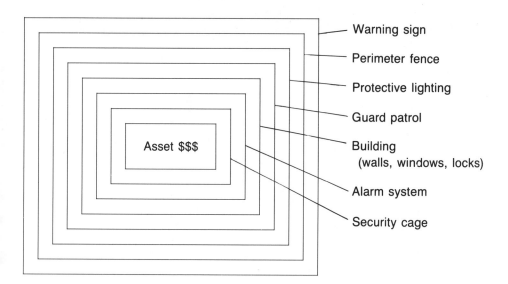

**FIGURE 10–3** *Physical security layering.*

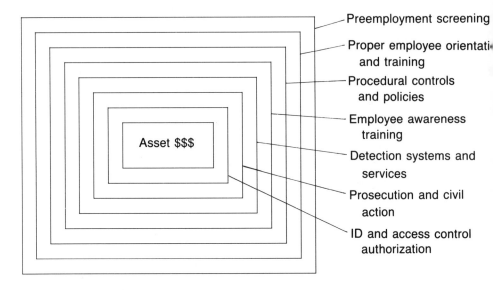

**FIGURE 10–4**  *Personnel security layering.*

The protection plan is just as important to the Loss Control Director as the business plan is to the CEO. The protection plan should guide the day-to-day activities of the security department. The comprehensive protection plan includes three elements—people, programs, and systems. These three elements should complement each other.

The next three chapters highlight some features of each of the three elements of the protection plan. Retailers can use the following chapters to select appropriate countermeasures and tailor them to their specific organization.

# Chapter 11

# People

The use of people to control losses is perhaps the most important loss prevention method and can be the most expensive one. *Because* of these two factors, this chapter is dedicated to this very important topic. *All* employees of any retail organization are responsible for controlling profit-draining loss. However, senior management generally designates one individual to be responsible for the administration of a loss control program. This individual may handle security duties in addition to other responsibilities or as their primary responsibility. Additional full or part-time individuals, whose main function is security, may be employed by the retailer or may be provided by an outside contract agency.

## IN-HOUSE EMPLOYEES

This section provides insight into the most common loss prevention positions held in retail operations of various sizes and their role in loss control. For the purpose of this book, titles or specific job positions will be used interchangeably, since there are many common names for each position.

### Director (Vice President) of Security or Loss Control

Every group needs a leader. For the security department, the director (or the vice president) is responsible for implementing and managing company loss control functions in larger retail companies. This individual normally reports to the CEO or high-level vice president to ensure that top decision-makers are kept abreast of loss control efforts and shrinkage problems. This reporting level is also important in maintaining companywide credibility for the loss control department and its efforts. Loss control must be viewed as a priority issue by all company employees.

Building on experience and education, the director sets loss control goals that fit into the overall corporate goals and designs the loss prevention program to accomplish these goals. In larger chains, subordinate managers implement and run the loss prevention program and the director acts as advisor and counselor to these subordinates to ensure and enhance the effectiveness of the program and the managers' efforts and abilities. To accomplish this, the director stays abreast of new control techniques and technologies by attending conferences, reading security journals, and exchanging ideas with peers (networking).

The primary role of the loss control director is to provide the direction and resources needed for cost-effective security.

## Shortage Control Committees

In an effort to get key company executives involved in reducing shrinkage, committees are formed at store and corporate levels to study the problems the company is experiencing and to ensure that loss control procedures are implemented and followed.

## Loss Prevention Staff

Depending on the size and type of retailer, the security staff can consist of one employee or hundreds. The staff may include a variety of personnel that have different responsibilities.

### Line Managers

Line managers (i.e., regional, group, and district managers) coordinate all loss control activities in their assigned geographic area. Their duties include monitoring variances such as cash overages and shortages, excessive voids, excessive refunds and price underrings; presenting loss prevention awareness courses to store employees and managers; acting as loss control consultants to district and store operations managers; and conducting store audits.

In larger retail chains, the district-level line manager represents the loss prevention department in the "field" and motivates store-level personnel to integrate prevention techniques into their routine activities.

### Investigator/Auditor

The investigator/auditor-level position is one that is being filled more often as we head into the twenty-first century. The investigator audits stores and distribution areas to determine vulnerable areas of the operation and to uncover crimes in progress. The investigator also sifts through computer data or paperwork and conducts interviews and surveillances to determine the causes and extent of suspected employee theft. Because of the civil liabilities involved in accusations of theft, and the more sophisticated nature of retail crime, the individuals in this position require extensive training in modern detection, investigation and interview techniques.

*Store Detective, Agent, Operative, or Specialist*

In larger chains, the store detective is generally considered the loss control department's first line of defense against shoplifting and employee theft. The loss prevention specialist is normally assigned to one or more stores, depending on the size of the company's stores. The primary responsibility of the loss prevention specialist is to detect and apprehend shoplifters. The training program for this position must be very comprehensive and well-documented. Violent incidents involving shoplifters and the threat of false arrest lawsuits are on the increase. Well-trained loss prevention specialists can be very effective at stemming store losses, especially when working in conjunction with well-trained, alert, non-security employees and EAS/CCTV technology.

*Uniformed Guard*

Some chains use guards who wear blazers or uniforms and station them at the front of the store or allow them to patrol in order to deter theft and serve customers. It is recommended that guards be part of a loss prevention program, but not be considered a prime theft deterrent.

*Fitting Room Attendant or Store Monitor*

Courteous, alert individuals should be assigned as fitting room attendants/ store monitors whenever possible. Store monitors can promote goodwill for the company while deterring theft. Usually, monitors report to the store manager, although they are trained and motivated by loss prevention personnel.

**Loss Prevention Department Organization**

A central reporting system is critical to maintaining a corporatewide, consistent, and focused loss control program. It is important to note that the most effective reporting system for a modern loss control department is vertical, not horizontal (as shown in Figure 11–1). District and store managers are rarely prepared to supervise store-level loss prevention specialists for three reasons.

1. Most operations managers lack the continuous training required to identify and reduce losses from the myriad of internal and external threats, and still run the store in a profitable manner.
2. Operations managers operate in an environment of constantly changing priorities and security agents may be assigned non-loss prevention duties at the expense of shrinkage.
3. Unfortunately, store managers themselves may be dishonest and could schedule store detectives opposite planned dishonest activity.

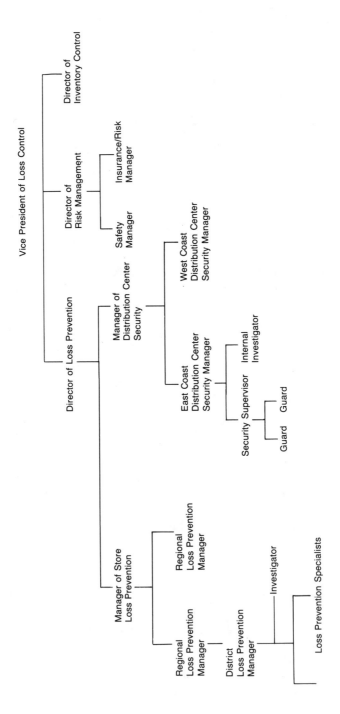

**FIGURE 11–1** *Loss prevention department organization.*

It is very difficult for a loss prevention specialist to effectively operate in this type of environment for obvious reasons.

## Non-Security Employees

As previously stated, all employees of the company should be trained to prevent theft and waste. These employees are the key to low shrinkage.

### Senior Management

The front line of any retail operation provides leadership and direction to the company in terms of what is to be done and how it should be done. The primary loss prevention role of senior management is to approve, endorse, and adhere to the security program. An endorsement from senior management legitimizes the personnel, procedures, and systems used to reduce shrinkage, and ensures that security remains a significant priority in the company.

Senior management can also infuse a sense of responsibility for shrinkage in subordinate managers by holding them accountable for their annual shrinkage and by reflecting shrinkage results on annual performance reviews, which also triggers incentive bonuses. However, remember that it is difficult to hold anyone accountable for shrinkage levels in their area of responsibility if a company's inventories are sporadic or poorly conducted. Good, sound management that pays attention to detail and motivates employees can simultaneously increase sales while reducing losses.

### Regional/District Operations Manager

In average to large retail chains, this individual implements corporate procedural and merchandising policies in the field, as well as supervises store managers. District managers influence the priorities of their store managers. For example, if clean floors and realigned display fixtures are stressed by the district manager during the store visit, these elements become the priority— sometimes at the expense of other operations. Therefore, district managers can help control shrinkage by continually stressing the need for loss prevention measures at the store level as well as supporting their counterparts (the loss control district managers) in their activities. District-level operations, and loss control and human resource representatives can form a triad by keeping each other informed of their activities and presenting an organized, unified front. This team approach helps to ensure that all company priorities are addressed and objectives are achieved.

### Store Manager

Store managers set the tone of operation in their stores. Whatever store managers stress and praise becomes important to their employees. If an employee detects a price switch, for example, the manager should compliment the individual. Loss control specialists assigned to stores must work in concert with all store employees. The store manager and loss control specialist on duty should check in with each other periodically and compliment the actions of one another. Safety and security are at stake and those issues far outweigh any petty differences that may exist. Store managers are responsible for their stores and their actions should be respected. Similarly store managers should foster a mutual professional respect between loss prevention and store operations personnel as both of these sources play an important part in boosting company profitability.

Store managers often receive bonuses based on quarterly results of their efforts. Profitability and shrinkage figures should be part of the requirement to receive an incentive bonus. If the store has tremendous sales figures but horrendous shrinkage, the company may not be making a profit. The shrinkage goals that are set must be achievable and store managers must be able to incrementally reduce their shrinkage or the concept of reward has little value.

### Store/Distribution Center Employees

While store detectives are the security deparment's first line of defense against shoplifting, store and distribution center employees are the company's first line of defense against theft and waste. As a group, store employees play the largest role of all in day-to-day control of losses. These individuals must be trained to recognize and report loss situations and rewarded by their supervisors.

### Miscellaneous Company Employees

Regardless of the size of the corporation, all employees from buyers to corporate office staff should be made aware of loss threats that exist within their span of control and be told what they can do to deter these threats.

## OUTSIDE PERSONNEL

Retail businesses of all sizes are attempting to maintain streamlined corporate staffs and supplement expensive in-house employee salary and benefit costs with cheaper security technology and contract services. By using contract services, the retailer can limit personnel costs to those times when it is specifically needed. This section briefly describes the most commonly used outside security personnel. Appendix 12 of this book will assist retailers in finding quality outside security personnel.

### Loss Control Consultants

Retail companies routinely use outside consultants or experts for services and advice. Outside corporate legal counsel, accounting firms, and management consultants are examples of non-employee advisors. Loss control consultants are called in to provide a fresh, objective view of corporate loss vulnerabilities and to make control recommendations. The in-house director of loss prevention should not feel the use of a consultant signals their inability to resolve shrinkage problems. The use of professional consultants is standard practice in government and industry around the world. The outside consultant may provide the recommendation that finally pushes senior management to authorize the installation of some key loss control program or system.

When selecting a loss prevention consultant, the retailer must first explain the area they want studied and/or improved. The following questions should then be asked of any consultant being considered:

1. Who will conduct the survey and make recommendations?
2. What are their qualifications?
3. What will you do for my retail business and how will you do it?
4. What are the anticipated long-term results of your services?
5. What is the total cost for using your services and following your advice?

The consultant should answer these questions, and more, in the form of a written proposal. See Appendix 6 for a sample consulting proposal. A standard proposal is as follows:

I.   *Scope*—This section should describe what the survey or audit will study and accomplish, such as review current security objectives, losses, policies, activities, personnel, and effectiveness.
II.  *Approach*—This section should describe the methods to be used and the areas to be visited while collecting data, such as a visit to three stores, the distribution center, and corporate offices to interview employees and observe systems and activities.
III. *Resolution*—This section should describe how the data analysis is to be conducted and should provide the results and preliminary recommendations.
IV.  *Considerations and Limitations*—This section should outline the need for confidentiality, low-key survey procedures, and the need for a positive, team approach to the consulting process.
V.   *Background*—This section should describe the qualifications of those being retained to conduct the security audit.
VI.  *Fees and Time Commitment*—This section should contain the time frame, estimated cost of the survey, and other expenses.
     Be aware that costs for consulting usually include

- manpower
- travel and expenses
- administrative overhead percentage

- miscellaneous administrative support expenses (e.g., copying, faxing, typing, postage)
- profit
- a contingency fee of approximately 10%, in case of unexpected expenses (used only if required)

The average fee for professional consultants is approximately $100 per hour or $1000 per day, plus reasonable expenses. A very good consultant can more than justify that cost in loss savings for the retail firm.

When receiving the proposal, the retailer should thoroughly evaluate it to ensure that the consultant is qualified to deliver satisfactory results and to ensure that the scope and methods to be used are acceptable.

### Expert Witness

As retailers increasingly find themselves the target of civil lawsuits alleging wrongful action or inaction, the need arises for an expert witness to do research and provide testimony before and during any trial proceedings. Like the consultant, the expert witness must have sufficient education, experience, and training to conduct a comprehensive study of the incident in question and to provide credible testimony.

### Featured Speaker/Trainer

Many in-house loss prevention or operations employees are experts in their field, but are poor public speakers or trainers. Because of the need for well-trained, motivated employees, loss prevention directors solicit expert speakers and security trainers to conduct workshops for key district and store personnel.

### Private Investigators

Small and average-sized retail chains often use outside private investigators to conduct background investigations on prospective employees, to investigate allegations regarding prospective employees, or to investigate allegations of employee theft. Because of the complexity of some employee theft incidents, retail companies that have no in-house investigators should consider the use of experienced, licensed investigators.

### Shopping Services and Plainclothes Agent Patrol

The use of "mystery shoppers" is very common by a variety of retail operations. These individuals, who are specially trained in observation techniques and dressed as ordinary shoppers, test the skill, courtesy, honesty, and procedure compliance of store employees, as actual store practices may be a far cry from stated policy. These shoppers then issue a detailed report that describes their shopping experience. Senior executives may use in-house or contract shopping teams to gauge the actual environment in their stores and to test suspected dishonest employees. Some retailers also hire highly trained plainclothes agents to patrol their stores for shoplifters.

### Uniformed Security Guards

Many local, regional, and national companies exist that provide businesses with armed or unarmed guards. These guards may be used to monitor specific locations during emergency situations such as power failure and special events (e.g., new store opening, large sale, celebrity visit), or used on a routine basis as a form of theft deterrent. The retailer should verify all training claimed by the guard company and scrutinize the guards sent. Ground rules must be established as far as detention of theft suspects and patrol procedures, since most contract guards are not qualified to detect and apprehend shoplifters or dishonest employees.

Retailers should ask for and contact retail client references of any outside agency offering security personnel before securing their services. A contract should also be drawn up and thoroughly reviewed by the retailer's corporate legal counsel before starting the service.

# Chapter 12

# Programs

This chapter highlights some programs retailers can implement as part of their loss control plan. As with personnel and systems approaches to loss control, programs must be selected on a priority basis and tailored to the specific needs of each retail organization.

Retailers should realize that their employees need direction and guidance. Standard operating procedures provide their managers, who are often isolated and thousands of miles from their supervisors, with a handy reference to guide their actions. The difference in having well-planned procedures versus being unprepared could impact the future of the business.

Programs designed to control losses can be categorized as policies, procedures, training, and follow-up.

## LOSS CONTROL POLICIES

Retailers should study loss control policies that have proven successful in other retail chains and design a similar policy based on the particular circumstances of their operation. These policies should have specific objectives, such as to control access, require supervisory verification of certain transactions, require that shoplifters and dishonest employees be prosecuted, etc. A policy tells employees where the company stands on specific issues and what the company will do if the policy is disregarded. All policies should be fair, consistent, and documented. Assemble a policy manual and distribute copies to all stores and department heads. Review and update these policies periodically. The following significant policies should be designed and implemented:

*Employee Searches*—the right to search employees, their packages, and their lockers or desks

*Employee Termination or Suspension Criteria*—the action or inaction that is serious enough to cause suspension or termination

*Non-disclosure of Proprietary Information*—the information that is not to be disclosed to anyone, unless specifically authorized

*Conflict-of-Interest Statements*—the company's position on outside employment and business with vendors

*Alcohol and Substance Abuse*—a policy for screening, detecting, and treating employees with abuse problems

*Expense Accounts*—accepted business expenses and established expenditure limits

*Contact with the Press*—restrictions on making public statements regarding company activities

*Ethics*—accepted and unaccepted ethical behavior

*Employee Preemployment Screening*—established criteria the applicant must meet prior to being hired

*Apprehension, Detention, and Disposition of Dishonest Employees and Shoplifters*—the company's stance on the detection and handling of theft suspects, including criminal prosecution, termination of employment, and civil action

*Evacuation of Premises*—criteria that must be met prior to ordering an evacuation of the premises and those individuals authorized to order such actions

*Auditing Payables*—importance of periodic audits of accounts payable activity

## LOSS CONTROL PROCEDURES

Security procedures build on the stated company policies by telling employees how to carry out the policies. Like policies, procedures should be researched and tested before implementation. They also should be included in the Operating Procedures Manual along with their corresponding policies. Some of the more common loss control procedures are discussed in the following pages.

### Procedural Controls

Procedural controls for cash handling, merchandise handling, paperwork routing, and safety are designed to limit risks by limiting access or vulnerability. Procedural controls include the following:

Cash-handling controls reduce loss of cash and negotiable instruments and include point of sale, cash office, or deposits. POS controls include voids, no sales, cash sales, check cashing, change requests, cash refunds, check acceptance, and credit card acceptance procedures. Cash office controls include limited access, money-counting, drawer and deposit-counting, deposit-reporting, impress fund-auditing, cash pick-ups, cash variance-tracking, and clerk error-tracking procedures. Deposit procedures indicate the techniques to use in depositing sales receipts in the bank.

*Paperwork controls* reduce shrinkage due to manipulation or errors when processing paperwork or data in the corporate office, distribution center, and store. Corporate controls include merchandise purchase orders, computerized data, payroll, accounts payable, and purchasing procedures. Distribution center controls include receiving, processing, pricing, transfering, and shipping procedures. Pricing controls include pricing and price changes (mark-ups and mark-downs), mark out-of-stock, refund slips, and discount coupon procedures.

*Merchandise controls* reduce loss of merchandise at distribution centers and stores. Distribution center controls include separating receiving and shipping areas, verifying purchase orders, separating items, hanging items, EAS tagging, store distribution assignment, protective packaging, and shipping. Store controls include receiving, individual item or carton count variances, processing, display techniques, secure storage of high-loss or high-risk items, protection from elements, return-to-vendor procedures, damaged merchandise log-in and disposal, clerk check-out of merchandise containers, and employee package checks.

*Safety controls* reduce losses from customer and employee accidents, and destruction of assets from natural or man-made disasters. Safety controls include storing and handling hazardous materials or chemicals, reducing fire hazards, eliminating slip-and-fall hazards, and correcting dangerous fixtures.

### Situational or Informational Procedures

These procedures provide guidance to employees at all levels and include the following:

*Shoplifting*—This procedure dictates the criteria an employee needs to satisfy in order to detain a shoplifting suspect and explains the steps to follow in processing the case. To avoid costly lawsuits, this policy and procedure must be well-designed and employees should be thoroughly trained in following this procedure.

*Employee Investigations*—This procedure dictates the steps to follow when conducting an employee investigation to substantiate or disprove allegations and to determine the extent and cause of a problem.

*Miscellaneous Crimes*—These procedures reduce the damages that can occur as a result of different crimes and facilitate the recovery of assets and successful prosecution/civil action.

*Bomb Threats and Hostage Situations*—These procedures detail how to deal with bomb threat or employee abduction situations.

*Natural and Man-made Disasters*—This procedure details disaster prevention, containment, and recovery plans.

*Reporting Structure or Chain of Command*—This procedure details the organizational structure and provides steps to avoid communication misunderstandings.

## PROTECTION PROGRAMS

Programs designed to control losses are an extension of established policies and procedures. For the purposes of this book, programs are broken down into three categories based on the objective of the program—deterrence, detection, and recovery.

### Deterrence Programs

Deterrence programs are primarily designed to prevent theft by discouraging criminal activity, making theft incidents less probable, or by providing data used to plan future prevention activity. A variety of deterrence programs are discussed in the following paragraphs.

#### New Store/Site Selection

The place to start when designing a loss control program is the site of a new store or other facility. Whether the new location is to be built from the ground up or remodeled from an existing structure, the security of company assets must be considered from the start of the planning cycle. Many factors are considered when new store sites are being evaluated and they include

- demographics (i.e., number of target customers in the area)
- visibility of the location
- accessibility of the site
- "anchor" or other stores in the same center if the site is located in malls or strip centers
- available support services
- expenses per square foot
- available advertising support
- area crime patterns

Crime potential is the primary concern of the loss prevention specialist when evaluating a new site. A security employee should conduct a survey of the area and gather input from other area merchants and law enforcement agencies regarding past and projected criminal activity in the proposed site area. The likelihood of crime in the area may not cause a particular site to be abandoned, but the information allows the company to plan and budget for appropriate security efforts.

## Store Environment Design

Just as stores are laid out to positively influence the customer's buying behavior, display fixtures and walls can be designed to discourage pilferage and theft by creating physical and psychological barriers, and surveillance opportunities.

The environmental design and physical layout of individual stores can impact the behavior of the retail shopper. Marein and co-workers noted,

> The retail store is a bundle of cues, messages and suggestions which communicate to shoppers. The retail store is not an exact parallel to the skinner box, but it does create mood, activate intentions, and generally affect customer reactions.[1]

Environmental cues that say "do not steal" or "buy this" are not necessarily mutually exclusive. Store planners can place interior walls and merchandise display fixtures in patterns that can accomplish the dual goals of increased merchandise visibility and protection. The goal of the environmental design concept is to minimize the opportunity to commit a crime in two ways. The first technique involves blocking access to specific areas or merchandise with physical barriers, such as cash registers, walls, display fixtures, locked doors, and merchandise tie-downs. Psychological barriers, such as "Employees Only" signs, also serve to discourage unauthorized personnel from entering into sensitive areas.

The second design technique, surveillance opportunity, opens up displays of high-risk merchandise to better observation by store employees and/or larger groups of customers. For example, by removing the large signs or 6-foot high merchandise fixtures from blocking the view of employees at POS locations, the chances of a potential shoplifter being spotted or deterred increase. Also, channeling the flow of customers near potential crime areas that have walkways is a form of a surveillance opportunity design technique. Other examples of crime control using environmental design include the following:

Eliminate blind spots by rearranging racks or by installing CCTV, domes, or mirrors.

Place high-risk merchandise displays near employee work areas and away from exits.

Keep aisles containing tall merchandise fixtures straight and wide enough to allow full observation.

Place opti-domes or smoked plexiglass panels over all POS stations and cash-counting areas to deter employee theft. Design these locations to readily accept live CCTV cameras.

Fit emergency exits with audible-sounding, observable, panic alarms to disccurage shoplifters from using them as covert exit points.

Limit the number of customer exits and entrances and control them by turnstiles, protect them by EAS sensors, and monitor them by POS stations whenever possible.

Install covert surveillance areas in walls, ceilings, or pillars where store personnel are able to survey the sales floor and use two-way mirrors, false airconditioning vents, and peepholes.

Design receiving and stockroom areas to eliminate hiding places and provide clear observation of the work area to prevent dishonest activity.

Ensure the exterior of the building and parking areas are well-lighted, fenced-off from potential problem areas (such as teen hang-outs, liquor stores, and bars), and readily observable from inside the store.

## Control Procedures

As mentioned earlier, control procedures may be considered a program. This type of program may, in fact, be one of the least expensive, since there is generally no capital requirement. Appendix 7 illustrates selected control procedures that should be integrated into the company's operations manual. This format reinforces the fact that loss prevention should be practiced every day.

## Employee Awareness

This type of program, when combined with procedural controls, is considered the minimum action a retailer should take to control losses.

## Public Awareness Campaigns

In many states, retailers band together to form retail associations to further their common interests. One program often promoted by these associations is a public awareness campaign aimed at making the negative result of a shoplifting arrest a high-visibility issue. Local law enforcement agencies also contribute to this effort by holding discussions with local groups, such as school children in all grades.

## Detection Programs

Detection programs are implemented to detect theft, indications of theft, or vulnerabilities to theft. Prominent examples of this type of program include exception reports, auditing, and store agent patrol.

## Exception Reports

Manual or computerized reports should be designed to detect voids, cash overages or shortages, refunds, and price ring-ups that vary from established company norms. At the point of sale, a system can be devised to report the number of occurrences of a particular type of incident as a percentage of sales. Incidents that can be tracked in this manner include voided transactions, refunds, cash overages and shortages, price variances, number of bad checks accepted, and other activities the retailer desires to track. Immediately, certain stores and clerks will stand out when compared with the average. The loss control department has determined the place to focus training and investigative efforts.

## Auditing

By setting up a planned and surprise auditing program, including a hands-on review of the paperwork and procedure compliance of specific departments or stores, the loss prevention department can spot areas that may develop problems or can uncover existing problems. More detailed information appears in Chapter 17. No retailer should operate without an ongoing audit program.

## Store Agent Patrol

By using plainclothes loss prevention specialists to supplement technology, retailers will detect shoplifters that previously went unnoticed. The use of store detectives is generally considered a reactive measure, but may actually be the ultimate form of deterrence, since it is difficult to steal while in the custody of store agents or police authorities. Any agents used by retailers should be carefully selected and thoroughly trained.

## Recovery Programs

Prevention of loss is the key to any loss control program, but the following programs allow retailers to recoup some of their losses. The following three programs are effective recovery programs.

> *Civil Action*—When retailers fall victim to theft, they may take tort action against offenders in an attempt to recover lost assets in the form of damages. By using civil demand, retailers can help offset some of their losses and security costs.
>
> *Insurance*—By adequately covering risk areas with insurance policies, retailers may be able to lessen the damage they sustain from theft and disaster.
>
> *Tax Write-offs*—State and federal tax laws allow deductions for many types of losses incurred by retail chains.

## POLICY AND PROCEDURE MANUALS

As the number of lawsuits against retail firms continue to increase, retailers are looking for ways to better protect themselves against adverse rulings. One of the most effective ways to protect retailers is to have a written policy and procedure manual—policies and procedures regarding the prevention of theft and error are among the most important. Every company should have a policy manual and security procedures should be an entire section in this manual. Some retailers also prefer to have a separate loss prevention manual (see Appendix 8).

Regardless of the format used, important points to keep in mind include

- document procedures
- update procedures periodically
- adhere to procedures as closely as possible.

While the establishment of sound procedures may greatly assist in defending a civil claim, these same procedures can cause the retailer to quickly lose the case if it can be shown they were not common knowledge or were not used in the field.

The policy and procedure manual is an integral part of any loss control program. The manual should reflect the policies of the organization and should detail how they are to be carried out. By implementing and following sound procedures, the retailer ensures a consistent, long-term approach to reducing losses.

## TRAINING EMPLOYEES

After procedures have been designed, employees must be shown how to implement and use them. Orientation and training are the keys to successful accomplishment of profit goals. Training is one of the most neglected facets of any organization. It is either ignored, underfunded, or assigned to individuals that have no training experience. Employees at all levels must strive to achieve competence in their field and become aware of those habits that make them good or bad at their jobs.

A good trainer must be both competent and conscientious, and training sessions must be well-planned and lively. Each workshop should combine a little entertainment with a lot of education. The trainer must interact with the trainees to allow for a two-way flow of ideas and methods.

Loss prevention training takes two primary forms in any retail company—orientation and training of non-security employees, at all levels, in tasks they can perform to reduce losses, and training security employees on their specific duties. There are several well-produced training videos, with workbooks, available to retailers. These programs may be presented by company employees or outside experts.

To train loss prevention employees, retailers must put together a comprehensive in-house, or solicit an outside, training program. There are training schools available that provide retail security training. Retailers may hire graduates of these courses, have instructors come to the retailer's facility to train employees, or send their employees to the training institute's facilities.

Suggested courses for entry-level training include: retail theft laws; detection, surveillance, and apprehension techniques; safety procedures; employee awareness training techniques; physical security; and report writing.

Appendix 9 provides a checklist that can be used when setting up an in-house training program or when evaluating outside training firms.

Training is the single most important factor in boosting productivity and reducing losses. It is also the least utilized technique. The realities of day-to-day business force retailers to postpone or cut back training programs. As a result, the entire organization is weakened and may never achieve its goals.

## FOLLOW-UP

Policies and procedures have been designed and implemented, and employees have been trained in their use. Now retailers must follow-up on these activities to ensure the success of their long-term loss control program. Follow-up occurs in three forms—testing and update, reward and recognition, and direction and discipline.

### Testing and Updating Policies, Procedures, and Programs

The retail industry is a rapidly changing industry. Because of this fact, no loss control program can remain completely relevant for very long. For example, a policy to control direct store delivery may become obsolete when vendors begin distribution center deliveries exclusively.

For these reasons, the retailer must periodically audit and alter procedures and programs currently in use. Some of the questions to ask about each policy, procedure, or program include, Does this policy fit our corporate or department objectives? Does this procedure unnecessarily hinder the flow of business? Is there a better way? Is the program working? Is this procedure being used?

### Recognition and Reward

Employees should be motivated by their leaders to follow procedures and prevent losses by having their supervisors recognize and reward their efforts.

Employee meetings and get-togethers are the perfect forum for recognizing the contribution of a certain employee to the company's profitability. By calling control practices to the attention of employees, a retailer may reward one employee and deter another from dishonest activity at the same time.

A formal reward program is recommended to ensure that loss control remains a priority with employees. Employees are in a position to make a significant difference in a company's annual shrinkage figure and in today's society, the businessperson must use proven incentives to accomplish their objectives.

One retail chain awards bonus points in the form of a "check" to employees who have been recommended by their supervisor for reporting or preventing a (security/safety) incident. These points are accumulated and used to purchase items displayed in a catalog based on their point value. For example, employees receive 50 points each time they deter a shoplifter or report an unsafe condition. After accumulating more than 500 points, they can purchase an AM/FM stereo. Because employees earn points each time they follow a procedure, they tend to be much more alert all year long. After experimenting with various options, this same chain reported that programs that award cash or gift certificates may actually cause employees (who feel slighted for not receiving a cash reward for *their* action) to take money from a cash register to compensate themselves. These programs keep loss prevention a daily priority, while reinforcing the idea that the only way any employee may receive cash or merchandise from the company is through a paycheck or legitimate purchase.

### Direction and Discipline

Supervisors must give their employees specific direction, in the form of training, to perform their jobs adequately and to follow company procedures. If employees fail to follow a particular procedure, supervisors should gain control by applying discipline.

Discipline is defined as training or instruction that corrects, molds, or perfects actions and is exercised to impose order and reasonable control. Supervisors must maintain some level of discipline in order to keep their groups focused and productive to accomplish corporate and department goals. All discipline should be applied in an objective and consistent manner.

### NOTE

1. R. Marken, C. Lillis, and C. Naranya, "Social Psychology Significance of Store Space," *Journal of Retailing* 52:43–45, 94–95.

# Chapter 13

# Security Systems

The final countermeasures a retailer can choose includes protective hardware and electronic systems. While the total cost of security labor increases, the cost of sophisticated protective systems is decreasing.

This chapter briefly highlights the large variety of available security hardware and electronic systems retailers can use to include in their total loss control plans. For more in-depth information on physical systems described in this chapter, refer to the *Handbook of Loss Prevention and Crime Prevention; second edition*, edited by L. Fennelly and published by Butterworth-Heinemann, New York, in 1989.

The security countermeasures discussed in this chapter generally work in three ways. They

1. limit or control access to sensitive or off-limit areas
2. limit the mobility of protected merchandise
3. physically or psychologically discourage dishonest activity

## ACCESS CONTROL SYSTEMS

The first line of defense in any program involves limiting access to sensitive assets such as cash, property, or information. ID and access control systems of all types are designed to limit or control access to specific areas. The following are examples of access control systems:

- *physical barriers*—fences, walls, and barred windows
- *Entrance hardware*—electric locks
- *Color-coded ID cards*
- *Turnstiles and gates*
- *guards*

Access control technology is constantly changing. Retailers interested in acquiring new systems should carefully review the available products, as well as carefully check references.

There are many miscellaneous control devices now available (or soon to be available) that retailers can take advantage of including

- *clear trash bags or shopping bags*—to discourage individuals from concealing items
- *devices designed to make high-loss items less concealable*—plastic attachments for compact discs and cassette tapes
- *tear-apart price tickets*—to make price-switching more difficult
- *fitting or dressing room tags*—with preprinted numbers or with hanger slots that correspond to the number of items being taken into the dressing room

### Physical Barriers

The following physical barriers are designed to delay or deter intruders:

*Doors*—The barrier at the point of entry must provide maximum delay time by forcing the perpetrator to pick the lock or use sophisticated tools to force entry. The construction must be sturdy enough to resist attack without tools. Door hinges must be inside the door or covered to prevent pin removal.

*Roof*—If a potential intruder can gain access to the roof of the premises, the roof must be sufficiently constructed to resist entry. Roof hatches, skylights, and vents or smoke stacks must be wired-off, locked, and alarmed.

*Floor*—If a perpetrator could gain entry through the floor, floor construction must be of material, such as reinforced concrete, designed to resist unauthorized entry.

*Fences*—Fences are used to define a specific area, deter accidental or non-criminal entry, prevent or delay entry by unauthorized individuals, and guide foot and vehicle traffic from specific areas. Fences should be at least 7 feet tall, anchored to the ground, and of sufficient strength to support a potential intruder.

*Windows*—Windows are natural entry points for burglars and should be kept locked, hooked up to the store's alarm system, protected by protective film or glaze-coated, illuminated by exterior lights, and barred.

### Locks

Locking systems are an important element of any loss control program. Security specialists must take the time to learn about the basic principles of locking mechanisms to select the brand suitable to their use. Some types of locks commonly used include

- *door locks* of all types (e.g., key, combination, electronic)
- *trailer fifth-wheel locks* to prevent the unauthorized removal of trailers
- *trailer door seals* to prevent/detect unauthorized entry into a merchandise trailer.

At this point, it is important to point out some techniques retailers can use to maintain control of keys.

1. Use a key cabinet, which is a cabinet that can be locked, to store all keys.
2. Use a key sign-out log to track keys. This document should also list those individuals who are authorized to check out specific keys. The key log should also be used as an inventory record.
3. Conduct audits of key usage to periodically check key locations.
4. Enforce the rekeying policy and change safe combinations whenever a manager leaves a specific location.

## Safes

Any company location at which more than $5000 is stored overnight should be equipped with a safe. Safes are rated by Underwriters Laboratories (UL) based on their fire and/or burglary resistance ability. Keep safes locked at all times. Use cash cache systems to take cash from the point of sale and place it in a secure container. Safes may be imbedded in the floor or mounted in a wall. Locking file cabinets should be treated like safes.

## LIGHTING

The use of lighting for security purposes dates back to the beginning of civilization. Protective lighting has evolved through the years to the highly efficient gas bulbs of today. Lighting is considered the single most cost-effective deterrent to crime, since it reveals to passersby the presence of individuals attempting unauthorized entry of specific locations.

Primary lighting sources are incandescent, mercury vapor, fluorescent, metal halide, and sodium vapor. These sources provide four general types of lighting.

*Continuous lighting*—provides glare projection or controlled lighting. Glare lighting projects out from a protected area to form a psychological barrier to intruders. Controlled lighting illuminates a specified area while controlling the amount of glare.

*Standby lighting*—the same as continuous lighting, but designed to back up or supplement primary lighting systems.

*Movable lighting*—portable or search light systems.

*Emergency lighting*—generally used during power failure.

Protective lighting can be used inside or outside of any area where a retailer wants to discourage unauthorized activity. High-pressure sodium (HSD) lights are generally regarded as the outdoor security light of choice since they provide fairly accurate color definition, are very energy efficient, and have a long lamp life. HSD lights do have a moderate to high front-end cost, but are more efficient in the long run.

## ALARMS

Alarm systems are designed to provide surveillance of or detect intrusion into an area or object without an expensive investment in manpower. It is much more cost-effective to have alarm systems installed in 100 stores than to station guards in every location. Retailers use a variety of alarm systems to protect stores, warehouses, and merchandise.

The primary function of any alarm system is to signal the presence of an intruder or to detect unauthorized removal of a targeted asset. Peripheral benefits include the deterrence of potential offenders by displaying notices of the use of an electronic protection system. The proper alarm system depends on the area and/or item to be protected. Some questions to be asked when selecting an alarm system include

- What is the asset to be protected?
- What is the asset to be protected against?
- What sensors are available to provide needed protection?
- How is the signal to be transmitted and who will respond?

Some of the more common types of alarm systems currently in use with retail operations worldwide include perimeter protection, area/space protection, and object/point protection. Sensors employed in the perimeter protection mode are designed to detect intrusion into a protected area. Doors, windows, hatches, and vents are protected by metallic tape, glass-break detectors, magnetic contacts, and shock sensors.

Area/space protection sensors are designed to protect outside zones or interior areas of a premises. This system should be separate from the perimeter system in order to act as a back-up system. If an intruder disables the perimeter system, or gains undetected access, the space protection system should detect the intruder. A space protection system is also very effective at detecting a stay-behind intruder or an individual that gains entry through a wall or the roof. Retailers must realize that interior sensors should be carefully and thoughtfully installed to gain maximum effectiveness and avoid false alarms. Common types of area/space protection sensors include the following:

*Photo-electric beams*—signal an alarm when their pulse beam is disrupted.

*Microwave detectors*—detect movement with high frequency radio waves, may be used indoors and outdoors, and may pass through building walls, doors, and windows (application is limited, because of false alarms triggered by movement outside of protected areas).

*Ultrasonic detectors*—sound an alarm when movement is detected by interruption of a radio wave pattern, but will not penetrate walls and may trigger false alarms by air conditioning or water movement.

*Infrared detectors*—are considered passive since they do not transmit a wave pattern, but sense a thermal object (human) moving in and out of their field of view, and may be used indoors and outdoors.

*Sound sensors*—either enable a monitoring guard to listen to noise in the protected area or automatically sound an alarm when the sound level increases above the normal pattern.

Object/point protection systems provide direct protection for a single location or specific object. Two types of object/point protection include the following:

*Proximity/capacitance detectors*—turn the object to be protected (metal) into a sensor (such as a safe) that sounds an alarm when a perpetrator approaches or touches it.

*Vibration detectors*—may be attached to movable objects or located near a wall or window to detect movement and breakage.

The alarm's sensor detects the intrusion and the annunciator (or alarm) signals it. The signal may be monitored or sounded in one of two ways—as a local alarm or at a central station. Local alarms sound an audio-visual signal that serves to warn local individuals and may deter amateur burglars. Central station-monitoring involves the alarm signal being transmitted over telephone wires to a monitoring station.

Before purchasing any alarm system, the loss control director or a qualified consultant should consider four factors—correct sensor selection, correct sensor placement, sensor defeat techniques, and alarm follow-up.

### Correct Sensor Selection

The security specialist, when evaluating the purchase of an alarm system, should consider the asset to be protected, the level of security required, the environment in which the system will operate, and the budget available. Ultrasonic, passive infrared, and capacitance sensors each have advantages and disadvantages that must be weighed before a selection is made. Ultrasonic sensors must be installed and monitored in the area in which they will be located to allow for adjustment of the sensor, since power surges and wind can trigger false alarms. Infrared sensor effectiveness can be downgraded by solid object blockage and confined spaces.

## Correct Sensor Placement

Sensors designed to protect a certain area or object must be correctly positioned to achieve maximum effectiveness. Microwave or ultrasonic sensors should be placed so that intruders must walk directly at them. Passive infrared sensors should be placed so that intruders walk across the collection paths. An intruder could consciously walk between the detection paths by slowly walking straight at the sensor. Because of these differences, a detector unit with both passive infrared and ultrasonic sensors is not usually recommended, since both sensors would not perform at maximum capacity.

Just as important as the position of the sensor is the proper aiming of the sensor and keeping the wave or detection path clear of obstruction. The following planning data will aid in the placement of exterior and interior intrusion detectors.

I.   Exterior Intrusion Detector Planning Data
  A.  Infrared Sensors
    1.  Place bottom beam no higher than 6 inches above the ground.
    2.  Place top beam at least 4 feet above the ground.
    3.  Overlap detection zones.
  B.  Microwave Sensors
    1.  Keep grass and snow lower than 4 inches in the zones between transmitters and receivers.
    2.  Keep sensors far enough away from fences and other obstacles to avoid interfering with the beam.
    3.  Overlap detection zones.
  C.  Fence Disturbance Sensors
    1.  Keep trees and brush from rubbing up against fences.
    2.  Secure any moving parts of fences such as signs, loose wires, and gates.
    3.  Tighten fence posts and fabric to avoid vibration.
II.  Interior Intrusion Detector Planning Data
  A.  Infrared Sensors
    1.  Avoid aiming a heat source or vent at the passive infrared sensor.
    2.  Avoid mounting sensors over, near, or toward any heat source.
  B.  Sonic Sensors
    1.  Avoid placing sonics sensors where an intruder might hear it before being detected.
  C.  Ultrasonic Sensors
    1.  Avoid placing sensor transmitters or receivers near any telephone bells.

2. Avoid air conditioning vents or registers when placing sensors.
3. Avoid aiming sensors at items or areas that might vibrate, such as movable partitions or large windows.
4. Do not aim sensors at each other.

D. Microwave Sensors
   1. Do not aim sensors at water pipes, walls, or windows that allow the beam to detect movement outside of the protection area.
   2. Avoid aiming sensors at vibrating objects or surfaces.

E. Glass Breakage/Vibration Sensors
   1. Mount sensors solidly to object.
   2. Adjust sensors for specific application.

F. Magnetic Opening Switches
   1. Beware of intruders using a magnet to disable the reed contact inside the switch.
   2. Tightly shut windows and doors being monitored to avoid false alarms.

G. Proximity/Capacitance Sensors
   1. Ground the reference ground plane to allow for proper detection.

H. Photo-electric beams
   1. Conceal transmitters, if possible.
   2. Don't use mirrors for detection of distances over 100 feet.

I. Audible Sensors
   1. Be careful not to locate microphones or sensors close to constant or sporadic noise sources.

## Sensor Defeat Techniques

Knowing the techniques some criminals use to defeat intrusion detection sensors is helpful when designing the protection system. For example, an ultrasonic sensor can be blocked by placing masking tape over the cover. Insiders working alone or in concert with others may block sensors or mark the detection patterns on the floor for later theft activity.

Infrared sensors can be defeated by blocking the emitter with objects, glass, hair spray, magazines, or plastic garbage bags. Another sensor defeat technique is to set the room temperature to 85–88 degrees Fahrenheit—the approximate temperature of human skin—and remain in the room until the system is turned on.

## Alarm Follow-up

To make an intrusion alarm system creditable, it must be responded to and kept in working order. If the individual responding to the alarm determines it was false, the cause must be found and corrected.

If a central station is used to monitor the protection systems of distribution centers and stores, an opening/closing report should be generated that lists the activity next to an employee identification number. This report may be used to indicate trends.

## Other Types of Alarms

In addition to intrusion detection systems, retailers use several other types of alarms to signal unauthorized activity. *Robbery duress alarms* are used to alert law enforcement agencies to a robbery or other violent crime in progress by tripping a switch. This type of alarm can be very dangerous since violent offenders may notice a clerk attempting to actuate a switch or may observe police officers responding and take subsequent violent action.

*Merchandise alarms* are hooked up to high-cost/high-loss merchandise (such as electronics). This alarm sounds when the circuit is broken by a shoplifter taking the protected item from its display case.

## EAS

EAS systems protect merchandise by sounding an alarm when tagged items are removed from a store or distribution center. The detection antennae at the store entrance have a deterrent effect, especially when combined with notification signs on the doors.

There are many types of EAS devices, including a dye tag that when tampered with will break a dye ampule and will ruin the targeted garment. Another factor to consider when evaluating EAS systems is to determine how it fits in with the total loss prevention effort. Should hard or soft tags be used? Can the system be integrated with other technologies, such as CCTC or bar coding?

Most EAS companies offer a choice between hard or soft tags, depending on the goods to be protected, the layout of the stores, and the technology used. Figure 13–1 illustrates the characteristics of different EAS technologies.

A growing trend is for merchandise manufacturers to implant dormant EAS circuits into their packaging. These circuits are converted to a live mode by passing through an activation device. By working in concert with manufacturers, EAS companies and retailers all win. The manufacturer moves more products by having their merchandise more openly displayed and retailers more effectively protect their merchandise while increasing sales.

Apparel retailers tend to prefer hard tags that are mixed with soft tags disguised as price tickers, "inspected by" cards that have been placed in pockets or hidden in clothing and shoes. Groceries, auto parts stores, supermarkets, and drugstores often use the soft tag systems.

| Characteristics | Technology | | | | |
|---|---|---|---|---|---|
| | Microwave (High Frequency) | Radio Frequency (Low Frequency) | Electro Magnetic (Very Low Frequency) | Dye Ampule (Non-electronic) | |
| Merchandise Application | Soft Goods | Hard/Soft Goods | Hard Goods | Soft Goods | |
| False Alarm Rate | Very Low | Frequency Splitting RF Very Good | Very Low | N/A: Susceptible to Vandals | |
| Detection or Rate | Good | Frequency Splitting; Excellent; RF Very Good | Excellent | N/A | |
| Defeat Techniques | Cover with body or foil, pressure on tag | Cover with foil; Pressure on tag | Sometimes cover with foil | Remove tag outside of store | |
| Antennae Width at Exit | +20 Feet | +8 Feet | +2 Feet | N/A | |
| Tag Application and Removal Speed | Fast | Soft Tag—Very Fast; Hard—Fast | Very Fast | Moderate | |
| Hard and Soft Tag Integration | Limited | Yes | Yes | N/A | |

FIGURE 13–1  *Electronic article surveillance operating characteristics.*

The following questions should be asked by any retailer investigating EAS systems:

- What technology is used?
- What is the detection or pick rate?
- What is the false alarm rate and what causes it?
- What types of tags are available?
- How can the system be defeated?
- How close to the alarmed exit can tagged merchandise be placed?
- What are the total costs (e.g., installation, training, maintenance, warranties)?
- What is the system's reputation?
- What are the applicable state laws regarding EAS alarm detection?

The cost of EAS systems can be expensive, but should prove effective. However, the effectiveness of EAS systems diminishes as time goes by if store employees fail to react to alarms or use other prevention methods. No technology can stand on its own. It must be supplemented with human surveillance and follow-up. In order for any EAS system to prove cost-effective over the long-term, senior management and store management must endorse its use and ensure that it is properly used. Employees must be trained in EAS system use and properly supervised to add creditability to the system. All targeted goods must be kept tagged and alarm situations must be responded to.

## CCTV

More and more retailers are using CCTV to prevent, detect, and document theft activity in their stores and distribution centers. In a back-up role, CCTV can verify fire, burglar, and robbery alarms, or other access control systems.

CCTV can be installed outside to observe parking lots and alleys, or installed inside to watch high-loss or unauthorized areas. Camera installation can be temporary or permanent. Portable camera kits are used by retail investigators to respond to suspected theft activity. The carrying case may include a small color-chip camera, two or three types of lenses, a portable monitor for aiming the camera, power cords, tools, mounting brackets, and a time-lapse VCR. These covert surveillance kits allow the investigator to respond to a location where theft activity is taking place and quickly install the equipment to record specific unlawful activity. By using this portable equipment, the retailer may avoid the investment of equipping an entire store. Smoked-glass panels or an opti-dome™ may be permanently installed and a camera may be swiftly installed when needed. Aim infrared sensors via lens' to detect movement. Movement triggers the VCR to turn on and the VCR records the target area.

When placing CCTV cameras in stores in an attempt to deter crime, it is important to realize that the pervasiveness of simulated CCTV cameras has negated their deterrent effect to some degree.

Cameras can be equipped with a variety of lenses, including zoom, split-image, night vision, covert (pin hole), right angle, and fixed focal length. The lens' used depends on the area or spot to be monitored, the distance to the target, and the environmental conditions.

Time-lapse VCRs allow the retailer to record a full day's activity on the tape. If a dishonest act is believed to have occurred, the investigator can quickly review the tape. It is possible to produce instant still photos from CCTV video with an attachment.

Date/time generators (DTG) display the current date and time on the screen and can be used as evidence in criminal or civil trial proceedings.

The following questions should be asked when selecting and installing a CCTV system:

- Is a color or black-and-white television required?
- What type of lens is required?
- What type of VCR is needed?
- What type and size of monitor is desired?
- How should the camera be mounted and where?
- What will the light level be during the surveillance?

## OTHER LOSS PREVENTION SYSTEMS

Alarms are a very cost-effective way of protecting assets of all descriptions in stores and storage facilities. However, other strategies and systems may be used to complement alarms to provide greater protection.

*Secure merchandise displays and tie-downs*—High risk merchandise, such as jewelry or handguns, should be kept in secure display cases. High-risk apparel, such as fur coats, leather jackets, and men's suits, should be kept on display fixtures that require a clerk to access them. While this can be very inconvenient, it should save a tremendous amount of merchandise from unauthorized removal. Radios and luggage can be tied down with metal cables to discourage easy grab-and-run thefts.

*Bar coding*—Bar coding allows a retailer to quickly receive, distribute, and ring-up merchandise. This technology makes price-switching and underringing more difficult and can be combined with other technologies, such as inventory trackers, price look-up and EAS systems.

*Subliminal messaging systems*—As advertised by their manufacturers, subliminal messaging systems allow a retailer to broadcast messages (about working safely, staying honest, and being a hard worker) to employees through their music system. These systems present a message to individuals on a level below their conscious awareness. Examples of subliminal messages include, "Be friendly—greet every customer," "Accuracy is important," "Hard work leads to success," and "I am an honest person." Systems now available are virtually tamper-proof and the volume level of the message adjusts to the ambient sound level of the store or distribution center. It is recommended that retailers considering these systems thoroughly check state or local laws that may regulate the use of subliminal messages.

*Lighting systems*—Designed to highlight merchandise the retailer wants featured, lighting systems can also be used to discourage shoplifting by overilluminating areas a shoplifter would normally use as a concealment area.

*Colored signs*—Since the beginning of time, different colors have symbolized different meanings. Red and black denote authority or signal the unknown. According to researchers Farrell and Ferrara, an example of the use of colors to discourage shoplifting is the placement of a stop sign in a high-loss area.

Researchers Farrell and Ferrara, in their book, *Shoplifting: The Anti-Shoplifting Guidebook,* suggest some of the following techniques to discourage shoplifting and employee theft:

- Distribute anti-theft pamphlets in the store or mall.
- Paint or display an eye or poster of an individual looking at customers to psychologically deter theft.
- Use intermittent, low sounds to put the potential shoplifter off balance.
- Display "Thou Shall Not Steal" buttons or stickers at point-of-purchase areas for sale.
- Display album covers of the rock group *Police.*
- Display a book with the word *shoplifter* in the title or display a bible.[1]

*Visual deterrents*—Some retailers find that in some instances, displaying likenesses of police officers or security agents tend to discourage shoplifting activity. Life-sized cardboard cutouts or holographic projections are two methods used to display these images. This practice is intended to remind potential shoplifters of the consequences of theft.

*Paper shredders*—Paper shredders are an important part of the protection program. Documents containing sensitive data, such as sales figures, should be shredded before being disposed. If enough paper is shredded annually, the bulk waste may be sold to recyclers. This extra income may eventually offset purchase and service costs.

*Identification dye sprays and marking pens*—Use inks that are normally invisible, but illuminate under ultraviolet or "black" lights to mark merchandise or documents as belonging to a specific owner. When subjects are detained with a targeted asset in their possession, the item is held under the special light. If the item is marked with the special ink, this indicates unauthorized removal. Examples of marked items include

- currency
- price tickets
- merchandise labels
- containers or cartons
- apparel of all descriptions

*Counterfeit currency detectors*—Many banks and retailers use a machine designed to detect counterfeit currency by variances in the reflection of light off of the ink used in printing bills. This technology is controversial and has staunch supporters and serious doubters. Retailers should confirm supporting research before purchasing any professed currency detectors.

*Computerized time systems*—Computerized time systems are a sophisticated version of the standard time clock. These systems record employee time totals and provide other benefits, such as

- reduce manual totalling and verification time
- fairly and consistently apply company policies, such as grace periods and averaging of uneven times
- restrict employees from punching-in outside of authorized work schedules
- speed up payroll service by transmitting data directly to paycheck generation facilities
- generate hard copy reports to be used as management tools, such as cost-to-sell and budget versus actual payroll hours

*Surveillance aids (mirrors and observation towers)*—Surveillance aids increase the retailer's ability to surveil the sales floor for shoplifters. Mirrors can assist an employee in viewing merchandise or aisles, but may also be used by the shoplifter to look for employees. Many retailers build observation towers in storage rooms, which enable store agents to observe sections of the sales floor from concealed positions. The observation opening may be an air conditioning vent or one-way mirror. These towers can increase the shoplifting detection rate, but the agent temporarily loses sight of the perpetrator while climbing out of the tower and "bad stops" may result. Towers are best used (as is CCTV) with two agents who operate with 2-way portable radios to avoid loss-of-sight incidents.

*Two-way radios*—Two-way radios can greatly enhance surveillance. It is difficult to covertly use radios while surveilling shoplifting suspects due to the obvious behavioral signs given off when talking into a "bag" or due to the appearance of a white earphone in an agent's ear. These systems are best used during dishonest employee surveillance. VHF or UHF radios are best-suited to business security use, since they have the range required and can penetrate through metal buildings. Federal regulations should be checked for any applicable licensing requirements.

Your physical security design should be based on an integrated approach. It should provide protection in depth, contain mutually supporting elements, and be coordinated to minimize gap or overlap in responsibilities and performance. An *integrated system*

- continuously analyzes existing protective measures.
- identifies possible interference with the operational capabilities of installations from any or all sources.
- carefully evaluates all measures that cost-effectively maintain security at the desired level.
- is tailored to the needs and local conditions of each location or activity.

*Mutually supporting elements* include

- physical perimeter barriers
- clear zones
- protective lighting
- entry control facilities
- detection, including the use of sensors and assessment systems
- warning systems
- CCTV

## NOTE

1. Farrell and Fervara, *Shoplifting: The Anti-Shoplifting Guidebook* (New York: Praegers, 1985).

# Chapter 14

# Selecting Protection Equipment and Services

The previous three chapters highlight protection equipment and services provided by outside sources or vendors. This chapter discusses the process retailers use to secure the best quality service or hardware at the best possible price. Retail and security executives are not required to know all the technical intricasies of specific systems, but appropriate purchasing is vital to a successful loss control operation. The systems or services purchased should not only perform to the standard set, but should provide retailers with a return on their investment in the projected length of time.

The process of purchasing security countermeasures basically consists of four equally important elements—specifications, bids, testing, and negotiating the contract.

## SPECIFICATIONS

The first step in the purchasing process is to detail what is needed in terms of performance on the part of the service or equipment. There are some very important performance questions that need to be answered when putting together the specifications for security countermeasures.

- What type of target is the system supposed to detect or deter (see Figure 14–1)?
- What kind of environment and conditions will the system work in?
- Who will install and maintain the system?
- How many personnel are required to support the system?
- Is the system expandable as the size requirements grow or new technology comes along?
- What is covered under the warranty or guarantee?
- Can this system be installed in increments, instead of one installation?

137

Store #

| AREAS: | Self-Service | Employee Lockers | Rest Rooms | Direct Delivery | Source Reps & Reorders | Service Work (Maint./Clean) | Employee Purchases | Control (Jewelry) |
|---|---|---|---|---|---|---|---|---|
| RISKS: | | | | | | | | |
| Shoplifting | | | | | | | | |
| Employee Theft | | | | | | | | |
| Vendor or Deliveryman Theft | | | | | | | | |
| Collaboration: Customer/Employee Delivery/Employee Supervisor/Employee | | | | | | | | |
| Break-In | | | | | | | | |
| Break-Out | | | | | | | | |
| Hold-Up | | | | | | | | |
| Records/Cash Manipulation | | | | | | | | |
| Unauthorized Access to Keys and Combinations | | | | | | | | |

Mark the appropriate control/action number or add any comments to appropriate risk box/area:

1. Authenticated Sales Documents
2. Approved Shipping Document
3. Surveillance
4. Security Device
5. Associate Training/Awareness

6. Receiving Register
7. Truck Seals
8. Lock/Combination Changes and Controls
9. Unobstructed Arrangements
10. Inspection

11. Posted Rules
12. Checklists
13. Location
14. Sensitive Item Control
15. Audit

16. Unannounced Cash Audits
17. Shopper Services
18. Undercover Operator

**FIGURE 14-1**  *Accountability control.*

- Should a reliable consultant or engineer be secured to draw up the specifications of all or part of the system?
- How much is the system likely to cost?
- Are there any hidden costs?
- Is the budget capable of supporting this purchase?

## BIDS

The next step in the purchasing process is to secure bids from competing vendors. In some instances, the only source for a particular product may be single distributors. It is recommended that the retailer accept bids or proposals from three to five companies, at a minimum. The old saying "Buyer Beware," should guide the actions of the retailer studying the qualifications and abilities of various vendors.

During the review process, consider both the technical capabilities of the vendor's product and its support ability.

The retailer's specifications should indicate the level of protection the security hardware or service must provide and the conditions of vendor/client relationship regarding delivery time frames, training, maintenance support. All of these elements are critical. A selection should not be based purely on initial purchase price.

Look into the vendor's background and reputation. What has been the track record of that company's product? Reliability, effectiveness, and access to key people in the security product company are all indicators of a company with which the retailer will want to do business. Ask for and check references from the vendor.

Many retail firms find bidder's conferences a very effective purchasing technique. This technique is used when collecting bids for a large project, such as EAS or access control systems, and involves calling all competing companies together for a single, well-organized, meeting. During the conference, the retailer gives the bidders either a personally guided tour or a slide/video show of the facility and holds an informal question-and-answer session. A short, private tour for each vendor is recommended to ensure receiving the best possible proposal.

The financial status of the vendor is important to the potential buyer since good, long-term support and future technological upgrades are dependent on a financially secure company.

When evaluating the various bids and proposals, it is very helpful to make up and use a simple matrix (see Figure 14–2). This matrix is used to simplify the key data being considered during the bid evaluation phase. All vendors are judged on an even, consistent basis.

|  | Vendor | | | | | |
| Performance Criteria | #1 | #2 | #3 | #4 | #5 | Comment |
| --- | --- | --- | --- | --- | --- | --- |
| Security Need Spec'd | | | | | | |
| On-time Bid Delivery | | | | | | |
| Proposal<br>  A. Technical<br>  B. Costs | | | | | | |
| Propsal Meets Needs | | | | | | |
| Contract Satisfactory | | | | | | |
| References Checked | | | | | | |
| Acceptable Installation<br>  Time Frame | | | | | | |

**FIGURE 14–2**  *Vendor bid analysis matrix.*

## TESTING

Before making a large purchase of equipment or a commitment to a service organization, it is recommended that a controlled test be conducted to determine if desired results and support are obtained. Any test conducted should be consistently applied to ensure that all vendors compete under similar conditions. It is important to allow the test to last a sufficient length of time. By testing the product or service over a period of weeks or months, the probability of discovering problems or ineffectiveness greatly increases before a major capital investment is made.

## NEGOTIATING THE CONTRACT

After all proposals are weighed and ranked, services or products have been tested, and a vendor with the best record and ability to meet specifications is selected, the contract must be negotiated. The retailer, not the vendor, should literally write the contract, specifying when the product is to be delivered, support activities, maintenance responsibilities, and payment schedules. The retailer's corporate counsel should be involved in the wording of the contract and/or its review before the documents are signed. The cost of a good lawyer's services will pay for itself over the long-term by avoiding conflicts over liability for nonperformance, maintenance, etc.

If vendors insist on using their contracts, be aware that their standard, or boiler-plate contract, is designed to place the vendor in the best possible position. The boiler-plate contract is the *starting* point for negotiation, *not* the *final* point. Vendors anticipate that most retailers will insist on modifications to the original contract, but also realize there are a few who may sign the first draft. Any contract should be specific and closely reflect the performance standards that have been established. The following points should be considered when negotiating a contract:

| **During Negotiation** | **Include in Written Contract** |
|---|---|
| • System expandability | • Legal technicalities |
| • System adaptability | • Performance descriptions |
| • Precise threats to be detected | • Equipment or personnel descriptions |
| • Environmental conditions | • Product or service delivery schedule |
| • Operating personnel required | • Security of equipment during installation |
| • Service and maintenance | • Implementation and installation details (i.e., who, what when, where, how) |
| • Spare parts or back-up personnel availability | • System testing plan |
| • Warranty and down-time acceptability | • Payment/lease plan |
| • Distance of vendor operations from retailer | • Maintenance agreement |
| • Access to key vendor personnel | • Warranties |
| | • Mutual indemnification clause |

Document the delivery and installation schedule. Any acceptable intallation plan should be realistic and take into account other activities and projects on the part of both the vendor and the retailer.

Working with the purchasing department, devise a procurement payment schedule with "out" clauses included, if possible, to avoid payment for faulty equipment or in case of adverse financial conditions.

Establish a credit line, if possible, to make final payments only upon complete implementation/installation and good system operation.

During negotiations, obtain purchase discounts, if possible, to cut unit costs and increase return on investment.

Devise a preferred payment method to pay x amount or percent upon awarding the contract, x percent upon installation, and x percent for total payment after a period of satisfactory operation.

It is recommended that at least 10–30 percent be withheld until the product has been judged satisfactory. It normally takes from 72 hours to 2 months before a system can be judged satisfactory. Small or local vendors may not be able to afford a large percentage being withheld.

## Installation and Follow-up

The time frame required to implement a service or install equipment should be detailed in the contract and the vendor should be held to those terms. The retailer should maintain contact with the vendor at regular intervals to make sure all is proceeding according to plan. The vendor's efforts should be supervised periodically to evaluate progress and assist where needed.

The contract should specify a system-check procedure itinerary, such as quarterly or annually, after final acceptance. This plan should be monitored to ensure detection and resolution of problems with performance or effectiveness. In addition to vendor checks, retailers should conduct their own objective surveys of all loss control countermeasures.

To ensure that any implemented program, service, or system achieves the intended results, it must be supported by thorough and ongoing training and reinforcement. In-house and contract personnel must understand the intent and procedures behind specific countermeasures and be motivated to use them properly if lowered losses are to result. In any case, the retailers and all vendors must operate as a team. There must be continuous open communication to gain desired results. Most vendors put their customers first to protect their reputation. Retailers should keep this in mind if problems arise.

# Chapter 15

# Sample Protection Program

Every retail company, regardless of its size, should develop annual business plans. These plans serve as written road maps for those individuals expected to execute them. The loss control plan is an integral part of the overall corporate business plan and, as such, its details must be coordinated with company employees involved in its execution or affected by its impact.

An effective and efficient comprehensive protection plan, begins with the determination of major loss areas and the best countermeasures to address those areas. The security director then selects the best people to implement and manage prevention efforts, as well as sets time tables for implementation and goal achievement.

## WHERE TO BEGIN

All retail companies must appoint a single individual who is responsible for corporate loss control efforts. Depending on the size of the company, or its losses, that position may be either full or part-time. The appointed person will be designated as the authority to plan the loss prevention effort as well as expend the funds required to execute it. No plan can be expected to work precisely as designed but by carefully surveying the company's problems and current prevention programs and establishing realistic prevention procedures, the eventual outcome should be positive.

The first step to take in developing a protection plan is to list the inventory of tasks, time lines, and assets available for the effort.

1. List the tasks to be performed in executing the plan (e.g., training meetings).
2. List all personnel in the company who will play a role in the plan (e.g., CEO, CFO, store managers, loss prevention staff, store employees).
3. List implementation and operational time frames (e.g., by second quarter).
4. List all administrative and support requirements, such as payroll, human resources, transportation or equipment, and use of company computers.

5.  Familiarize staff with corporate and loss control goals and objectives. Reinforce your message with a similar one from the CEO.
6.  Assess the status of any collective loss control efforts already in place.
7.  Establish priorities for countermeasures. Attack your biggest problems first; address secondary concerns later.
8.  Identify individual, collective, and leadership tasks that support loss control efforts. Regardless of the organization's size, every department must get involved. Those individuals in leadership positions must understand their roles and responsibilities. Don't assign a responsibility to someone unable to carry it out because of a lack of time, expertise, or ability.

## HOW TO PREPARE A LOSS CONTROL PLAN

Using an annual/quarterly calendar and a list of individual and leader tasks, the plan can be designed in six basic steps. A sample Loss Control Plan is included in Appendix 10.

### Step 1: Select Priority Countermeasures to be Implemented

As mentioned in previous chapters, selected countermeasures should be the most cost-effective available and should be aimed at those risks deemed the most likely and costly. After reviewing the three previous years' incident reports of the company, it may become apparent that shoplifting is increasing and a combination of awareness training, store detectives, and EAS and merchandise tags may solve major loss problems. This decision may also be based on the fact that the review also indicated only one burglary incident the same period. Therefore, the purchase of new safes can be delayed.

### Step 2: Identify all Collective, Individual, and Leader Tasks Associated with Planned Loss Control Efforts

Each employee involved with the loss prevention effort should be identified and their tasks described, including

- *Collective tasks* of both loss prevention and non-loss prevention employees associated with priority countermeasures
- *Individual tasks* associated with the collective tasks
- *Leader tasks* (implementation and follow-up) associated with the collective tasks

These task lists only need to be prepared once, although they will be updated periodically. Copy the lists and distribute them to each member of the loss control team. Input from company employees at all levels should be actively sought when designating specific tasks.

## Step 3: Identity Collective, Individual, and Leader Tasks to Be Trained and Evaluated Before and During Loss Control Efforts

No individual should be assigned a task or responsibility without first being properly trained. The planners of collective training must sort through all the individual, leader, and collective tasks to determine tasks that need training (based on the best estimate of the current training status derived from observation and reports) and tasks that need evaluation. It is impossible to gather enough evaluators to observe all the tasks being trained. Therefore, those tasks that require special attention should be selected, such as proper techniques to use when counting cash for deposit or changing prices on merchandise. If the director of loss control or the training coordinator is sufficiently aware of training needs, that individual can personally identify these tasks. Otherwise, their identification can be delegated to capable subordinate leaders. A copy of the task list can be used as a worksheet to record the identified or delegated tasks. This step doesn't need to be overly complex, but it is absolutely critical to the success of the overall plan.

The second part of Step 3 is to decide whether the selected tasks are to be trained and evaluated before or during the collective exercise. The following procedure may prove useful in reaching this decision:

1. List the tasks to be trained prior to implementing specific countermeasures, including tasks that are required to implement priority countermeasures.
2. List the tasks that may be trained after total program implementation. Good candidates for this list are tasks that require that specific countermeasures be in place before training can occur, such as monitoring a CCTV system.

## Step 4: Check Resources and Support Availability

There are a great deal of resources and support required to implement and manage an effective protection program. Sources for needed services and assets must be identified and contacted. In addition to budget dollars, examples of resources required include the following:

*Time*—Sufficient time must be allocated for training, implementation, and management of loss control operations. Be realistic.

*Manpower*—The avoidance of building up large staffs is paramount. A streamlined work force should be the goal of any security organization, but there must be enough quality manpower available to effectively control losses.

*Authority*—All the planning in the world will prove fruitless if the employees charged with the responsibility of protecting corporate assets are not taken seriously or have no real authority to accomplish stated goals. Support and backing of security efforts must originate at the very top of any retail company. By the same token, loss prevention employees are cautioned to keep their overall importance to the company in perspective. Loss control is but one of several means to increased profits.

Just as a variety of resources is required to effectively control losses, so is support and cooperation required by groups or individuals inside and outside of the organization. Examples of groups or individuals that can provide needed support of security efforts include the following:

*Legal counsel*—During planning phases, it is important to confer with the company legal counsel on certain matters where action or inaction on the part of company employees could pose a civil liability. It is also important to report any incidents to the company attorney that may develop into a lawsuit against the company.

*Finance/accounting*—Individuals in finance and accounting can be very helpful in putting together budget forecasts, assisting in evaluating vendor bids, and assisting in fraud investigations by spotting or explaining financial documents and paper trails.

*Human resources personnel*—Human resources employees can provide invaluable support by recruiting and selecting top-quality security applicants, providing expertise in matters involving the employment life cycle (such as policies and procedures), and supporting investigations of employee theft or fraud.

*Planning and construction*—Store design and layout play an important role in discouraging and detecting theft. Individuals involved in this type of work can assist in the set up of special observation areas or can prewire surveillance setups. Also, store designers can include psychological barriers when plotting fixture layouts.

*Buyers or merchants*—Buyers and planners have a vested interest in the flow of merchandise from the vendor to the point of sale. They can provide information on the recorded location of particular items or on incoming high-loss merchandise, such as leather jackets or designer jogging suits.

*Distribution center*—Distribution center employees can assist in investigations of missing merchandise.

*Outside firms*—Outside firms, such as consultants, investigators, and guards can all assist in a total protection program without adding to the permanent staff.

*Government agencies*—Police, fire, and government agencies should be contacted and plans established for their support of routine or emergency loss control activities, such as bomb threats, major fires, earthquakes, etc.

## Step 5: Prepare the Training and Implementation Schedule

The training and implementation (T&I) schedule illustrates, for all parties involved, the tasks that are to be performed and when they are to be performed. Supervisors at all levels should participate in creating this schedule, especially if lower level supervisors have been authorized to select individual and lower level collective tasks and training scenarios. If subordinate departments require time for training or evaluation prior to implementing specific countermeasures, an appropriate time frame must be made available.

The T&I schedule has several uses. Subordinate leaders use it to plan training and operations for which they are responsible. Senior leaders and evaluators use it as a basic reference in preparing to evaluate and make adjustments to performance. Supporting departments use it when planning their schedules and budgets.

To prepare a realistic T&I schedule that efficiently uses time and other resources, the security specialist must have a clear mental picture of the daily, real-world conditions under which the loss control effort operates. Manpower shortages, high-crime areas, and the skill of local managers are examples of conditions that vary from location to location and can significantly impact the results of a protection program. These varying and changing business conditions must be planned for. Forecasted results and time frames should be optimistic, yet realistic.

Consider the following points when preparing the T&I schedule:

Use time efficiently. Training and operations should be scheduled to allow for the simultaneous accomplishment of more than one task, if possible. It is also important to attempt to place the right individuals in the right positions. A certain employee may have considerable skill or knowledge in a particular area, but may not have the personality or the desire to become a good leader.

Resource availability should not drive the entire program. If certain services or equipment are absolutely required to reduce shrinkage, the needed resources should be proposed and vigorously lobbied. If desired systems, manpower, and training needs can't be secured in the indicated quality or quantity, this must be planned for.

A critique should be scheduled after each phase of training or implementation. These critiques can be used to discuss the successful and unsuccessful performance of all participants and equipment. This will help ensure that employees remember the correct things they did and will help identify incorrect procedures. The critiques will also provide ideas for future training and how it should be conducted. Evaluators and employees taking part in the programs should be included in any critiques. The extent of the critique depends on available staff and time.

Realism in training is key to a successful profit protection program. Actual conditions should be simulated whenever possible and a moderate degree of stress should be introduced to determine if specific personnel or programs will prove effective over the long-term.

When estimating the time required for training or implementation, leaders who will be conducting the training or supervision should be consulted. These estimates will guide the determination of time requirements. The actual schedule must remain flexible.

Evaluators and observers will use the schedule to be at the proper location to evaluate assigned tasks or training.

### Step 6: Write the Actual Loss Control Plan

Each retail security manager will have a preferred style (or the company will dictate the style) to be used when documenting the annual loss prevention plan. Regardless of the style used, the plan should state, at the minimum, the objectives of the program, the tasks to be performed and the equipment to be used, the individuals to carry out these tasks, the support and resources required to accomplish the stated objectives, and the time needed to accomplish the plan. It may be advisable to design the plan so that it can be implemented in phases (e.g., training, evaluation, implementation, operation, reevaluation, operation).

# Annex  A

## Loss Control Departmental Goals

This annex outlines the goals of the Loss Control Department and the objectives to meet those goals for this fiscal year.

1. **Goal**—Reduce shoplifting losses to under an estimated $6 million annually or .079 percent of gross sales.
   **Objectives to meet goal**—Install EAS systems in all stores. Tag, and keep tagged, 95 percent of high-loss merchandise. Assign one loss control agent to each store. Train 90 percent of all store employees in shoplifting prevention techniques.
2. **Goal**—etc.

# Annex  B

## Loss Control
## Training Objectives

Prioritized listing of training requirements for this fiscal year.

1. Employee awareness training in all stores—At least 90 percent of the employees in each store must complete the Loss Control Workshop.
2. Store management training—All managers must complete the Loss Control Workshop.
3. Store-level agents—etc.

# Annex   C

## Director's Program— Four "A"s for Loss Control

In an attempt to focus our loss control efforts on high-priority risk areas while keeping our program simple, we have organized these efforts into four main areas—Awareness, Auditing, Apprehension, and Area focus. Subordinate leaders will be issued checklist/activity forms to help keep themselves and their employees on track throughout the fiscal year.

### AWARENESS

Employee awareness and training is the single most important issue in dealing with reducing theft and waste in any business. Our ongoing program will show all employees what the problems are, how these problems affect them, and what they can do to reduce these problems. Apathy, changing priorities, and high-employee turnover are realities in any retail setting. Our three-tiered program keeps these facts in mind; it consists of employee workshop packages, awareness bulletin boards, and an incentive award program.

A seminar series for our store employees has been put together and consists of three topics—shoplifting/external theft, employee theft, and safety. Each topic is a separate workshop. The seminar can be given by any manager, assistant manager, or loss prevention specialist and should consist of the custom video and facilitator's guide that shows, step-by-step, how to present the program. Also included are workbooks and handouts. Each workshop can be presented in less than an hour to allow for maximum floor coverage at all times. These workshops can be part of new employee orientation, can be given to a group of employees as reinforcement training, or can be presented according to the manager's wishes.

Each store is provided with a loss prevention awareness bulletin board that is posted either in the employee lounge or central meeting area. The board serves as a constant reminder to employees and is an important part of the program. Three topic updates can be posted on the board monthly—

theft prevention techniques, safety techniques, and congratulation notices to employees who prevented a loss or potential accident the previous month.

To reinforce positive loss prevention actions on the part of our employees, the third part of our program consists of incentive awards. All employees are taught to acknowledge all customers, make add-on sales through subtle suggestive selling techniques, and verify questionable prices. These activities not only increase sales and customer satisfaction, but are proven theft deterrents. When an employe deters an incident, recovers merchandise, or provides information that results in an apprehension, a request for bonus points can be submitted. A "check" for 50–100 bonus points will be issued to that employee. Employees save their points to purchase merchandise from a catalog. With this program, awareness remains a priority with employees.

We will also provide a toll free, 24-hour hotline for employees to report suspicious incidents anonymously or to suggest ways we can improve our security efforts.

## AUDITING

After employee awareness, the second most critical issue in reducing loss is to establish controls on money and merchandise. For the purpose of this plan, we have included the establishment and verification of compliance to loss controls in one section.

We studied procedural controls, used by different retailers, that apply to all aspects of store operations. From these studies, we selected those controls that not only prove most effective, but that fit in our hassle-free customer service atmosphere. All procedures were thoroughly researched, tested, and documented. Employees and supervisors who will practice these procedures will be taught the reasons for these controls and allowed to practice them before going back to the sales floor.

Controls can be internal or external and can be designed to protect either cash or merchandise. In addition to procedural controls, we will also emphasize external controls such as high-quality locks, safes, burglar alarms, glass film, CCTV, and EAS. Our EAS system has been invaluable in reducing the bottom line shrinkage figures in EAS stores. If properly used, EAS can be very effective and presents a positive return on investment. More pre-tagged high-loss items will be requested from the vendor to reduce store labor requirements for this effort.

Once controls are implemented and adjusted to fit in the real-world work flow of daily business, they must be continually tested and reinforced. The best controls in the world are useless if employees don't practice them on a consistent basis (as is very often the case).

Procedures that control voids, refunds, and cash register access are absolutely essential. Our Store Inspection Report is similar to an audit that our loss prevention managers perform with store managers twice annually. The report is used as a positive management tool.

Managers set the mood, as well as the priorities, in their stores. If employees perceive that management doesn't emphasize or enforce procedure compliance, the morale and theft activity reflects this mood. The inspection report will indicate specific problems to the store and district managers, so that a concentrated effort can be made to reduce them.

## APPREHENSION

If a customer or employee steals cash or merchandise from your store, what, if any, action should be taken? A lot of research and deliberation went into our decision to combine criminal and civil action against the majority of apprehended shoplifters and dishonest employees. We felt that arrest and prosecution still provide a degree of deterrence for certain categories of offenders, since "the word" still travels in schools and some neighborhoods. If Store A has EAS, highly trained, effective store agents and/or employees; and prosecutes perpetrators, a thief will most likely steal from Store B.

Civil action against dishonest employees and shoplifters has been made relatively easy with the advent of civil demand laws that exist in at least 44 states. Civil demand has not only proven itself effective in our stores as a deterrent to repeat offenders, but is a deterrent to juvenile theft as well. Parents tend to keep a closer eye on their children when their theft acts begin to impact the household budget.

When dishonest employees or shoplifters are taken into custody for commiting a crime, they are deterred from theft activity for as long as they are detained. Other potential criminals who hear of the situation may think twice about committing a similar crime in that establishment. The detention also may result in a recovery of assets.

A third benefit of apprehension is the opportunity to interview the suspect. Interviews often provide the retailer with valuable intelligence. Information collected from these sources can reveal break-downs in controls or morale, implicate others involved in criminal activity, and can provide insight into methods and motives of shoplifters and dishonest employees. For these reasons, we will not be discouraged from pursuing the apprehension of offenders.

## AREA

All merchants have high-loss stores and high-loss departments. Our comprehensive exception report tells us, on one page, which stores, employees, or merchandise areas are experiencing the majority of the problems in voids, refunds, price variances, cash overages and shortages, bad checks, and shrinkage percentage. We will combine these data with a trend analysis report that indicates type of incident, high-loss time, and high-loss location to allow our loss prevention resources to be quickly and efficiently applied.

# Annex   D

## Individual Departmental Tasks

The following guidance is provided for training and operation of individual departments within the company.

1.  Loss Control—will concentrate on the tasks listed in Annex C.
2.  Human Resources Department—will implement sound preemployment screening techniques and will provide advice and support during dishonest employee investigations.
3.  Finance Department—etc.

# Annex   E

---

# Follow-Up
# Interdepartmental
# Meetings

In order to ensure effective two-way communication and conflict resolution to achieve ultimate corporate objectives, a follow-up meeting is scheduled between the Loss Control Department and each of the departments that play a significant role in the corporate loss control effort. This schedule is flexible to allow for additional meetings, if required.

is fiscal year.

- Human Resources—March 15, 1991; Meeting Room C; three representatives
- Finance—etc.
- Store Operations—etc.

# Annex  F

---

# Fiscal Year T&I Calendar

This schedule provides the anticipated start and completion dates for training and implementing loss control countermeasures. This schedule should be used as a guide for all departments and supervisors when planning resources and activities required to successfully implement an effective control program.

**FIRST QUARTER**

- Feb. 1–3; Install EAS ssytems in stores 14, 28, and 29–31.
- Feb. 5–8; Provide training on EAS procedures in applicable stores.
- Mar. 2–5; Provide loss control training to store managers in Region 2 etc.

# Chapter 16

# Implementing the Program

Once the protection program has been designed, it must now be implemented. The task of beginning a corporatewide loss control program can be very complex. The security specialist must understand the objectives and methods, and gain the support of senior executives and peers if the control effort is to be a success. Everything possible should be done to ensure a near, problem-free implementation of the total loss control program.

## JUSTIFICATION OF THE CONTROL PROGRAM

Once a total asset protection program has been developed, it must be justified to those individuals who pay for it. Retailers must justify the program in terms of the need for protection of assets to control costs and, therefore, ultimately to increase gross profit margins. The tendency, for most retailers, is to consider the security function to be, at best, a "necessary evil" that displays little tangible benefit. Therefore, the loss control specialist should strive to demonstrate that shortage control programs *can* play a positive role in the business and need not always be viewed as a negative activity.

While the programs are being designed, the loss prevention specialist should ask and answer the questions that will, or should, be asked by senior management regarding the plan. Do the expected results of countermeasures justify the expense? Is this countermeasure the most cost-effective technique available? Is this countermeasure absolutely necessary? Can the company afford to capitalize requested security equipment purchases? Can a positive return on investment be shown for each countermeasure?

All countermeasures do not need to be cost justified. Few corporations would require a security director to justify the need for fire or safety protection, but they may question the methods and equipment used.

### Cost Justification

When funds are spent on security efforts, those funds are not earning income by investment. The security specialist can use three methods to demonstrate to top decision-makers, in economic terms, the need to protect assets.

159

*Cost avoidance*—Cost avoidance shows the losses that will most likely occur if the security program is not implemented or is only partially implemented. If the amount of the loss exceeds the cost of the program (and the capital cost of the money spent on the program), then the program can be justified. For example, if the cost of locking 100 leather jackets, which cost $250 each, with cables is $1200 and the estimated loss of these *protected* jacks is zero (compared to the projected loss of $10,000 if the jackets are not cabled), this indicates that the proposed cabling program should result in a savings of $8800.

*Recovery of Assets*—Recovery of assets includes the projected dollar amount of total merchandise and cash recovered due to security efforts in a fiscal year. Examples of recoveries include

1.  an employee who is apprehended for writing a false refund for $170. The cash taken from the register is recovered. Additionally, the cashier admits to taking $3500 over an 8-month period and begins paying that money back in monthly payments.
2.  three shoplifters are arrested carrying $1800 worth of athletic shoes out of a store in plastic garbage bags
3.  a sales clerk notices that a customer is attempting to purchase $198 worth of merchandise for only $58 because the price tickets have all been switched

*Return on Investment (ROI) or Expenditure*—ROI includes totalling calculated avoided losses and their resulting costs, and counting the cost of merchandise and cash recovered. The retailer then subtracts the projected cost of the loss control program from the above ROI figure (or the combined total of avoided loss and recoveries), which includes all losses to be avoided and the dollar amount of recoveries projected. It is not possible to precisely project the ROI of any protection program, but the program should show an acceptable return over the specified time frame.

### Selling the Protection Program to Senior Management

In addition to the cost justification, there are some other methods that loss control directors can use to convince top managers that their loss control program is worth the proposed costs.

Conduct (or have a consultant conduct) a thorough survey and analysis of the company.

Document the protection plan in clear, concise terms.

Open, and keep open, lines of communication with all key decision-makers and the individuals that influence those decision-makers.

Deal in principles, not personalities, when collecting data to support the proposed program.

Be aware of the feelings about security that many retailers have. These feelings range from support, to indifference, to outright hostility and may be due to previous exposure to obnoxious or incompetent security "types." At all times, loss control executives or their staffs should dress and act like competent professionals.

Maintain an air of neutrality and professionalism, and avoid a narrow, self-serving view of corporate goals and objectives.

Maintain a fresh and focused view of the department's methods and objectives by reading books and journals on retail and retail loss control. This activity on the part of the loss control executive will become apparent to key decision-makers.

After the security manager (and/or the security consultant) has analyzed all obtainable data and structured the protection plan, the following sequence of events is recommended:

1. Prior to scheduling a meeting with senior management, start a public relations program within the company to determine the feeling most emplcyees have about safety and security at the work place. Personally visit stores and key corporate employees to discuss their perceptions of the current loss control effort to make your plans for better control clear and to attempt to gain their support of loss control efforts.
2. Timing is important in any situation and presenting a loss control plan and budget at the appropriate moment is beneficial. If at all possible, the loss prevention director should time the initial submittal when the executive committee is most receptive. It may be very difficult to judge this, but, often times, either a very positive or very serious incident may create a favorable atmosphere for making the loss control pitch. Always be prepared for the presentation.
3. When presenting the proposal, keep it short and to the point. Discuss the highlights and the projected results of the plan. Make sure that issues that are based on educated guesses are described as such. Do not over or underexaggerate the capabilities of the program.
4. Keep in mind that very few programs are accepted in their initial form. Remember that thorough research and a well-prepared plan is appreciated.

## TEAMWORK

Any loss control program is doomed to failure if all individuals concerned are not brought into the planning and implementation "loop." A concerted effort must be made by loss prevention specialists to present their educated views as well as to listen to the views of others. No effort will be conflict-free; human nature will not allow for all individuals to agree on every issue or method. However, it is possible to rise above misunderstandings and personality clashes to achieve shrinkage control goals.

# PART IV

# Testing and Follow-Up of the Loss Control Programs

# Chapter 17

# Auditing and Follow-Up

Any loss control program should be continually inspected to ensure it is relevant to the current situation and effectively achieves its goals. The inspection process should have a well-conceived structure in order to collect the specific data required to give the most accurate picture of the shrinkage situation. This inspection will also help judge the efforts that control shrinkage. This chapter demonstrates some of the tools available to retailers to help evaluate their loss control efforts.

It is important to note the fact that many people resist change. Because of this resistance, recommendations resulting from an inspection may be difficult to implement.

Another factor to consider when designing the company audit/inspection program is the natural defensive posture taken by anyone or any department that comes under close scrutiny. Any inspection program must be tempered with diplomacy and tact. No program that reflects a "gotcha" attitude will succeed. The plan, as well as those chosen to promote it, must reflect the true intent of the exercise—to gain an accurate picture of problems so that those problems can be fixed.

The purpose of an audit and follow-up plan is to determine the level of compliance to company policies and what would happen if changes are required to better achieve full compliance. The next step in the audit process is to design the changes. Finally, those changes must be implemented. The programs appear sound, but the individuals being inspected may be reluctant to cooperate in any or all of these phases. It then follows that senior corporate managers must understand and wholly endorse the program in order for it to succeed. It is the responsibility of the loss control manager to ensure that key members of company management are aware of the risks that exist if such a plan is not carried out. Once the top managers understand the cost-to-benefit ratio of this activity, they can make an educated decision about any phase of the loss control plan, including the audit and follow-up phase. The true support of senior management will be tested at some point—either an influential employee or a significant event will force the issue. By keeping the lines of communication open between the loss control manager and senior management, misunderstandings can be kept to a minimum.

## INSPECTIONS

The audit/inspection program can take many different forms. It can be a formal, structured program; informal; unstructured; or a combination of all of these. All inspection programs should be continuous, as the organization and its problems are constantly changing, and new technology and procedures are being developed and made available periodically.

Perhaps the best design for the inspection program is a combination of formal and informal events. By asking senior managers to accompany the security specialist on scheduled and announced inspections, the three following objectives can be reached:

1. Key company managers become personally familiar with loss control vulnerabilities and countermeasures.
2. When senior executives are seen actively inspecting current loss control initiatives, rank-and-file employees realize loss control is a priority issue with top management.
3. People, programs, and systems are reviewed and evaluated. If the program is proving successful, future security proposals tend to be easier to "sell" to senior management.

    Informal or unannounced audits are just as important as formal inspections. These visits can be preplanned or purely spontaneous. Informal inspections should be the norms, since it is imperative that the loss control manager get a realistic view of normal routines and practices. As stated earlier, security personnel must go to great lengths to avoid turning company employees against them by using unannounced audits as weapons against selected or targeted individuals. All audits/inspections should be fairly and consistently applied. This does not mean, however, that high-loss stores or departments should not receive closer scrutiny or special attention. These stores are a logical place to start concentrated control activities. Sometimes, certain managers may be capable of covering shrinkage problems by "playing games" with merchandise or paperwork (such as temporarily changing prices to increase revenue). It is for this reason, as well, that audits should be conducted of all areas of the company.

    Inspections and audits should be conducted by different people, depending on the data to be collected and/or the objectives of the inspection. If the data to be collected are procedural and financial, internal auditors or specially trained loss control inspectors would be designated to conduct the audit. If, however, a strong message is to be sent to the managers and employees being visited, higher ranking managers are the appropriate personnel to carry out the inspection.

    The use of a qualified security consultant is recommended in cases when there is no in-house security department or when the loss prevention director needs an objective, "fresh" perspective on current activity.

Outside consultants can also bring new solutions to problems encountered by different retail operations.

## EFFECTIVENESS ANALYSIS

The point of conducting program inspections/audits is to measure loss prevention program impact and effectiveness. All indicators studied should be end-oriented and should relate to loss control program strategies, goals, and objectives. By evaluating end-oriented data, the results of an effort, rather than the effort itself, can be determined and the effort's effectiveness can be gauged. It is at this point that procedures and systems can be evaluated for necessary fine-tuning or elimination.

## DATA COLLECTION

Data collected and used in the formulation of the protection program can be compared to data collected during inspections conducted at planned intervals. Examples of this type of data include

- inventory shrinkage figures
- reported incidents (quantity and distribution)
- comments and perceptions from rank-and-file employees

These data, when compared to similar data collected earlier, should indicate an upward or downward trend in problem areas. The trend direction indicates success or failure of implemented countermeasures. Trends must be studied in relative terms. In other words, new store locations or new risk problems may distort the numbers. If all numbers are given as a percentage of sales, or a fairly constant percentage, then comparison of trends will be much more accurate.

## INSPECTION/AUDIT REPORTS

Every retailer will have a preferred procedure for auditing their operation, as well as a preferred method of documenting their efforts. The objective is to implement a fair and consistent procedure that stands the test of time. An example of a standard store inspection report is included in Appendix 11.

# Chapter 18

# Inventories*

## RETAIL METHOD OF INVENTORY

As every retailer knowns, an annual physical inventory of all merchandise is required by federal income tax law. However, this should not be your only reason for taking inventory. A physical inventory serves several purposes that are as important as satisfying the legal requirement. But unless it is meticulously taken to ensure its accuracy, you will find that the information obtained is worthless and misleading.

By comparing the actual physical inventory with the book inventory, the retailer is able to check the accuracy of the record keeping that is being done, not only in the office but in the receiving and marking department and on the sales floor. Many things will affect the accuracy of the book inventory, such as unrecorded markdowns, unrecorded markdown cancellations or markups, merchandise sales that are recorded in a wrong class due to carelessness, or merchandise received and counted in the physical inventory without its invoice being recorded in the books. The list can go on an on. The important thing to remember is that careless record keeping and the resulting "paper shortage" will hide real shortages caused by shoplifting and theft.

If the retailer will keep unit inventory information in addition to cost and retail, he/she will have a tool to be used to analyze the amount of shrinkage that has occurred since the last physical inventory was taken. This shrinkage can tell the retailer many things if he/shewill take the time to analyze it. By comparing the average retail dollars of shrinkage with the average retail price of merchandise sold and merchandise in the actual ending inventory, he/she will be able to determine how much of the shrinkage is due to unrecorded markdowns, merchandise recorded in a wrong classification, missing merchandise or employee theft.

Of course, if the physical inventory count is inaccurate, the information obtained will be useless. An inaccurate physical inventory has many far-reaching consequences that retailers often do not consider when actually

*This chapter was contributed by retail management consultant Gerald H. Smith and is printed with the permission of Gerald H. Smith and Associates of Dallas, TX.

preparing for and taking a physical inventory. An inaccurate physical inventory that overstates the total amount of merchandise actually in inventory at year-end will result in overstated gross profit and net profit for the current year, which in turn can result in the paying of excess income tax. This misstatement of gross profit and net profit will distort the company's financial statement for two years, the year in which the inaccurate physical inventory took place, and the following year, when the inaccurate physical inventory is corrected by the taking of a correct physical inventory. Many retailers base their store manager's and/or buyer's compensation, in part, on the achievement of certain gross profits, stock turn rate and shrinkage goals. When the physical inventory is incorrect, this causes the amount of compensation to be computed incorrectly. While one manager could be overcompensated, another could be unfairly penalized.

A bad physical inventory can also seriously affect a company's merchandising decisions by causing erroneous information at the classification level, even though the overall store figures look valid. If the actual inventory counts taken in the store for each class are incorrect, the buyers will be basing their purchases on figures that are distorted. For example, if the physical inventory erroneously shows that a particular classification's inventory level is too low, the buyer will mistakenly buy merchandise the store doesn't need. This can simultaneously work the other way, with the inventory showing that a class has too much inventory. In this case, the buyer will avoid placing needed orders and sales can be lost.

## THE INVENTORY PROCESS

As shown in the above examples, it is easy to see that a physical inventory carelessly taken is worse than not taking one at all. Instead of bringing the book inventory back in line with what is actually in stock, a bad inventory just causes extra work and confusion, and results in a wealth of misleading information. Fortunately, there are steps the retailer can take to ensure the accuracy of a physical inventory.

The taking of a good physical inventory involves almost all of the store's employees, whether they work on the sales floor, in the receiving and marking department or in the office. It is also requires careful advance preparation. The merchandise on the sales floor must be checked to verify that the information on the garment tags is correct. Personnel must be scheduled for the actual count. The numbered inventory count sheets must be ordered, and written procedures must be established to ensure a clean cut-off of all movement of merchandise and the resulting paperwork. A store meeting must be held to review the procedures and emphasize their importance.

No matter how careful the retailer and his/her employees are, there are items that may be overlooked, which can result in a poor count. Following are some of the things to be aware of and watch out for in preparing for and taking a physical inventory. You can most likely add more based on your own experiences.

- Merchandise held for evidence
- Merchandise out for repair
- Merchandise on display
- Merchandise taken out of the store for use in developing advertising
- Hold merchandise
- Owned merchandise being repaired in the alteration shop
- Merchandise being stored in a seldom-used storage area
- Improperly counted interstore transfers
- Merchandise in the receiving area that is not counted, even though the paperwork was processed, or vice versa
- Merchandise taken off the sales floor by a buyer and left in the buyer's office
- Damaged merchandise that was taken off the sales floor for which the RTV has not been processed
- Merchandise returned by customers but not put back into stock
- Merchandise left in the layaway room, even though the paperwork has been processed to return it to return it to stock
- Merchandise stored in what inventory counters assume is an ''empty'' box
- An inaccurate cut-off of paperwork: receipts, interstore transfers, price changes and return-to-vendors

On the day the inventory is taken, inventory teams must be carefully instructed concerning the appropriate manner for counting the merchandise and filling out the inventory count sheet. If outside help and non-sales employees are used, it is important that the person doing the actual counting is familiar with the merchandise, and can therefore spot any mismarked merchandise that otherwise might go unnoticed. All teams should be checked during the first half-hour to verify that the forms and being filled out correctly, as this will prevent a large number of recounts. Finally, it is of the utmost importance that all count sheets be left on the fixtures until unit counts are verified and the store manager is ready to begin picking them up. This helps to ensure that everything is counted.

The taking of an accurate physical inventory, because of the many details that must be attended to, can be an awesome task. But it is not impossible. Remember, it takes no longer to take a good, accurate physical inventory than it does to take a sloppy, inaccurate physical inventory.

## INVENTORY TIPS

- Conduct an inspection tour and prepare a listing and timetable of things to do in preparation for inventory.
- Train all personnel on inventory procedures.

- Develop a floor plan—a drawing of the selling and stock areas.
- Arrange merchandise in the stockrooms and on the selling floor to facilitate a timely and accurate inventory.
- Perform a careful review of store paperwork to be sure that all adjustments and corrections have been made.
- Clear up problem receipts before inventory.
- Do not allow merchandise to be moved during inventory.
- Provide adequate supervision for all inventory counting teams.
- Verify counts made on a random basis.
- Remember, *communication and training are key elements to an accurate inventory!*

# Chapter 19

# The Future

No book on loss control would be complete without a chapter discussing what lies ahead for retailers and, specifically, for security specialists. The forecasting of future trends is an inexact science, but it is also one of the most important tasks a competent executive can perform. Strategic as well as short-term activities should be planned with an eye toward the future. The world is rapidly changing, demographically and geopolitically, as seen by the radical changes taking place in eastern Europe. These changes have a dramatic impact on the way retailers do business. They also determine the way crime and loss affect the retail industry.

## INDUSTRY TRENDS

### General Trends

Retailers are taking more time to carefully plan their future business moves. This trend should continue as chains reevaluate company images, pricing strategies, and customer convenience practices, and target customer profiles. Many retailers are forced to service mounting debts that are a result of leveraged buy-outs and acquisitions.

Another significant trend that must be recognized is the shrinking labor pool, which provides entry-level employees.

Most retail chains are beginning to apply more and better training resources to their lower level managers. These managers must cost-effectively run the business. In order to remain flexible and responsive to rapidly changing needs and problems, decision-making authority must be granted at a much lower level. Merchandise mixes, employee-hiring needs, advertising requirements, and security levels will vary greatly from region to region and even neighborhood to neighborhood. Centralized command and control will become obsolete. Overall company goals and objectives will be based on more realistically achievable goals that are set by the various store managers. Goals and objectives will not be set solely by an executive committee that is isolated from the day-to-day operations and realities of the store.

Also, be aware that the use of technology is decreasing the manpower requirements in the central office, distribution facility, and stores. This decrease will significantly decrease "paperwork" shrinkage and employee theft. The downside to this trend is the resulting loss of personal service to the customer and an increase in shoplifting losses.

### Drug Abuse

As the use of illegal drugs increases, theft incidents increase. Employees and shoppers who abuse drugs constantly need a supply of available cash to purchase their drugs and associated paraphernalia. A retail store or warehouse is the ideal source of ready cash, as merchandise can be easily converted to cash. Liberal store refund policies provide the best source of cash to the hardcore shoplifter. As substance abuse testing procedures become less obtrusive, they will become more routine.

### Employee Theft

As the labor pool decreases, retailer's preemployment screening efforts will become increasingly futile. The merchant will be forced to hire whatever applicants show up. Also, as lower level managers are forced to handle more and more tasks, the level of employee theft will rise as supervision and policy enforcement decreases.

Companies must make a concentrated effort to recognize and reward employees for sound loss control behavior. Morale levels in stores and distribution centers must be kept high. Employees must be made to feel an important part of the operation. Managers at all levels will be held more accountable for their focus on procedural controls, which directly affect year-end shrinkage levels.

### Shoplifting

Store pilferage is, unfortunately, a fact of life in our society. This practice will continue to increase. Merchandise display methods will directly determine the amount of shoplifting losses a retailer can expect. The trend of extended store hours and fewer store employees will continue and these practices will boost theft losses for obvious reasons. As store designers cram more items into each square foot of the display floor and create blind spots, theft levels will increase accordingly.

All store operations must implement and maintain employee awareness and reward programs to positively impact theft losses from shoplifting. No other technology is more important than employee involvement.

As technology improves, it will provide retailers with the tools they need to significantly reduce theft losses. By integrating EAS with CCTV and with access control, merchandise and access to that merchandise can be more effectively controlled. As EAS tags are implanted by manufacturers in their products or on their product's packaging, the systems become much more effective. The systems also become less costly to operate, since the tags are included with the product and do not need to be purchased separately. Manufacturers generally absorb this cost because their merchandise will be displayed more openly—which means more sales.

By using civil recovery, retailers can further reduce the cost of EAS and other protective technology by generating revenues from apprehended offenders.

### Paperwork Errors

Technology improvements will reduce errors in pricing mark-downs and inventory manipulation. UPC-scanning, DSD, and price look-up technologies will steadily improve and will result in more efficient and accurate purchasing, accounts payable, delivery verification, and point-of-sale transactions.

### SUMMARY

As always, the future holds much uncertainty and much excitement for the retailer. This is especially true for those employees, or outside experts, charged with the responsibility of protecting corporate assets. It is no longer someone else's job to plan for and adapt to our rapidly changing world. The businesses that survive the next two decades will do so because of their strategic, flexible approach to doing business.

The bottom line is to get back to basics. Clearly define problems and goals, and devise and implement simple, plainly stated strategies to reduce the negative impact of loss control problems. Swiftly changing technologies will greatly enhance loss control efforts, but good, sound leadership and management provides the ultimate resolution to loss control problems.

# Appendix 1

# Sample Conflict of Interest Policy

1. OBJECTIVE

   The purpose of this policy is to provide to key employees of the Company basic principles and guidelines to aid in avoiding conflicts of interest. The Company is committed to conducting its business in accordance with the best interest of its shareholders and the highest ethical standards. The Company likewise expects all its employees to conduct themselves in accordance with the highest standards of integrity, honesty, and fair dealing, including avoidance of any conflicts between the interests of the Company and the personal interests of the employee.

2. DEFINITION OF CONFLICT OF INTEREST

   A conflict of interest occurs when an employee allows the prospect for direct or indirect personal gain to influence his or her judgment or actions on behalf of the Company.

3. STATEMENT OF POLICY

   a. Each employee with be free of any investment, association or connection which interferes, or may be considered to interfere, with the independent exercise of his or her judgment on behalf of the Company.

   b. The fulfillment of this obligation shall include, but not be limited to, the following:

      i) No employee or his or her family * may own, directly or beneficially, any financial interest in any supplier if the employee is in a position to influence decisions with respect to the Company's business with that supplier.

      ii) No employee or a family member may hold a position of director, officer, employee or agent with any supplier or potential supplier.

      iii) No employee may accept cash, gift certificates or trips for any reason whatsoever from any vendor or supplier. Token Christmas gifts of $25.00 or less and vendor promotional gifts (containing vendor's name) may be accepted. The acceptance of conventional business courtesies, such as an occasional lunch or dinner, is not considered capable of influencing an employee to disregard the best interests of the Company.

---

* For this purpose, the employee's family includes the employee's spouse, parents, children, siblings, mothers- and fathers-in-law, sons- and daughters-in-law and brothers- and sisters-in-law.

    iv) No employee should use information which comes to them in the course of their employment for personal investment or gain. This would include dealing in the Company's stock while possessing insider information. **

    v) Any employee who becomes involved in, or becomes aware of any situation which represents a possible conflict of interest, is to immediately report that situation to their supervisor or the Chief Financial Officer.

4. REPORTING REQUIREMENTS
   a. The attached conflict of interest certificate should be completed annually by all:
      i) Employees of Director level and above, including buyers
      ii) Any other employee requested to do so by the President, an Executive Vice President, Senior Vice President or Vice President.
   b. Certificates are to be sent to the Chief Financial Officer, or designee. New hires may be requested to complete a certificate when hired.
   c. Any questions should be directed to the Chief Financial Officer.

---

** For this purpose, insider information means information about the Company which is not generally available to investors and which would be substantially likely to affect either (1) a reasonable person's investment decision regarding the Company's stock; or (2) the market value of the Company's stock.

    The definition of insider information and trading on insider information are defined in much greater detail by *Regulation of the Security and Exchange Commission.* The definition given in the above paragraph should be sufficient to provide guidance to most individuals. If further clarification or assistance are required, please contact the Chief Financial Officer.

# Appendix 2

# How-To Manual for Shoplifters

According to police intelligence, two schools for shoplifters were found—one in Casper, Wyoming, and the other in Dallas, Texas. Printed material provided by the Texas school was also confiscated and is very similar to material which was taken from a shoplifter in Southern California in 1983.

Read this document carefully. Reprint it for your store employees. Discuss it in store meetings. This is how store personnel and security people are perceived by professionally trained thieves. Only by understanding shoplifters and their methods, and by being constantly aware, can the retailer defend against professionally trained shoplifters.

The following is the unedited text of what appears to be a procedure manual for shoplifters. The "manual" was taken from a shoplifter who was arrested in Southern California during the summer of 1983.

## DRESSING ROOM

This method should not be used unless you can't "do it off the floor," or the opportunity is obvious. Of course, many stores have dressing room counters and this prevents their use. The most important thing to remember in working the dressing room is to make sure no one can tell how many and what specific pieces you have taken in; needless to say, if you are planning to take 4 or 5 pieces, it is necessary to take into the dressing room at least twice that many. Of those that you take in, it is essential that the pieces be similar; this is because if a salesperson or security sees you, they see a certain print or style go into the dressing room and if it is not there when you are finished, it will tip them off. So whatever pieces you decide to take, make sure you have at least one other of that print. A good way of disguising how many pieces there are, is to hang the piece you want to take on the one you're not going to take.

Never wander around with any of the pieces you are planning to take because not only will the salespeople want to help you or hold them for you or put them in a dressing room for you, all of which defeat your purpose, but it gives security a chance to count how many you have.

Figure out which pieces you want to take and either swing them around to one rack or when the salespeople are not paying any attention to you, quickly gather them up and go into the room. Try not to look too obvious about this because you never know if security is watching. Once in the dressing room, separate out which pieces you want to take and try to hide them by putting them on a chair, covered by your jacket. Often saleswomen will come in and check on you and when this happens, your pieces are protected. Most dressing room doors have slits in them which face in your direction; these allow people on the outside to see in. These were designed specifically for this purpose because before security can make a bust, they have to be absolutely sure that you have taken something and the best way to do this is to observe you.

One way to guard against this is to hang some clothes on the door itself so they cannot see in. You can see if someone is observing you by bending down low and looking up through the slits or open the door and see if someone is out there. Once you have taken your pieces, leave the remaining ones in the dressing room.

This gives you more time to leave the store undetected because by the time someone goes back there to see what's left, you will be on your way out.

If you feel uneasy about something and you want to test if security is suspicious, take the remaining pieces out and see if they are paying attention or acting funny. One thing to your advantage is that when a salesperson is suspicious, they will almost always show it by acting rude or looking you up and down, etc.

## OFF THE FLOOR

This seems a lot more nerve-wracking than in the dressing room because you are practically doing it in front of people around you. The best ones are those that block you from view of any and all people around you; the best ones are those that shield you from both sides. Of course, you can't have anyone close by, but as long as no one can see you, don't be stopped by other people in the department. The only thing you have to worry about is observation windows and 3-sided mirrors. Also, many stores have disc shaped mirrors in the corner which reflect down; however, these are not too dangerous unless you are standing close by them, besides which somebody has to be looking close and you should notice if they are. The last thing you must be concerned with is a 2-way mirror observation windows, these are usually small dark little holes located towards the top of the wall. Most of the time there is never anyone in there, but if they can be avoided, do so. If not, you can usually tell if someone is behind them by standing directly under them.

One nice thing about working off the floor is that if someone has seen you, they will let you know because they get crazy. If it is a customer, they will usually look twice to make sure they saw what they thought they saw, and then run and find a salesperson to tell. If a salesperson sees you, they will have a suspicious expression on their face and either go tell someone, or pick up the phone to call security. Security can be contacted by three methods: phone the security office and tell them where the suspected thief is; or they have walkie-talkies; or a system of dings will go off in the store to notify them. I'm sure you've heard them and in a large department store, they are going off constantly. Unfortunately, no one has the code to be able to figure out which department is calling them and most of the time you should ignore the bells; however, if you think a salesperson is suspicious and you see them pick up the phone or push something and you hear the bells go off, then be aware because they could be for you.

If you have gotten your pieces all right and there are no detachers, you can get ready to leave the store. Check in a mirror to see if you look all right and there are no belts or tags hanging out. Remember, because you know those pieces are there, you can see them but nobody else can. As you're getting ready and getting closer to the door to leave, be double-checking security because they will not grab you until you are out that door. How to spot security will be described later, but be suspicious of anyone who is around you a lot or following you; if they were around when you took the pieces and they are around you when you're leaving, watch them. Security almost always gives themselves away by using their walkie-talkie which will be in their purse or some shopping bag. They will stare at you from behind racks, they will keep looking at you, follow you, etc. Never, ever leave the store without checking for them no matter how cool you thought you were. If for some reason you think someone is onto you, don't panic because they can't do anything unless you leave that store.

Keep walking around from department to department just casually shopping and if they're still around, give them back their merchandise. Quickly go behind a rack and dump it or go into a dressing room and leave it. At that point, security knows what you're doing and you know who they are, but you haven't broken the law. They might even say something to you but just act like you don't know what they are talking about and leave. Do not go directly to your car because they know you are a pro and that you probably have other pieces in your car, so if they can get your plates, they will call the police and get you searched. Just walk around and see if someone is following you and if no one is, then go to your car. If someone is, call "J.S." and arrangements can be made. Your car is very important; it can keep you from getting busted. Always park it as close to the store entrances as possible, the further away it is, the further you may have to run. Leave the door unlocked so you can jump in as fast as possible and as soon as you get in, close and lock the door. Make this a reflex action because once you are in that car, you are almost home free.

After you leave, put the pieces in the trunk and take your trunk key off the ring and put it somewhere else. This way if you do get pulled over and they want to search your trunk, tell them you don't have the key. The police can then either take you and the car in and get a warrant and search your car and you're sunk; or, they will probably bust open the trunk and this is an illegal search and seizure and though you might go to jail, the case will not hold up in court. Always check for people tailing you. Sometimes, they will let you leave the store but a plainclothes will follow you from store to store, waiting for you to finish so they can bust you and get more charges against you.

If you are being tailed, get out of the city and if they try to pull you over, ignore them; you could always claim you didn't believe they were police. If you have pieces in the car, rip off the price tags, and throw them out because without these, they have no proof.

## DETACHERS

These are a royal pain in the ass. They are designed to sound an alarm as you leave the store. As I'm sure you have seen, they are white plastic and must be taken off with the proper tool. At one time, only about 50% of the stores had them, but now all of them do so they must be dealt with. When working off the floor, take your pieces as usual and then go into the dressing room, but make sure you take some clothes in with you. This is necessary when you take the detachers off—you will have no place to put them. Put them on the clothes you have taken in, they clip on. Put them in the seams because that is where the stores place them. Don't put more than one on if there already is one there; if for some reason you don't have enough clothes to put them on, put them in your pocket and then put them in pockets of clothing out on the floor.

Quite often, you can sort through the pieces and find some that are undetached but always feel the pieces because you may not be able to see them. This brings up another point, there are other forms of this; little pieces of cardboard; however, these can be ripped off. These usually say inventory control on them but sometimes stores, especially smaller ones, try to disguise them by putting them in plastic and putting the store name on them. Because they are small, they are tricky to find, so make sure you check the garment inside and out. Be extra sure and if you're not, go into the dressing room and double check.

Finally, some stores have really slick methods; always check the door to see if they have alarms, they will take different forms: white or wood pillars, overhanging ones, or things that sort of resemble gates—if you see any of these, be clued that there is something on the clothes. If you can't find anything on them, hang out by the cash register and see what they do to the clothes when something is bought. If the beeper does go off, you have to make a decision whether to run for it or give back the pieces. In a department store, if you can walk back into the store and drop off the pieces without too much attention, go ahead; if you car is real close, run; but that is a decision you have to make.

## SECURITY

As I mentioned earlier, security almost always gives themselves away, but nevertheless, there are some that are as slick as you are. The one thing most of them have in common is their mentality. I mean, it takes a certain type of person to have a job where you suspect everyone and send people to jail. This mentality expresses itself—most security look like real "pricks"; they get off on the power they think they have. When they're working, they will be sneaking looks at people, looking over racks, or hiding behind things, trying to spy on whoever. Most often security works in couples because they can see more that way and more importantly, a man has the strength to grab you and keep you. They almost always carry a walkie-talkie, so if you see a woman sort of talking into her purse, be careful. The men carry theirs inside their jacket or a bag, like they bought something. They also try to dress down and usually wear blue jeans because they are trying to look like your average shopper. If you see a supposed customer talk to a salesperson like they know them, be suspicious; or if you see two customers who aren't together, stop and briefly talk to each other, that is another good sign. When they're suspicious, they will keep looking because they have to make sure that you have taken something. Sometimes they will even bump into you to see if they can feel something on you. If you act cool, however, there is no reason for them to be suspicious of you, unless of course, they see you doing something. Security looks for people who look nervous, minorities. They are always suspicious of blacks, chicanos, etc., sometimes this works against you because if there are some around you in a store, you can be pretty sure security is around; however, most of the time security will be so worried about them, they won't be paying any attention to you. One should be more careful when working the dressing room because security is real aware of this method. When you go into a dressing room, stop and check real fast and see if anyone is watching you go in. If you see someone and then they come into the dressing room, be aware; and if they leave when you do, the odds are real high that is who they are. I try and make it a practice never to leave through the men's department. This is because if you are being followed by a man, he will be much more obvious if you're in the women's department than in a man's. The reason this is important is as I mentioned earlier, he can grab you. If a woman tries to bust you by herself, you will probably be so scared that you will have the strength to get away and if that involves kicking her or hitting her, do so because you really don't want to go to jail. Some stores also have security who wear red jackets and although they are obvious, they should be paid attention to. Also, some of the smaller stores have armed guards, and if you can avoid dealing with these, it would probably be better.

## WHERE TO GO

You should have a list of stores; when you are first starting out, go to the smaller stores until you build up your confidence for the bigger stores. Remember, you have to keep going back into these bigger stores every couple of weeks so the less attention you draw to yourself, the better. The bigger stores have different departments which helps because you can go in one department one week and a separate department the next.

Mostly, you have to use common sense and act cool and you shouldn't really have any trouble. If you are careful and alert, you should never get caught. Remember too that it is better to come home with no pieces than to get arrested, don't force it. If, God forbid, you do get caught, don't panic. You will be out in several hours. Do not tell security or the police anything about your name. They will try to get you to confess, or tell them who you work for, etc. They will also ask you who the pieces are for. Tell them they are for yourself.

# Appendix   3

# Civil Recovery Laws

Civil recovery is not a new concept; it is as old as common law. What *is* new are the civil demand laws being passed across the nation. These statutes are written to make it easier, administratively, for merchants to collect for damages incurred as a result of increasing losses due to theft.

The first civil recovery statute was enacted in Nevada in 1973. Prior to this, the legal damages awarded to the retailer for incurring shoplifting offenses were small, if any. Attorney's fees were generally not recoverable and such fees would typically outweigh any recovery of damages. This situation placed the financial burden of pursuit of the shoplifter (and security costs in general) on the retailer and ultimately, through increased prices, on the non-shoplifting customer.

By establishing automatic, preset ranges of penalties directed at the shoplifter, civil recovery statutes shift this financial burden from the consumer to those who commit acts of shoplifting and theft. Civil recovery statutes were enacted in order to compensate the retailer *and* provide for theft deterrence.

By 1986, 16 states had adopted civil recovery statutes. Since then, that number has more than doubled and now includes 41 states. Civil demand arose in and spread among the western states. Currently, only a few of the northeastern states have civil recovery laws. The states that currently use civil recovery include

- Alaska
- Arizona
- California
- Colorado
- Connecticut
- Florida
- Georgia
- Hawaii
- Idaho
- Illinois
- Indiana
- Iowa
- Kentucky
- Louisiana
- Maryland
- Massachusetts
- Michigan
- Minnesota
- Mississippi
- Missouri
- Montana
- Nebraska
- Nevada
- New Hampshire
- New Jersey
- New Mexico
- North Carolina
- North Dakota
- Ohio
- Oklahoma
- Oregon
- Pennsylvania
- Rhode Island
- South Dakota
- Tennessee
- Texas
- Utah
- Virginia
- Washington
- West Virginia
- Wisconsin

## INTENT OF THE LAWS

1. The laws help offset the tremendous costs of theft and security by placing the cost burden on the offenders, not by raising consumer prices.
2. The laws serve as a deterrent—especially to repeat offenders.
3. In some states, the laws are viewed as a possible alternative to criminal action—although they can be used simultaneously. The state of Ohio is the only exception. In Ohio, retailers can either pursue the criminal *or* seek civil remedy—not both.
4. The laws provide a source of revenue to retailers for funding loss control training, programs, and equipment.

## CIVIL ACTION FOR THEFT

When a customer or employee steals from a company, that action is both a crime *and* a civil tort. In 41 states, a retailer can take not only criminal action, but also civil action in the form of civil demand. In both cases, a third party with legal expertise is generally used. In the case of criminal action, the state or district attorney files an information or secures an indictment to prosecute the offender.

In a civil action, a civil recovery firm (with a staff attorney) screens all incident reports sent by a client (retailer) and issues carefully written letters of demand to theft subjects. These firms also answer questions posed by demanded subjects, their attorneys, and parents.

The following information explains some of the differences between criminal action and civil (tort) action and references the attached figure.

I.   Burden of Proof—"What is required to get a conviction or judgment?"
  A.   *Criminal Action*—The state must prove beyond any reasonable doubt that the individual is guilty. This is sometimes difficult to prove.
  B.   *Civil Action*—Burden of proof is preponderance of evidence. If a retailer has stopped an individual for theft, with good reason, that is enough. Preponderance of evidence is much easier to prove than guilt beyond any reasonable doubt.

II.   Restitution—"How will my company be compensated for our losses due to theft?"
  A.   *Criminal Action*—Retailers must rely on the state to determine if they will receive restitution. If some sort of restitution is granted to the retailer, it is usually for the value of the merchandise. Due to high workloads or politics, a prosecuting attorney may drop a retailer's case, regardless of the merchant's wishes.
  B.   *Civil Action*—Retailers control from whom they demand restitution (through the civil demand process). In most states, a retailer can recover not only the value of the merchandise, but also general, special, and/or punitive damages. Since the retailer is in control, a case can be dropped at any time.

III.   Deterrent—"What provides the best deterrent to future theft in my stores?"
  A.   *Criminal Action*—Although prosecution is a good deterrent, it is most effective when used in conjunction with civil action. Since criminal courts and jails are overcrowded, the chance of incarceration or serious penalty is virtually nonexistent.
  B.   *Civil Action*—Crime prevention is sometimes best described as crime "displacement." If thieves know that stealing from your company will result in

their arrest, recovery of the merchandise from them, *and* a fine of $150 payable to the retailer, thieves will probably avoid stealing in your retail establishment.

IV. Corporate Image—"How will my customers view the use of criminal/civil action?"

    A. *Criminal Action*—Criminal prosecution is a necessary evil. Although it is a good deterrent, the retailer is sometimes looked upon as the "bad guy." Also, criminal action is a public issue as arrest reports are public record.

    B. *Civil Action*—The high cost of security should be passed along to the offender *not* to the good-paying customer in the form of higher prices. Therefore, customers should be outraged if a retailer is not practicing civil recovery! Unlike criminal action, civil action in the form of demand letters is a private issue. The offender is not fingerprinted, photographed, or incarcerated. Therefore, the public does not have access to the records.

V. Variance in Processes—"How complex is a criminal/civil action program?"

    A. *Criminal Action*—There are as many different statutes and policies regarding the handling of apprehended shoplifters as there are cities in the United States. Every municipality has different criteria that retailers must follow.

    B. *Civil Action*—There are only 41 different variations since 41 states have civil demand laws. All that is needed to civilly demand is a civil demand law in your state, a correct subject name and address, and preponderance of evidence. (Note: A certain degree of legal expertise is required to research civil laws, write appropriate demand letters, and respond to inquiries from demanded subjects and their attorneys.)

The merchant, and ultimately the customer pays for losses incurred as a result of shoplifting and internal theft. Civil recovery laws help offset higher prices due to theft and enable retailers to offer the competitive prices customers expect.

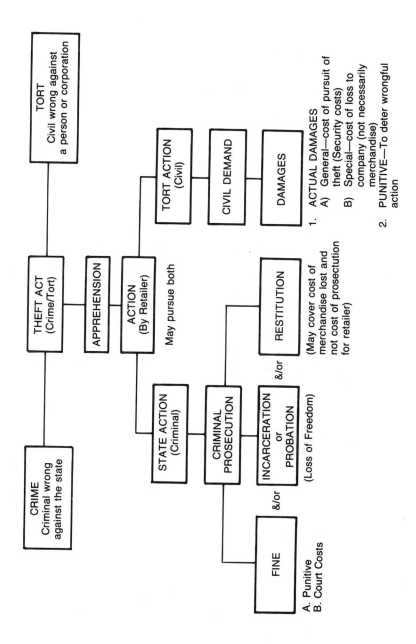

# Appendix 4

# Abbreviated Retail Security Survey

I. People
   A. Security or Loss Control Coordinator/Director
      1. If part-time, list the percent of time spent on security.
      2. Describe the chain of command from the Security Coordinator to the CEO.
   B. Number of full-time (non-clerical) loss control employees
   C. Number of part-time (non-clerical) loss control employees
   D. Is a Loss Control Training Program in effect?
      1. Hours of initial, annual, and in-service training
      2. Briefly describe the content of the training course, the quality of the instruction, and testing.
   E. Based on visual observation of work activity and interviews with store management and employees, are loss control policies and procedures
      1. published?
      2. taught to security personnel?
      3. followed routinely?
      4. reinforced by supervisors?
      5. audited and updated?
   F. Do these policies and procedures appear to be well-focused on total loss control efforts?
   G. Is an Employee Awareness Training Program in place?
      1. Briefly describe the content and frequency of workshops, the quality and technique of instruction, information reporting procedures, and any incentive programs.
   H. Are loss control briefings given to senior management?
      1. What is the frequency with which they are given? Daily? Weekly? Monthly? Quarterly?
   I. Personnel Screening
      1. Is a written, signed employment application required?
      2. Are all candidates interviewed twice?
      3. If a job classification requires the following screening procedures, verify and cite exceptions to the following conditions:
         a. Previous employment
         b. Education

  c. Criminal convictions
  d. Credit history
  e. Driving record
  f. Workers' compensation history
J. Comments

II. Programs
  A. Are all incidents reported?
  B. Are incidents documented and compiled for review?
  C. Are detected incidents investigated?
  D. Is there a criminal prosecution policy?
  E. Is there a civil action/recovery policy?
  F. Is there a restitution policy for DE cases?
  G. Is there a bad check follow-up policy?
  H. Has top management established loss control policies?
  I. Are these policies published, issued, and updated?
  J. Are managers accountable for the success of these policies?
  K. Are disciplinary procedures published?
    1. Are they taught to employees?
    2. Are incidents recorded?
    3. Are actions uniform in nature?
  L. Are emergency plans published?
    1. Do they cover natural and man-made disasters?
    2. Are responsibilities listed?
    3. Are responsible employees designated? Notified? Trained?
    4. Are periodic drills held?
    5. Are critical areas and operations protected?
    6. Are emergency communications and notifications planned for?
    7. Have public emergency services been planned for and notified?
    8. Have mutual-aid pacts been established?
    9. Is a post-disaster recovery plan established?

III. Systems
  A. Are purchase order management systems in place?
  B. Is a vendor verification system in place?
  C. Are accounts payable notices verified?
  D. Is payroll verified?
  E. Are distribution and corporate office facilities secure?
    1. Proper fencing?
    2. Proper lighting?
    3. Alarm systems in place and tested?
    4. Keys controlled?
    5. Access controlled?
  F. Are store shipments verified?
  G. Are stores tested periodically on overship reporting?
  H. Are EAS systems installed?
    1. Are they being used?
    2. Is targeted merchandise kept tagged?
    3. Is proper usage rewarded?
    4. Is the system checked daily, prior to use?
  I. Are display areas observable?

J.   Is high-loss merchandise specially controlled?

K.   Are inventories taken periodically?

L.   Are interstore transfers controlled and reconciled?

M.   Are price changes verified and checked?

N.   Is a clear refund policy posted?

O.   Are suspicious refunds tracked?

P.   Are cashiers limited to one per register during work periods for accountability purposes?

Q.   Are cash variances tracked?

R.   Are cash pick-ups made periodically?

S.   Are deposits verified?

T.   Are adequate safes in place and equipped with alarms?

U.   Is the store equipped with an effective alarm system?

1.   Is the system tested periodically?

V.   Are fitting rooms controlled?

X.   Comments.

# Appendix 5

# Sample Completed Store Audit Report

### LOSS PREVENTION INSPECTION REPORT

### CASH CONTROL

Cashier - General Office

1. Is daily cash register tracking chart in use?   Yes _×_ No_____

2. Is the register sign in/out sheet being used?   Yes _×_ No_____

3. Are current shortages over $3.00 entered on the
   daily tracking chart? *Cash office mgr advised*
   *on 2/16/90  × Mrs. Cash Smith 2/18/90*   Yes_____ No _×_

4. Overages in any amount entered?   Yes _×_ No_____

5. Problem over/shorts found?  (Enter names of problem
   operators)

   Name _Mary Smith_

   Name _Jon White_

6. Are item correction forms stapled to recap sheets?   Yes _×_ No_____

7. List corrective action taken on problem operators: _discussed with_
   _Store mgr. will conduct verbal review w/ both operators_
   _Discussed w/ Human Resources_

8. "Shotgun" shortages found?   Yes_____ No _×_

   Action taken:_____

   _____

9. Price variance report reviewed with Manager?
   Problems found? *Mary Smith*                    Yes _x_ No _____

   Corrective action taken: *to be discussed w/ Smith as*
   *per mgr. Verbal corrective action to be taken*
   *and copied to Personnel file.*

10. Adding machine tapes on pick-up saved?            Yes _x_ No _____

11. Are all bank deposits being verified? Adding
    machine tapes on deposits signed?                 Yes _x_ No _____

12. Bank deposits agree with call-in sheet?           Yes _x_ No _____

13. Bank deposits made daily?                         Yes _x_ No _____

14. Cash office door locked? Office door locked?      Yes _x_ No _____

15. Access restricted?                                Yes _x_ No _____

16. Safe locked when not in use? *advised cashroom*   Yes _____ No _x_
    *mgr. on 2/16/90 signed: Ms Cash Smith .*

17. Petty cash fund being handled per policy?         Yes _x_ No _____
    (Review petty cash slips - last 90 days)

18. Any petty cash discrepancies found?               Yes _____ No _x_

    If yes, explain: *However, Petty Cash slip was made out*
    *and signed 3 days after receipt of item purchased*
    *was attached. Receipt dated 2-1-90, signed slip*
    *was made out on 2-4-90. Mgr. advised*

19. Any IOU's or employee personal checks found in
    the safe?                                         Yes _____ No _x_

    If so, who? (explanation given): _____

    _____

    _____

## VOIDS

1. Are void stamps used?  Are reasons and signature on back of receipt?  Yes_____  No _✗_

2. Are post-voids of $5.00 or more, with reasons stating, "no money", "not enough", "didn't want", "check refused", looked up on the detail tape for re-ringing?  Yes _✗_  No_____

3. Are all void slips being defaced?  Yes _✗_  No_____

4. Are all reasons for void accurate for tracking purposes?  Yes _✗_  No_____

5. Are H.C.S. and register operator signing all voids?  Yes_____  No _✗_

6. Is the void profile sheet done per policy?  Yes_____  No _✗_

Exceptions Found:  Comments/Addendum - Void Profile Sheet:_____

① Mary Smith prime violator (3 occasions) counseled at verbal review, as discussed.

⑤ Mary Smith, 3 voids as discussed in #1

⑥ ARPM did void profile this month reviewed w/ cash office mgr. signed: Ms. Cash Smith 2/16/90

VOID PROFILE CHART

Store Number.

| DATE | REG. NO. | AMOUNT | VOID RERUNG YES | NO | REGISTER OPERATOR | AUTHORIZING PERSON | REASON FOR VOID | AMOUNT TENDERED CHANGE GIVEN YES | NO |
|------|----------|--------|-----------------|-----|-------------------|--------------------|-----------------|----------------------------------|-----|
| | | | | | | | | | |
| | | | | | | | | | |
| | | | | | | | | | |
| | | | | | | | | | |
| | | | | | | | | | |
| | | | | | | | | | |
| | | | | | | | | | |
| | | | | | | | | | |
| | | | | | | | | | |
| | | | | | | | | | |
| | | | | | | | | | |
| | | | | | | | | | |
| | | | | | | | | | |
| | | | | | | | | | |
| | | | | | | | | | |
| | | | | | | | | | |

## CUSTOMER SERVICE DESK

1. Refund handled per policy?  Yes __x__  No _____
   (Separated and matched back)

2. "No Receipt" refund over $25.00 recorded in
   "No Receipt" refund book?  (Check 10?)  Yes _____  No __x__

3. Merchandise cleared from customer service
   desk on a timely basis?  Signed for?  Yes __x__  No _____

4. Is green slip being separated and attached
   to merchandise?  Yes __x__  No _____

5. Refunds being checked by phone to customer
   for validity?  Yes _____  No __x__

6. Is refund slip being defaced?  Yes __x__  No _____

   Exception : _____

   _____

7. Are refunds being filled out by H.C.S?  Yes __x__  No _____

8. Employee log being kept?  Yes __x__  No _____

9. Package checks:  Handled per policy?  Yes __x__  No _____

   Exceptions/Comments/Addendums : ② 5 refunds $25. and /over were
   found not in book. Asst. Mgr. John Doher advised on 2-16-90
   x Mr. John Doher 2-16-90  ⑤ not consistent. Reviewed w/ Cash
   office mgr on 2-16-90 x Ms. Cash Smith, DOPM made 10 calls
   on 2-16-90

**STORE** _307_

**REFUND PROFILE**

**DATE** _3-1-88_

LIST **ALL** REFUNDS OVER $5.00

| REFUND DATE | REFUND AMOUNT | CHK REG # | REGISTER RECEIPT DATE TRANS. NO. | REFUND ISSUED BY | REFUND AUTH. BY | MDSE. SKU DESCRIPTION | REASON FOR RETURN | CUSTOMER'S NAME | PHONE NUMBER | STREET ADDRESS |
|---|---|---|---|---|---|---|---|---|---|---|
| 2-1-88 | 38.00 | 2 | 2-1-88 5100 | Susan F. | | 6130 3615 | | MRS. BILLY KENT | 657-1990 | 2719 PARKSIDE L |
| | 16.45 | 1 | 1-15-88 1918 | Susan F. | | 5650 5489 | | MRS. KEN NEVES | 471-9747 | 329 BLUEBIRD LANE |
| | 32.00 | 2 | 2-1-88 5108 | Susan F. | | 1114 0232 | | Mr. CAROL TIDWELL | 275-4903 | 4151 DOYER ST |
| | 37.15 | 2 | 2-1-88 5119 | Susan F. | | 8976 0468 | | MRS. WALTER COCHRAN | 471-4462 | 24050 SILVA AVE |
| | 7.95 | 5 | 1-27-88 014 | Susan F. | | 1135 1470 | | ANGELA DAVIES | 638-7127 | 4737 THORNTON AVE |
| | 41.00 | 2 | 2-1-88 5131 | Susan F. | | 4912 3637 | | JANET GUYER | 471-1477 | 216 BANYAN |
| | 33.80 | 2 | 2-1-88 5145 | Susan F. | | 1711 3342 | | PRISCILLA NEVILLE | 656-9850 | 4631 BENEDICT RD. |
| | 18.18 | 7 | 1-24-88 3379 | Glenda M. | | 6140 8026 | | DIANE SHANEY | 657-9674 | 4193 CENTRAL |
| | 22.00 | 5 | 1-30-88 245 | Glenda M. | | 5750 1221 | | CHARLES SMITH | 447-5874 | 2298 STILWELL DR. |
| | 79.00 | 8 | 1-26-88 4189 | Glenda M. | MR. O. | 1114 0232 | | VANA BAKER | 796-9255 | 4603 MIRA LANE |
| | 17.99 | 1 | 12-29-87 1615 | Glenda M. | | 6120 6938 | | MAE MARGO | 537-6191 | 5005 BRANDON ST. |
| | 24.30 | 11 | 1-27-88 495 | Glenda M. | | 7110 0957 | | YVONNE PENTER | 582-4180 | 2255 NINA ST. |
| | 9.99 | | NONE | Glenda M. | MR. O. | 9540 0826 | | ROBERTA TIERNEY | 651-5373 | 685 MONTANA ST. |
| | 51.99 | 5 | 1-14-88 768 | Susan F. | | 1117 1677 | | JOHN ADAMS | 278-0196 | 2651 OLIVER ST. |
| | 20.99 | | NONE | Susan F. | MR. D | 3190 0436 | | GAIL GATES | 481-5428 | 5310 FARWELL LN. |
| | 7.60 | 3 | 1-29-88 831 | Susan F. | | 1231 1905 | | JUDITH CAPP | 471-5366 | 2117 TUXEDO CT. |
| | 16.66 | 2 | 2-1-88 5167 | Susan F. | | 4940 0932 | | CHRIS CANALTA | 487-2224 | 1520 VIA GARRETT |
| | 37.95 | 6 | 1-29-88 2116 | Susan F. | | 1231 1905 | | DORIS LIVELY | 651-8270 | 4616 SLOAT RD. |
| | 11.95 | 7 | 1-25-88 3516 | Glenda M. | | 1314 0760 | | JOSINE RANICK | 538-4599 | 35253 LIDO BLVD. |
| | 14.00 | 3 | 1-16-88 795 | Glenda M. | | 7112028 | | ANITA TRONICO | 637-2699 | 3529 LANCERO DR. |

Follow the arrows:

### In the register receipt column.

Six receipts from customers who had all been in the store the previous day.
Transaction numbers 5100, 5108, 5119, 5131, 5145 and 5167 - all from register
number 2!!

### Refund issued by column

All refunds processed by Susan F.!

### Customer name column

Five different customers!

### Street address column

Five different addresses!

## REGISTER OPERATION

1. Is register balanced daily?                                    Yes _✗_ No _____

2. Register operator entering register per policy,
   before ringing - using proper code and employee
   number?                                                        Yes _✗_ No _____

3. Post-voids reported by register operator and
   handled quickly by H.C.S.? *Mary Smith problem*               Yes _____ No _✗_
   *2/16/90*

4. Operator using wand?  On <u>Price</u>, if SKU
   number does not take?                                          Yes _✗_ No _____

5. Operator looking to see if the right price
   is appearing after wanding?                                    Yes _✗_ No _____

6. Register drawer closed, except when recording
   sales?                                                         Yes _✗_ No _____

7. Making change per policy?                                      Yes _✗_ No _____

8. Improper or careless register operations
   observed?                                                      Yes _____ No _✗_

9. Operator calling for price checks, where
   applicable?                                                    Yes _✗_ No _____

10. Package checks being held per policy?                         Yes _✗_ No _____

11. Operator checking for concealed merchandise?                  Yes _✗_ No _____

12. Checks being processed per policy?  (Checks and
    bank name must be preprinted, date must be correct,
    changes must be initialed by customer and must
    have correct micro number entered)                           Yes _____ No _✗_

*2 checks noted that did not have
proper identification. Mgr. advised on
2-16-90  X Mr. Pete Noonan mgr. 2-16-90*

## SALES FLOOR

1. **Store making periodic security calls using "genderless" name?**                    Yes __✓__  No _____

2. **Pricing guns found on sales floor?**                    Yes _____  No __✗__

3. **Safety hazards found?**                    Yes __✗__  No _____

4. **Fitting rooms: Manned at all times?**                    Yes __✗__  No _____

5. Fitting room booths checked regularly?                    Yes __✗__  No _____

6. Pick ups of clothing done frequently by departments?                    Yes __✗__  No _____

7. Broken hangers, etc., kept picked up?                    Yes __✗__  No _____

8. Flash lights kept in store? Location of flash lights known? *Cash office, customer service area, fittingroom.*                    Yes __✗__  No _____

9. Numbered tag system being used?                    Yes __✗__  No _____

10. Number of 1 and 2 tags missing?

    Last 30 days? _____

11. Number of 1 and 2 tags gained?

    Last 30 days? _____

12. Rate fitting room attendant for:

    A.  Garment inspection before issuing number:  Good _✗_ Fair ___ Poor ___

    B.  Niceness to customer:  Good _✗_ Fair ___ Poor ___

    Comments: _____

    *② fire exit blocked in corner, cleared within 20 minutes*

    _____

    _____

    _____

    _____

### RECEIVING/STOCKROOM AREA

1. Receiving door locked?  Rollaway doors locked at the bottom, on both sides, when not receiving freight?                                    Yes __✗__  No _____

2. Blocked fire exits found?                          Yes __✗__  No _____

3. Review stockrooms for signs of shrinkage, empty packages, etc.?                         Yes __✗__  No _____

4. Receiving freight checked in by carton number and total carton count?                         Yes _____  No __✗__

5. Loose merchandise found in stockrooms?             Yes _____  No __✗__

6. Manifests in order?  Exceptions noted?
   *see #4*                                           Yes _____  No __✗__

7. Storage trailers used? Locked? Keys secure?
   How many?_____                          Yes _____  No __✗__

8. Outgoing shipments handled per policy?             Yes __✗__  No _____

9. Trash being handled per policy?                    Yes __✗__  No _____

Exceptions/Comments/Freight Delivery Observations: _____

② Cleared fire exit immediately. advised mgr.
✗ Mr. Pete Noonan 2-16-90 ④ found 3 discrepancies
not checked off but received. advised mgr. ✗ Mr. Pete
Noonan 2-16-90

## PHYSICAL SECURITY

Alarm systems - when tested last? (Date shown on alarm door
inspection tag.) __1-21-90__        Infra-red? __1-20-90__     Battery? __11-16-89__

Alarm problems found? __none__

_____

_____

Evidence of known theft found around the exterior of the building? __none__

_____

_____

Is trash handling procedure being followed?                     YES __+__   NO ____

Dumpster check - plastic bags intact or broken open? __yes, intact__

If intact, check. Any merchandise found? __no__

_____

Exterior building lights broken?                                YES ____   NO __+__

Trash or weeds found around building?                           YES __+__   NO ____

COMMENTS: _advised Mgr. of weed, land scaping problem. Said_
_he would handle with week x Mr. Pete Noonan 2-16-90_

_____

_____

## SHOPLIFTING

Store using incident report?                                    YES __+__   NO ____

Number of incidents reported in last 30 days __3__

Manager's comments on shoplifting activity in his/her store: _Mostly evenings_
_and weekends are the problem. Shoe dept. and young_
_Mens area. x Mr. Pete Noonan 2-16-90. DLPM will_
_chedule coverage for proper attention, x Ms. DLPM 2-16-90_

ADDITIONAL COMMENTS: _____

As per Review, Mrs. Mary Smith cashier seems to be a potential problem. A verbal counseling will be done on 2-17-90 to address the void and price variance issues.

Problem will be reviewed and follow-up done with compliance and also reviewed in Triad Meeting with O.M. and DHRM to consider initiation of Internal investigation. See Triad Meeting Review.

x Mrs. District LPM  2-16-90

# Appendix 6

# Sample Consulting Proposal

Consulting Service X proposes to conduct a study for Corporation Y to determine loss vulnerabilities and study loss control practices. The overall objective is to answer the questions, "What is the retail operation doing to maintain a healthy gross profit margin?" "Are these measures reasonable and sufficient to achieve their purposes?"

## I. SCOPE

The security audit will cover

- security measures presently used, with respect to the buying, receiving, processing, and distributing of merchandise
- efficiency of security hardware currently in use in stores and distribution facilities
- considerations involved in screening, hiring, orienting, training, and motivating company employees
- study of the quality and extent of the rapport between individuals responsible for loss control and senior management
- store vulnerabilities to employee, vendor, and customer theft, with major emphasis on employee theft

## II. APPROACH

Current practices in merchandise control, especially in the receiving, marking, processing, and distributing portions of the distribution operation, will be observed. Interviews will be conducted and a survey completed.

Security and inventory control practices and equipment will be evaluated. The effectiveness of loss control people, programs, and systems in the stores and distribution facilities will also be evaluated. The study will determine prioritized risks and high-loss areas in the operation.

Cost-effective countermeasures and shrinkage control programs will be designed and an implementation plan, which includes recommended practices, will be submitted.

## III. RESOLUTION

At the conclusion of the information-gathering phase, we will analyze our findings and prepare tentative recommendations. Thereafter, these recommendations will be discussed with your selected committee to ensure that the recommendations meet standards of reasonableness and feasibility.

Our discussions will be documented in a written report that contains our findings. The report will contain our recommendations. Two copies of the report will be produced by the release date.

## IV. CONSIDERATIONS AND LIMITATIONS

The study will be conducted in a professional, low-key manner. It is understood that this review does not denote any dissatisfaction with Corporation Y security operations or its management. Rather, the study is a positive effort to ensure that reasonable provisions have been made to protect the company and its assets.

Consulting Service X reserves the right to use the services of other consultants only if the requirements of the project establish this need. Any expenses would be included in the standard fees.

## V. BACKGROUND

Consulting Service X is a retail security consulting and training firm. We are a company that has been created by retailers for retailers. Our retail background and experience gives us the ability to provide you with the best evaluation and plan of action possible.

Our principal consultant, Mr. Z., is also our Vice President. Mr. Z. is a Certified Protection Professional (CPP) and a Certified Security Trainer (CST). He has more than x years of retail loss prevention experience and has served as Deputy Sheriff for the Alachua County Police Department.

Mr. Z. has been a featured speaker for many organizations, including the American Society for Industrial Security (ASIS), the International Mass Retail Association (IMRA), the International Security Conference (ISC), and the Florida Attorney General's Office.

## VI. FEES AND TIME COMMITMENT

Our fee for this study will be based on our standard rates. The estimated cost of our services for this project is $x.

It is noted that charges are not assessed for travel time. Only time spent on-site, time spent off-site in analysis, or time spent preparing written materials is charged.

Cost of travel expenses is estimated at $x. Miscellaneous expenses are projected at $x, for a total of $x. These costs include expenses and fees for two trips to your location.

We will bill Corporation Y in two installments for services, submitting the initial statement at the end of 30 days and the final statement when the report is delivered.

If any follow-up visits or surveys are indicated in the future and any additional fees are required, these issues will be negotiated at that point.

The dates for the project will be secured, by agreement, between Corporation Y and Consulting Service X.

# Appendix 7

## Recommended Control Procedures

**OPENING THE STORE**

At the start of the day, make sure you

1. turn off the alarm
2. turn on the lights, music, and paging system
3. inspect the floor for problem areas that need attention either before the store opens or during the workday

List problem areas and assign your employees to handle them. For example, you may notice an empty feature rack in the Men's Department that needs to be filled before the store opens. Complete the following steps either simultaneously or in a different order than listed here. Make sure you complete all the steps properly.

1. Supervise the front door to let employees into the store.
2. Ensure the head customer service clerk opens the registers. Direct any problems to the cash office person.
3. Oversee garbage removal by walking with the stock person to remove garbage through the back door. Supervise everything that leaves the store through the back door.
4. Identify any problem areas for the janitorial service to handle before the store opens (e.g., revacuum the Children's Department).
5. Complete the daily personnel schedules (this can be done the night before).

**HANDLING PERSONAL CHECKS**

Acceptable checks must have

- preprinted customer name and address (in case of change-of-address, customer must delete old pre-printed address and write in correct, current address)
- current date
- numeric amount equal to the written amount
- preprinted bank name
- preprinted magnetic ink character recognition (MICR) account number

Out-of-state checks are acceptable only when they are on-line. Note that employees must have a supervisor deny a check. The following criteria apply to unacceptable checks:

- second-party checks
- check written in pencil
- check with alterations not initialed by customer in cashier's presence
- check that has an illegible amount
- **check written or presented by a juvenile on an account other than their own**
- **check presented by intoxicated or out-of-control customer**
- **traveler's check in foreign money**
- check that has a rubber-stamped bank name
- **check payable to "cash"**
- government check
- payroll check
- business check made out to or endorsed by a second party
- check with a P.O. Box address

1. Ask customer for a valid driver's license with a photograph.
2. If customer has a driver's license, enter the following information on the front of the check, to the right of the name and address:

   - license expiration date
   - birth date
   - telephone number
   - state on the license
   - license number
   - approval code

   The approval code is entered later, only when a "2" or a "9" appears on the terminal.
3. If the customer does *not* have a driver's license, the cashier should call a supervisor who will determine whether or not to accept a secondary ID. Secondary ID includes

   - Visa card
   - MasterCard
   - American Express card
   - Diner's Club card
   - Carte Blanche card

   Be cautious when accepting any identification without a photograph.
4. If identification is accepted, your cashier should

   - press "check tendered" on the terminal.
   - line up the MICR reader to the personal check and enter the check's MICR number in the terminal.

5. A code will appear on the terminal. If the last digit in the code does not appear, the check has been approved and the cashier should complete the transaction.

## TASK: HANDLING CUSTOMER RETURNS AND EXCHANGES

### Handling Cash or Check Without Receipt

The customer service clerk follows the basic return and exchange procedures, along with these additional steps:

1. After printing the customer's name, address, telephone number, and obtaining customer signature, ask to see a current driver's license.
2. Write the driver's license number in the identification box of the charge slip.
3. Ensure that the check ID information matches the information the customer previously stated.
4. Print "Without Receipt" on the charge slip.

- Call a supervisor for approval.

While waiting for the supervisor to reach the Customer Service Desk, the customer service clerk should discreetly check the unmarked folder to see if the customer's name appears on the "No Refunds" list. If name does not appear on the list, the clerk should put the list away and hand the supervisor the refund slip. The supervisor should check the refund and ID. If they are OK, endorse the charge slip and let the customer service clerk complete the transaction.

If the customer's name appears on the "No Refunds" list, the clerk should put the refund slip in the folder and hand the folder to the supervisor. The supervisor should politely tell the customer,

I have been instructed to give no more refunds or exchanges to you. If you have any questions, please contact the Director of Loss Prevention at the Central Office.

### Watching Out for Refund Fraud

If you have reason to suspect a fraudulent return

1. Tell the customer you will mail the check in one week.
2. Apologize and emphasize, if necessary, that the store is not refusing the refund.
3. Give the customer a receipt for the merchandise and retain the merchandise.
4. After the customer leaves, contact the Loss Prevention Office with the customer information.
5. Write "customer-owned goods; holding for approval" on the yellow copy of the refund slip and staple the slip to the top of the bag with the items inside. Keep the items at the Customer Service Desk.
6. If the refund information checks out positive, send cashier's check to the customer within one week. Ring up a refund and endorse the slip. Write "check sent to customer" on the refund slip.
7. If refund information checks out negative, the Loss Prevention Office will instruct you further.

## PAGING CUSTOMERS, EMPLOYEES AND MANAGEMENT, AND SECURITY

### Paging Customers

When paging customers, summon them to a specific location. Do *not* state the content or nature of the request. Announce the page by saying, "Mr./Ms. (*surname*), please come to the (*location*)." For example, you might say, "*Mr. Jones, please come to the Customer Service Desk.*" If there is no response, repeat the page after 30 seconds.

### Paging Employees and Management

Always page management by title or surname only, never by first name. Page other employees and management for business reasons, only. Do not make personal pages. Page by name, department, or title and request the individual to report to a location. Do not page an individual more than twice; leave 30 seconds between pages.

### Paging Security

Page Security on a regular basis throughout the day to discourage shoplifters. Increase the number of pages during the holiday season. Also, page security when you suspect a shoplifter is in your store. Change the department locations at random.

# Appendix  8

# Standard Operating Procedures—Sample Employee Investigation Policy

## PURPOSE

This policy is designed to protect the company's assets and ensure proper handling of the employee/employer relationship.

## SCOPE

This policy is to be implemented when the Loss Prevention Department, while protecting the physical assets of the store, finds an alleged perpetrator to be an employee.

## POLICY

The Loss Prevention Department will protect the assets of the company via effective loss prevention methods, including the counsel of the Human Resources Department. When an employee is suspected of theft (i.e., when suspicious behavior has been observed or reported), a representative of store management, the Loss Prevention Department, or the Human Resources Department will document the reason for suspicion. One of these representatives will then contact the District Loss Prevention Manager, who will review the documentation. If an employee investigation is to be started, the District Loss Prevention Manager will meet with the District Manager and the Human Resources Representative, in person or by telephone, to develop an agreed-upon action plan. This plan must be documented and must include the following items:

- the individual who will document the action (Primary responsibility for loss prevention documentation normally belongs to the District Loss Prevention Manager)
- the investigation strategy and the time frame for the investigation
- the names of the individuals who may access the confidential personnel documents and the reasons why they may do so
- the names of the individuals who will be told of the investigation and who will tell them

- the disposal procedures for the original and all copies of the documentation if the employee is not prosecuted
- the investigation start and completion dates

The Human Resources Representative will be advised of any employee surveillance plan. This representative will ensure that the reason for surveillance is clearly documented by the Loss Prevention specialist *before the surveillance takes place.* The Human Resources Representative will also ensure that the time frame for the surveillance is clearly indicated, the reason for the surveillance does not conflict with the employer/employee relationship, and, that if sufficient evidence leading to prosecution or disciplinary action is *not* obtained on videotape or any other media, the videotapes or other surveillance media are erased, destroyed, or sent to the Central Office Records Department in a sealed package to be destroyed within 1 year of the investigation.

The Human Resources Representative will cooperate and take direction from the District Loss Prevention Manager in regard to assisting in the interrogation, preparing documentation, and supplying employee background information. Any employee interrogations should be held in the presence of a Human Resources Representative (or a member of the employee management team or another loss prevention employee). This action is to ensure that the employee meets with someone who represents both the company's and the employee's interests. The Human Resources Representative must ensure that the employee's rights, as well as the company's rights, are protected during an interrogation. It is the responsibility of this representative to thoroughly document (personally or by receiving the notes of the loss prevention specialist) all activities and conversations with the employee regarding the alleged theft, *even if the Human Resources Representative was not present* at those meetings.

The Human Resources Representative must also ensure that the documentation for investigations that do not result in a clear indication of theft or violation of company policy on the part of the employee, are sealed and sent to the Central Office where the custodian of records will automatically destroy the records after 12 months (if the investigation is not resumed by the Loss Prevention Department).

# Appendix 9

# Training Program Checklist

## WHAT ARE THE TRAINING GOALS?

The questions in this section are designed to help the designated loss prevention trainer define the objective or goals to be achieved by a training program. Whether the objective is to conduct initial training, provide for upgrading employees, or retrain employees changing job assignments, goals should be spelled out before developing the plan for the training program.

1. Do you want to improve the performance of your employees?
2. Will you improve your employees' performance by training them to perform their present tasks better?
3. Do you need to prepare employees for newly developed or modified jobs?
4. Is training needed to prepare employees for promotion?
5. Is the training goal to reduce accidents and increase safety practices?
6. Should the goal be to improve employee attitudes, especially about theft and errors?
7. Do you need to improve the understanding of theft techniques in order to better deter potential incidents?
8. Is the goal to orient new employees to their jobs?
9. Will you need to teach new employees about the overall operation?
10. Do you need to train employees so they can help teach new workers in an expansion program?

## WHAT DOES THE EMPLOYEE NEED TO LEARN?

Once the objective or goal of the program is set, you will need to determine the subject matter. The following questions are designed to help you decide what the employee needs to learn in terms of duties, responsibilities, and attitudes.

11. Are there certain skills and techniques that trainees must learn?
12. Are there standards of quality that trainees can be taught?
13. Can loss prevention techniques be broken down into steps for training purposes?
14. Are there hazards and safety practices that must be taught?
15. Have you established the methods that employees must use to avoid or minimize error and waste?

16. Are there proper cash and merchandise-handling techniques that must be taught?
17. Have you determined the best way for the trainees to operate point-of-sale equipment?
18. Are there loss prevention performance standards that employees must meet?
19. Are there attitudes that need improvement or modification?
20. Will information on your merchandise help employees do a better job?
21. Should the training include information about the location and use of fire and first-aid equipment?
22. Do employees need instruction about departments other than their own?

## WHAT TYPE OF TRAINING?

The type of training to be offered has an important bearing on the balance of the program. Some types lend themselves to achieving all of the objectivs or goals, while others are limited in scope. Therefore, review the advantages of each type of training in relation to your objective or goal.

23. Can you provide on-the-job training so that employees can produce while they learn?
24. Should you have classroom training conducted by a paid instructor?
25. Will a combination of scheduled on-the-job training and vocational classroom instruction work best for you?
26. Can your goal be achieved with a combination of on-the-job training and correspondence courses?

## WHAT METHOD OF INSTRUCTION?

One or more methods of instruction may be used. Some are better for one type of training than another. For example, lectures are good for imparting knowledge and demonstrations are good for teaching skills.

27. Does the subject matter call for a lecture or series of lectures?
28. Should the instructor follow-up with discussion sessions?
29. Does the subject matter lend itself to demonstrations?
30. Can operating problems be simulated in a classroom?
31. Can the instructor direct trainees while they perform the job?

## WHAT AUDIO-VISUAL AIDS WILL YOU USE?

Audio-visual aids help the instructor to make points and enable the trainees to grasp and retain the instructions.

32. Will an instruction manual—including job instruction sheets—be used?
33. Will trainees be given an outline of the training program?
34. Can outside textbooks and other printed materials be used?
35. If the training lends itself to the use of videos, overheads, or slides, can you get ones that show the basic operation?

36. Do you have drawings or photographs of the equipment or products that could be enlarged and used?
37. Do you have miniatures or models of equipment that can be used to demonstrate the operation?

## WHAT PHYSICAL FACILITIES WILL YOU NEED?

The type of training, the method of instruction, and the audio-visual aids will determine the physical facilities needed for training. In turn, the necessary physical facilities will determine the location of the training. For example, if a certain processing machine is necessary, the training should be conducted in the distribution center.

38. If the training cannot be conducted on the sales or processing floor, do you have a conference room or a lunch room in which training can be conducted?
39. Should the training be conducted off the premises—in a nearby school, restaurant, hotel, or motel?
40. Will the instructor have the necessary tools, such as a blackboard, lectern, TV, VCR, and microphone, if needed?
41. Will there be sufficient seating and writing surfaces, if needed, for trainees?
42. If equipment is to be used, will trainees be provided with their own?

## WHAT ABOUT COURSE LENGTH?

The length of the training program will vary according to the needs of your company, the material to be learned, the ability of the instructor, and the ability of the trainees to learn.

43. Should the training be conducted part-time and during working hours?
44. Should the sessions be held after working hours?
45. Will the instruction cover a predetermined period of time (e.g., 4 weeks, 6 weeks, 3 months)?
46. Can the length of each session and the number of sessions per week be established?

## WHO WILL BE SELECTED AS INSTRUCTOR?

The success of training depends, to a great extent, on the instructor. A qualified instructor can achieve good results even with limited resources. On the other hand, an untrained instructor may be unsuccessful even with the best program. You may want to use more than one person as instructor.

47. Can you fill in as an instructor?
48. Do you have a personnel manager who has the time and the ability to instruct?
49. Can your supervisors or department heads handle instructing?
50. Should a skilled employee be used as the instructor?
51. Will you have to train the instructor?

52.  Is there a qualified, outside instructor available for employment on an as-needed basis?

## WHO SHOULD BE SELECTED?

Employees should be selected for training on the basis of the goals of the program as well as their aptitude, previous experiences, and attitudes.

53.  Should new employees be hired for training?
54.  Should the training of new employees be a condition of employment?
55.  Would you prefer trainees with previous experience in the work?
56.  Are there present employees who need training?
57.  Will you consider training employees presently in lower rated jobs who have the aptitude to learn?
58.  Is the training to be a condition for promotion?
59.  Will the training be made available to handicapped employees whose injury occurred while employed by the company?
60.  Will employees be permitted to volunteer for training?
61.  Should employees displaced by job changes, departmental shutdowns, automation, etc., be given the opportunity to be trained in other jobs?

## WHAT WILL THE PROGRAM COST?

It may be beneficial to compute the cost of your training before starting the program. Thus, you can budget sufficient funds for the program and use the budget as a tool for keeping training costs in line.

62.  Should you change the program for the space, the equipment, and materials used?
63.  Will trainees' wages be included?
64.  If the instructors are employees, will their salaries be included in the training costs?
65.  Will the time you and others spend in preparing and administrating the program be part of the training costs?
66.  If usable products result from the sessions, should they be deducted from training costs?

## WHAT CHECKS OR CONTROLS WILL YOU USE?

The results of the training program need to be checked to determine the extent to which the original goal or objective was achieved.

67.  Can you check the results of the training against the goal or objective?
68.  Can standards of learning time be established against which to check the progress of the trainees?
69.  Can trainee performance data be developed before, during, and after training?

70. Will records be kept on the progress of each trainee?
71. Will trainees be tested on the knowledge and skills acquired?
72. Will the instructor rate each trainee during and at the end of the course?
73. Will the training be followed-up periodically, by a supervisor or department head, to determine the long-range effects of the training?
74. Should you personally check and control the program?

## HOW SHOULD THE PROGRAM BE PUBLICIZED?

Publicizing the company's training program in the community helps attract qualified job applicants. Publicity inside the company helps motivate employees to improve themselves.

75. If the program is announced to employees, will the announcement be made before the program starts? During the program?
76. Are pictures to be taken of the training sessions and used on bulletin boards and in local newspapers and newsletters?
77. Should employees who complete the training be awarded certificates?
78. Should the certificates be presented at a special affair, such as a dinner or lunch?
79. When the certificates are awarded, will you invite the families of the trainees?
80. Should local newspaper, radio, and TV personalities be invited to the "graduation" exercises?

# Appendix 10

## Sample Loss Control Plan

### I. PURPOSE

This plan provides the goals, priorities, and guidance for all employees involved in the planning and implementation of the corporatewide loss control effort.

### II. APPLICABILITY

The provisions of this plan apply to all departments assigned tasks designed to reduce corporate losses.

### III. DOCUMENTATION

To better protect customers, employees, and other assets, this plan and other documents will be retained. These documents serve to act as road maps or reference lists of current and future activity, and provide historical data for future planning or explanation of past activity. The following is a listing of required documents:

A. Updated lists of prevention tasks for the training plan
B. A written assessment from each Loss Control District Manager of their reporting area, including training requirements, resources needed, communications problems or conflicts, and high-loss areas or stores
C. Updated training schedules that include actual training and reflect additions, deletions, and other changes
D. Copies of training files for each employee
E. Work schedules of loss prevention specialists
F. Monthly reports on incidents that occur in individual districts
G. Results of store audit/inspection reports
H. Copies of investigative notes of all current and past dishonest employee investigations.

All documents will be secured and monitored by the designated custodian of records. Records will be destroyed per company policy.

## IV.  RESPONSIBILITIES

A.   The director of loss control is the corporate security manager and has the principal responsibility for planning, scheduling, and supervising all company loss prevention efforts and training. The determination of specific training or operational needs rests with supervisors most familiar with their group's primary job, personnel, levels of proficiency, and availability of loss control resources and constraints.

B.   The regional loss control manager is responsible for ensuring that all assigned districts comply with the policies and instructions listed in this plan or issued by the director of loss control.

C.   District loss control managers are the primary loss control trainers and supervisors. They are responsible for implementing company security policies and for ensuring, through close and continuous supervision, that training and operations are conducted in accordance with company policy.

D.   All loss control supervisors enforce the standards of training and operations contained in this plan.

E.   The duties and responsibilities of operations (i.e., non-loss prevention personnel are listed in Annex D.

## V.  MISSION

Our mission is to reduce losses suffered by the company through coordinated, simultaneous action on the part of every company employee. Specifically, we will reduce losses by identifying major current or potential loss areas and implementing cost-effective countermeasures to prevent and detect problems, educating and motivating all company employees to recognize and reduce loss problems, and recovering assets or lost revenue where possible.

## VI.  PROGRAM ANALYSIS

The policies, goals, and objectives outlined in this plan are based on analysis of this company's current shrinkage and loss control program status. Surveys of risk areas, questionnaires completed by employees, annual shrinkage figures, incident trend reports, and a consultant's report were all used in this analysis. These analyses are good indicators of our current status and provide future direction.

The quantity and quality of store-level loss control specialists needs to be increased by better recruiting efforts. The quality of these critical personnel will improve by sending each agent to a comprehensive training course. The leadership and management skills of district loss control managers can be improved by requiring additional intensive training. Awareness programs will be presented quarterly, in all stores, by loss control personnel to heighten employee awareness. All store managers and assistant store managers will attend a loss control workshop presented by the loss control director.

All stores will receive EAS equipment and it will be used to its fullest potential. High-loss merchandise, such as health and beauty aids and athletic shoes, will be pretagged by the manufacturer to achieve maximum sales by open display and maximum protection. High-loss leather jackets will be cabled to fixtures. The top ten high-shrink stores will have subliminal messaging systems installed.

## VII.  FY LOSS CONTROL GOALS

A.  The goal for this fiscal year is to trim the annual shrinkage figure to 1.55% of sales across the board, while spending only .52% of sales on this effort.
B.  Annex A contains the goals and objectives to meet the shrinkage goal for this fiscal year.
C.  Priority control efforts are outlined in Section VIII.
D.  Annex B contains fiscal year training objectives.
E.  Annex C contains the major control directions to be used in achieving the overall goal.
F.  Annex D identifies individual tasks to be emphasized during this fiscal year.

## VIII.  PRIORITY CONTROL EFFORTS TO MEET GOALS

There are many areas that the director and staff recognize as being deficient or needing emphasis.

A.  Store pilferage/shoplifting is believed to be increasing, particularly in new stores in the northeastern United States and Florida. By increasing the use of EAS, employee training, and well-trained store agents, the upward trend should decrease by the second quarter.
B.  Employee cash pilferage is also on the rise, particularly in the south and central Florida stores. Paper and pencil honesty testing, better interviewing, and background checks will help reduce this problem. A greater emphasis on procedural controls will result in fewer incidents or at least in quicker discovery. A combined effort with the Human Resources Departments in all of these areas should result in a reduction of employee theft.
C.  Interstore transfers are creating paper and real shrink problems. Due to lack of compliance by store managers in this area, it has become very difficult to determine exactly where certain stock keeping units (SKUs) are located. District store managers have been briefed on this matter and will closely supervise interstore transfer procedures.
D.  Mark-down error is believed to be very common and has an error rate in some stores as high as 20% of marked-down items. Again, district managers will pay close attention to this matter.
E.  Accidents by both customers and employees are at the same level as the previous year and must be reduced by better awareness training and motivation.
F.  Vendor error is increasing in some merchandise classes. Better receiving procedures have been implemented to quickly discover errors and to follow-up with the appropriate vendor.
G.  Individual training of store agents and managers will receive priority attention.
H.  Leadership development training for loss control supervisors is a very important issue during this fiscal year.

I.  Employee awareness training will be continued since this program proved very successful in the previous fiscal year. Due to natural employee turnover, these efforts must continue on a regular basis.

J.  Enhanced communication between different departments within the company must be emphasized. Annex E outlines the schedule of interdepartmental meetings for this purpose.

K.  Physical fitness is an issue to be dealt with this fiscal year, since fewer loss control agents will be used relative to the number of stores. Injuries and sick leave have increased, in part, due to poor physical fitness on the part of field loss control personnel.

## IX. PERFORMANCE EVALUATIONS AND INSPECTIONS

To ensure that loss control activities remain focused on priority risk areas and that programs and personnel are operating as expected, evaluations and inspections will be conducted periodically.

A.  Personnel reviews and counseling sessions will identify and assist individuals that are not performing to company standards.

B.  Spot surveys will determine perceptions and actual activities of store and distribution center employees.

C.  Inspection and audit reports will indicate to managers at all levels where loss problems exist or are likely to begin due to lack of adherence to procedural controls. These audits also tend to uncover suspicious trends.

D.  Listening to employees will assist in determining what is working and what isn't.

## X. SUPPORT

The ability of the Loss Control Department to achieve its objectives is dependent on the availability of support by other departments within the company, such as

- store operations (e.g., the director, district and store managers)
- human resources (e.g., the director of personnel, district representatives, and benefits coordinator)
- finance (e.g., chief financial officer, accounting, accounts payable, payroll, and internal audit personnel)
- store planning and real estate
- marketing
- corporate staff

## XI. RESOURCES

Sufficient resources required to keep losses to an acceptable level must be identified and allocated.

A. Authority and cooperation are key ingredients of any successful shortage control program. Senior management has designated the director of loss control as the lead figure in the company's efforts to increase profitability by decreasing losses. As the lead, the loss control director may assign control tasks to subordinates and employees in other departments. This plan identifies those personnel, in departments other than loss control, that fall under this category.
   1. Example 1
   2. Example 2
   3. Example 3
B. A recommended general and administrative (G&A) budget and a capital expenditure (CAPEX) budget have been approved and are sufficient to fund the activities listed in this plan.
C. Time is a very valuable resource that must be carefully used. Annex F outlines the time frame for program implementation.

# Appendix 11

# Sample Loss Prevention
# Inspection/Audit Report

## CASH CONTROL

### Cashier—General Office

1. Are the daily cash register tracking charts in use?
2. Are current shortages of $3 or greater entered on the chart or accounted for by the cash office?
3. Are overages in any dollar amount entered?
4. Were problem overages/shortages found? If yes, list the names of the problem operators.
5. Describe the corrective action to be taken regarding the problem operators.
6. Were "shotgun" shortages found? If yes, list the action taken.
7. Was the price variance report reviewed with the manager? Were any problems found? If yes, what was the corrective action taken?
8. Are adding machine tapes on pick-ups saved?
9. Do bank deposits agree with call-in sheets?
10. Is the Cash Office door locked? The office door locked?
11. Is access restricted?
12. Is the safe locked when not in use?
13. Provide comments.

### Register Operation

1. Is each register balanced daily?
2. Is the register operator entering the register, per company policy, before ringing?
3. Is the operator using a wand? Is the bar coding functional?
4. Is the register drawer closed, except when entering sales?
5. Is the operator making change per company policy?
6. Are improper or careless register operations observed?
7. Is the operator calling for price checks, when applicable?
8. Is the operator checking for concealed merchandise?
9. Are checks processed per company policy?
10. Provide exceptions/comments on observation.

## Cash Control (Possible Addendum) Photocopy of Tracking Chart and Price Variance Profile Sheets

1. Provide additional comments.

## Voids

1. Are void stamps used?
2. Are void reason and signature on the back of the receipt?
3. Are post-voids of $5 or more, with the reasons, "No money," "Not enough," "Didn't want," and "Check refused," checked on the detail tape for evidence of reringing?
4. List exceptions found and add any other comments. Attach the void profile sheet.

## Customer Service Desk

1. Are refunds handled per company policy?
2. Are "No Receipt" refunds over $10 recorded in the No Receipt Refund Book?
3. Is the store using a round-robin reporting system?
4. Is the manager checking refunds, by phone, with the customer, for validity?
5. Is refunded merchandise cleared from the Customer Service Desk on a timely basis? Is it signed for?
6. Are refunds being defaced?
7. Note exceptions.
8. Are package checks handled per company policy?
9. Are employee purchases handled per company policy?
10. List exceptions, add comments, and attach the refund profile sheet.

## RECEIVING/STOCKROOM AREA

1. Is the receiving door locked?
2. Are roll-away doors locked at the bottom and on both sides when not receiving freight?
3. Are blocked fire exits found?
4. Search stockrooms for signs of shrinkage. Are any found?
5. Is receiving freight checked in by carton number and *total carton count*?
6. Is loose merchandise found in stockrooms?
7. Are manifests in order and exceptions noted?
8. How many storage trailers are used?
9. Are storage trailers locked?
10. Are keys secure?
11. How many keys are there?
12. Are outgoing shipments handled per company policy?
13. List exceptions and add any comments on freight delivery observations.

## SALES FLOOR

1. Is the store making periodic security calls, using a "genderless" name, when no specialist is present?
2. Are pricing guns found on the sales floor?
3. Are safety hazards found?
4. Are blind areas containing high-shrink merchandise observable with mirrors?
5. Are clerks using mirrors?
6. Are display alarms installed and functional?
7. Are displays orderly?
8. Is it easy to spot missing merchandise?
9. Are salespeople preventing theft with good customer service?
10. Are sales people familiar with security codes?
11. Provide comments.

## PHYSICAL SECURITY

1. When were the alarm systems last tested? Note date shown on alarm door inspection tag.
2. What type of alarms are being used? Infrared? Battery?
3. Any alarm problems found?
4. Is there evidence of theft around the exterior of the building?
5. Are trash-handling procedures being followed?
6. Check the dumpster. Are plastic bags intact or broken open?
7. If plastic bags are intact, check them. Is any merchandise found?
8. Are exterior building lights broken?
9. Is trash or weeds found around the building?
10. Is the inventory disposal log complete? Any problems?
11. Provide comments.

## SHOPLIFTING

1. Is the store using incident reports?
2. What is the number of incidents reported in the last 30 days?
3. What are the manager's comments on shoplifting in the store?
4. Provide additional comments, from the store manager and district manager. Describe the corrective action planned.

# Appendix 12

# Security Resources

## SECURITY MAGAZINES, NEWSLETTERS, AND JOURNALS

This listing provides addresses of security periodicals published around the world. You may want to select and subscribe to three to five of them. A continuous source of new information in the loss control field is invaluable.

### Major United States Publications

*Assets Protection*, Box 5323, Madison, WI 53705

*Computers and Security*, 52 Vanderbilt Ave., New York, NY 10017

*Corporate Security*, 817 Broadway, New York, NY 10003

*Corporate Security Digest*, 3918 Prosperity Ave. Suite 318, Fairfax, VA 22031

*Corrections Today*, 4321 Hartwick Rd. L-208, College Park, MD 20740

*Criminal Justice Newsletter*, 443 Park Ave. S., New York, NY 10016

*Data Security Letter*, 764 Forest Ave., Palo Alto, CA 94301

*The Educator/ASET*, York College, York, PA 17403

*Executive Briefing/Bi-monthly Retail Security News*, 5471 Lake Howell Rd., Suite 236, Winter Park, FL 32792

*Forensic Accounting Review*, 150 N. Main St., Plymouth, MI 48170

*Fraud & Theft Newsletter*, P.O. Box 400, Boynton Beach, FL 33425

*Guardsmark, Inc.*, 22 S. 2nd St., Memphis, TN 38103

*Hayes Report*, 405 Prevention Way, Stanfordville, NY 12581

*IAPSC Newsletter*, 835 Deltona Blvd. Suite 77, Deltona, FL 32725

*International Drug Report*, 112 State St., Albany, NY 12207

*International Risk Control Review*, 4547 Atlanta Hwy, PO Box 345, Loganville, GA 30249

*Investigative News*, 13575 Martinique, Chino Hills, CA 91709

*Journal of Security Administration*, P.O. Box 164509, Miami, FL 33116–4509

*Law & Order*, 1000 Skokie Blvd., Wilmette, IL 60091

*Law Enforcement Product News*, 100 Garfield St., Denver, CO 80206

*Law Enforcement Technology*, 210 Crossways Park Dr., Woodbury, NY 11797

*Lloyd's Corporate Security International*, 611 Broadway, #523, New York, NY 10012–2608

*Loss Prevention Forum*, 1 Woodfield Lake, Suite 139, Schaumburg, IL 60173

*NAPSI Watch*, 2711 LBJ Freeway, Suite 356, Dallas, TX 75234

*NCPI Hotline*, University of Louisville, School of Justice Administration, Louisville, KY 40202

*NIJ Reports*, Box 6000, Rockville, MD 20850

*Parking Security Report*, 403 Main St., Port Washington, NY 11050

*The Peter Berlin Report*, 380 N. Broadway, Jericho, NY 11753

*Police*, 6300 Yarrow Dr., Carlsbad, CA 92009–7596

*Police & Security Bulletin*, P.O. Box 88, Mt. Airy, MD 21771

*The Police Chief*, 1110 N. Glebe Rd., Arlington, VA 22201

*Police Collectors' News*, 2392 U.S. Highway, Baldwin, WI 54002

*Prevention Connection*, 711 G Street, Sacramento, CA 95814

*Private Security Case Law Reporter*, 1375 Peachtree St. NE, Suite 235, Atlanta, GA 30367

*Protection Officer News*, IFPO, 4200 Meridian St., Suite 200, Bellingham, WA 98226

*Security*, P.O. Box 5080, Des Plaines, IL 60018.

*Security Case Law Reporter*, 2 Midtown Plaza, Suite 2000, 1360 Peachtree St. NE, Atlanta, GA 30309

*Security Dealer*, 210 Crossways Park Dr., Woodbury, NY 11797

*Security Distribution & Marketing*, P.O. Box 5080, Des Plains, IL 60017–5080

*Security Law Newsletter*, 1063 Thomas Jefferson St. NW, Washington, DC 20007

*Security Letter*, 166 East 96th St., New York, NY 10128

*Security Magazine*, 1350 E. Touhy Ave., Des Plains, IL 60018

*Security Management*, 24 Rope Ferry Rd., Waterford, CT 06386

*Security Management—ASIS*, 1655 North Fort Myers Dr. #1200, Arlington, VA 22209

*Security Monitor*, 50 S. Service Rd., Jericho, NY 11753

*Security News Syndicate*, 5471 Lake Howell Rd., Suite 236, Winter Park, FL 32792

*Security Personnel NewsLetter*, 3400 SE 35 St., Ocala, FL 32671

*Security Systems*, 210 Crossways Park Dr., Woodbury, NY 11797

*Security Systems Digest*, 7820 Little River Turnpike, Annandale, VA 22003

*Smith & Wesson NewsLetter*, 2100 Roosevelt Ave., Springfield, MA 01101

*Spain Report*, 4426 Mulberry Ct., Suite J, Pittsburgh, PA 15227

*Theft Trax*, P.O. Box 150310, Longview, TX 75615

*Training Aids Digest,* 7043 Wimsatt Rd., Springfield, VA 22151–4070

*White Paper,* 716 West Ave., Austin, TX 78701

## Major International Security Publications

*Antifurto;* Livio Colosanti, Editor; EPC S.P.A.; Via dell' Acqua Traversa; 187/189–00135 Roma; Italy

*Canadian Security;* Jack Percival, Editor; P.O. Box 430, Stn. "0"; Toronto, Ontario; M4A 9Z9

*Esse Come,* Edis SrL; Paulo Tura, Chairman; Via Emilia Ponente 20/4; 40133 Bologna; Italy

*International Security Review;* Queensway House; 2 Queensway; Redhill; Surrey RH1 1QS; England

*Police Review;* Brian Hilliard, Editor; 183 Marsh Wall; London E14 9FZ

*Protector Magazine;* Grah & Neuhaus AG; Daniel Beer, Editor; Mohrlistrasse 69; Postfach 205; CH-8033 Zurich, Switzerland

*Revue Suisse de la Securité;* Editions Marcel Meichtry; Chemin de la Caroline 22; Petit-Lancy, Genève, Switzerland

*Security & Fire News Asia;* David Slough, Editor; Elgin Consultants Ltd.; Tungnam Bldg., 5D; 475 Hennessy Road; Causeway Bay; Hong Kong

*Security Focus Magazine (Pty) Ltd.;* Godfrey King, Editor; Suite 4, Matruh Bldgs.; Westville Road; Westville 3630; Natal, P.O. Box 414; Kloof 3640, South Africa

*Security Gazette;* 33–35 Bowling Green Lane; London EC1R ODA; England

*Security Times;* see *International Security Review.*

*Sedep-Alarmes Protection Securité;* Peter Hazelzet, Editor; 8 Rue de la Michodiere; Paris 75002; France

*Selecciones de Security Management;* Estebanez Calderon 3; Madrid 20, Spain

*Sicurezza,* Via Statuto, 2–20121 Milano, Italy

*Wirtschaftsschutz Und Sicherheitstechnik;* Kriminalistik Verlag GmbH; Anzeigen-abteilung; Postfach 102640, Im Weiher 10; D–6900 Heidelberg 1; FRG

## SECURITY ASSOCIATIONS

Part of any true profession is becoming an active member of career-oriented associations. This list includes most of the larger security associations.

**Academy of Security Educators & Trainers (ASET),** Rte. 2, Box 3645, Berryville, VA 22611

**AIPROS,** Associazione Italiana Professionisti Della Sicurezza, Via Carlo Conti Rossini, 115, 00147 Roma, Italy (Members of ANIE, ANCISS)

**AIPROSEIN,** Iberamerican Association of Security Safety & Fire Professionals, c/o IFEMA, Avda. Portugal s/n, 28011 Madrid, Spain. (Tel. 34–1–470–1014; Telex 44025 IFEMA-E; Contact: Sr. Rafael Calderon)

**American Society of Amusement Park Security,** Cedar Point, P.O. Box 5006, Sandusky, OH 44871–8006

**American Society of Industrial Security (ASIS),** 1655 N. Ft Meyers Dr., Suite 1200, Arlington, VA 22209

**Associacao Portuguesa de Tecnicos de Prevencao e Seguranca,** APTPS; Rua Angelina Vidal; 57–1; 1100 Lisboa; Portugal (Tel 814–4969)

**Associacion Espanola de Instructores de Seguridad Int'l "Professional,"** (A.E.D.I.S.), Sede Central Int'l, Mozzen Xiro n 5 Bjos. 08006 Barcelona, Spain. (President—Jose M. Martinez Barrera, Tel. 237–55–12)

**Associacion des Industries de l'Alarme a.s.b.l.;** Avenue d'Arderghem, 320; 1040 Bruxelles; Belgium (Tel. 02–647–35–47; Fax 02–648–60–96; Belgian Alarm Ind. Assoc.)

**Association for the Prevention of Theft in Shops—APTS,** The Quadrangle, 180 Wardour St., London W1V3AA (Chairman—Sir Kenneth Newman; Dir. & Sec.— The Baroness, Phillips, JP.; Contact: Mrs. Marie Easby, Tel. 01–741–4815)

**British Safety Council,** National Safety Centre, 62 Chancellors Road, London, W6 9RS (Tel. 01–741–1231, or 01–741–2371, Director-General—Sir James Tye)

**British Security Industry Association (BSIA),** Witco House, Barbourne Road, Worcester, WR1 1RT (Tel 0905–21464, Fax 0905–61325, Chief Executive—David Fletcher, Director General—Sir John Wheeler)

**British Standards Institution,** 2 Park Lane, London, W1A 2BS (Tel. 01–629–9000)

**Chambre Syndicale Nationale des Entreprises de Securité;** 7, rue Louis le Grand; 75002 Paris, France (Tel. 1–42–61–56–29)

**Comité Europeen Des Assurances, CEA;** 3-bis, rue de la Chaussee d'Antin; F–74009 Paris, France (Tel. +33–1–48–24–6600, Fax +33–1–47–70–0375, Telex 281829)

**Crime Concern,** Level 8, David Murray John Bldg., Brunel Centre, Swindon, Wilts, SN1 1LY (Tel. 0793–514596, Fax 0793–514654, Chief Exec.—Nigel Whiskin, Press Officer—Peter Topper)

**Electrical Contractors Assocn.,** ESCA House, 34 Palace Court, Bayswater, London, W2 4HY (Tel. 01–229–1266, Press Off.—Tania Mattock, Tech. Off.— Peter Greenwood

**Euralarm,** Sekretariat, c/o ZVEI, Postfach 700 969, D–6000 Frankfurt 70, FRG (Tel. 49–611–6302–250, Fax 49–611–6302–317, Telex 0411035)

**European Locksmith Federation,** Huddingevagen 107, S–121.43 Johanneshov Sweden

**European Television Surveillance Assocn. Ltd., (ETSA),** P.O. Box 19, Shepperton, Middx., TW17 8RN (Sec.—Peter Goddard)

**Forschungs-und-Profgerneinschaft,** Geldschranke und Tresoranlagen e.v., 6 Frankfurt—Niederrad 1, Postfach 109, FRG

**Fraud and Theft Bureau,** Box 400, Boynton Beach, FL 33425, USA

**Home Office Crime Prevention Centre,** Staffordshire Police HQ, Connock Road, Stafford, ST17 OQE (Tel. –785–58217, Fax 0785–41082, Dir. Asst. Chf. Constable—Bob Neville, Dep. Dir. Ch. Spt.—Philip Veater)

**Iberamerican Association of Security,** Avda. de Portugal, s/n, 28011–Madrid, Spain

**Instituto Latinoamericano de Seguridad, 'INSELA';** Calle 72A, No. 16–57; A.A. 10850 Bogota, Colombia, Suramerica (Tel. 2–171963 or 2–173338)

**Institute of Retail Security,** 33 Barnwell, Stevenage, Herts, SG2 9SJ (Tel. 0438–358713 or 01–221–6211/6120)

**Institute of Security Management,** 3 Cavendish Road, Halesowen, West Mid. B62 0DB (Tel. 021–422–958, Chairman—E. Slater)

**International Association of Credit Card Investigators,** 1620 Grant Avenue, Suite 1, Novato, CA 94945

**International Maritime Bureau,** Maritime House, 1 Linton Road, Barking, Essex. IG11 8HG (Tel. 01–591–3000, Telex 8956492 IMB LDN-G, Director—Eric Ellen)

**International Professional Security Administration (IPSA),** 292A Torquay Road, Paignton, Devon. TQ3 2ET (Tel. 0803–554849, Fax 0803–529203, Int. Sec—Mr. Pat Rabbitts, Asst. Sec—James C. Tappin)

**International Society of Crime Prevention Practitioners,** 1560 Fifinger Rd., Columbus, OH 43221

**Jewelers Security Alliance U.S.,** Suite 1601, 45th Street, New York, NY 10017

**Loss Prevention Council,** 140 Aldersgate Street, London, EC1A 4HY (Tel. 01–606–1050, Fax 01–600–1487, Chairman—Peter Duerdon, CEO—John Hill)

**Master Locksmiths' Association,** Units 4 & 5, Woodford Halse Busn. Park, Gt. Central Way, Woodford Halse, Daventry, Northants NN11 6PZ (Tel. 0237–62255)

**N.V.O.B.,** Secretariat, Postbus 1092, 4700 BB Roosendaal, Netherlands (Tel. 31–1–650–51915, Sec.—Theo. J. Horsthuis)

**National Association of Certified Fraud Examiners,** 716 West Ave., Austin, TX 78701

**National Center for Prevention and Protection;** 5, rue Daunou; F. 75002 Paris, France (Tel. 1–42–61–5761, Fax 1–49–27–09–43, Telex 217522 F CNPP)

**National Supervisory Council for Intruder Alarms,** (NSCIA), Queensgate House, 14 Cookham Road, Maidenhead, Berks. SL6 8AJ (Tel. 0628–37512, Fax 0628–773367, Dir. Gen.—Michael Vann)

**Risk and Insurance Management Society Inc.,** 205 E. 42nd St., New York, NY 10017

**S.T.E.L.F.,** Station D'Essais, 65 avenue de General de Gaulle, 77420 Champs-sur-Marne, Paris (Test Lab.—Burglar Alarms)

**Security Association of South Africa,** SASA, P.O. Box 31882, Braamfontein 2017, South Africa (Tel. 011–724–3027, 725–1695, or 724–3268)

**Security Industry Association,** (SIA), 2800 28th Street, Suite 101, Santa Monica, CA 90405, USA (Tel. 213–450–4141, Fax 213–452–7524, Exec. Dir.—Mrs. Donna Gentry)

**Security Lock Association (SLA),** Penfold House, Brent Street, London NW4 2EU (Tel. 01–202–7821, Sec.—Shirley Barnett)

**SIGSAC,** 10160 Snowbird Dr., Rancho Cucamongo, CA 91701, USA

**Six S Society-Retail Protection Specialists,** 5471 Lake Howell Rd., Suite 236, Winter Park, FL 32792; USA

**Swedish National Association of Insurance Companies,** Strandvägen 5B, 11451 Stockholm, Sweden

**Union Professionelle des Belgium,** Enterprises d'Assurances de Belgique, Square de Meeus 29, B. 1040 Bruxelles, Belgium (Tel. 02–513–6845)

**UNETO,** Parkstraat 32, 2514 JK Den Haag, Holland (Tel. 070–624–491)

**Verband der Sachversicherer e.V., VdS.** Postfach 10 20 24, D–5000 Koln 1, FRG

## ANNUAL LOSS CONTROL WORKSHOPS AND CONFERENCES

It is absolutely vital that the loss control specialist stay abreast of the current available technology and services. Also, interacting with professional peers is essential to any successful career. The list in this section highlights conferences for the loss control specialist.

**Academy of Security Educators & Trainers (ASET),** Rte. 2, Box 3645, Berryville, VA 22611

**Academy Security Ed. & Trainers,** 4007 Arcade Ct., Chesapeake Beach, MD 20732

**ACRA,** Marketing Dept., Miami of Ohio, Oxford, OH 45056

**AEA,** 2311 Pontius Ave., Los Angeles, CA 90064

**AFIO,** 6723 Whittier Ave., Suite 303A, McLean, VA 22101

**AFSB,** 407 S. Dearborn St., Chicago, IL 60605

**Akron Food Dealer Association,** 1386 Allendale Ave., Akron, OH 44306

**Alabama Retail Association,** P.O. Box 1909, Montgomery, AL 36103

**American Management Association,** 135 W. 50th St., New York, NY 10020

**American Retail Federation,** 1616 H Street NW, Washington, DC 20006

**American Society of Amusement Park Security,** Cedar Point, P.O. Box 5006, Sandusky, OH 44871–8006

**American Society of Industrial Security,** 1655 N. Ft. Myers Dr., Suite 1200, Arlington, VA 22209

**Arizona Retailers Association,** 6915 E. Main St., Suite 201, Mesa, AZ 85207

**Arkansas Retail Grocers Association,** 1123 S. University Ave. #1000, Little Rock, AR 72204

**Arkansas Retail Merchants,** University Ave. at 12th St., Little Rock, AR 72204

**ASIS-Orlando,** 4713 Southhold St., Orlando, FL 32808

**ASLET,** 9611 400th Ave. Box 1003, Twin Lakes, WI 53181–1003

**Associated Food Dealers,** 10700 Old County Rd. 15 #270, Plymouth, MN 55441

**Association of Federal Investigators,** 1612 K St. NW, Suite 202, Washington, DC 20006

**Association of Iowa Merchants,** P.O. Box 22040, Des Moines, IA 50322

**Association of Oregon Food Industry,** 3000 Market St., Plaza Suite 541, Salem, OR 97309

**ASTD,** 1630 Duke St., Alexandria, VA 22313

**Cahners Publications,** 1350 E. Touhy Ave., Des Plaines, IL 60018

**Connecticut Retail Merchant,** 60 Washington St., Suite 1308, Hartford, CT 06106

**Cornahan Conference,** ICST, ETh-Zentrum, CH–8092 Zurich, Switzerland

**Corpus Christi Retail Grocers,** P.O. Box 6052, Corpus Christi, TX 78411

**Crime Control Corporation,** 1063 Thomas Jefferson, NW, Washington, DC 20007

**D-FW Grocers Association/DBA,** 1515 W. Mockingbird Lane, Dallas, TX 75235

**Delaware Retail Association,** 2 East Eighth St., Wilmington, DE 19801

**Delaware Retail Council,** 1 Commerce Center, Wilmington, DE 19801

**Direct Marketing Association,** 6 E. 43rd St., New York, NY 10017

**Do-It-Yourself Retailing,** 770 N. High School Rd., Indianapolis, IN 46214–3798

**East Central Ohio Grocers,** 1200 Rear North Main St., North Canton, OH 44720

**Effective Law Enforcement,** 5519 N. Cumberland Ave. #1008, Chicago, IL 60656–1471

**Executive Protection Institute,** Arcadia Manor, Rt. 2, Box 3645, Berryville, VA 22611

**Federation of Retail Merchants,** 185 Great Neck Rd., Suite 300, Great Neck, NY 11021

**Florida Retail Federation,** P.O. Box 10024, Tallahassee, FL 32302

**Food Industry Association,** 1001 Connecticut Ave. NW #800, Washington, DC 20036

**Food Marketing Institute,** 1750 K St. NW, Suite 700, Washington, DC 20006

**Food Retailers Association,** P.O. Box 7007, Columbia, SC 29202

**Footwear Retailers of America,** 1319 F Street NW, Washington, DC 20004

**Fraud and Theft Bureau,** Box 400, Boynton Beach, FL 33425

**FRET (FL Food and Fuel),** 209 Office Plaza, Tallahassee, FL 32304

**Georgia Grocers Association,** 2150 Parklane Dr., Suite 160, Atlanta, GA 30345

**Georgia Retail Association,** 100 Edgewood Ave., Suite 1804, Atlanta, GA 30303

**IFSEC, IFSSEC Ltd.,** Blenheim House, Ash Hill Dr., Pinner, Middx. HA5 2AE, UK

**Illinois Retail Merchants,** 36 South Wabash Ave., Chicago, IL 60603

**IMC,** 2250 E. Devon, Suite 318, Des Plaines, IL 60018

**Indiana Retail Council,** 1 North Capitol, Suite 430, Indianapolis, IN 46204

**Indiana Retail Grocers Association,** 201 North Illinois, Suite 1720, Indianapolis, IN 46204

**Institute of Internal Auditors Inc.,** P.O. Box 1119, Altamonte Springs, FL 32701

**International Association of Chain Stores,** 3800 Moore Pl., Alexandria, VA 22305

**International Association of Chiefs of Police,** 1110 N. Glebe Rd., Suite 200, Arlington, VA 22201

**International Association of Credit Card Investigators,** 1620 Grant Avenue, Suite 1, Novato, CA 94945

**International City Management,** 1120 G St. NW, Washington, DC 20005

**International Council Shopping Centers,** 665 5th Ave., New York, NY 10022

**International Executive Association,** 122 E. 42nd, Suite 1014, New York, NY 10017

**International Loss Control Institute,** P.O. Box 345, Loganville, GA 30249

**International Mass Retail Association,** 570 7th Ave., New York, NY 10018

**International Security Exhibition,** Trade Fair Authority of India, Pragati Bhawan, Pragati Maidan, New Delhi, 110 001, India

**International Society of Crime Prevention Practitioners,** 2204 Basset St., Suite 400, Alexandria, VA 22308

**Iowa Grocer,** 2894 106th St., Suite 102, Des Moines, IA 50322

**Iowa Retail Federation,** 520 35th St., Suite 100, Des Moines, IA 50312

**IPTM/UNF,** 4567 St. Johns Bluff Rd. S., Jacksonville, FL 32216

**ISCPP,** 2204 Bassett St., Suite 400, Alexandria, VA 22380

**ISMA,** Lewis Plaza, 1155 Battery St., San Francisco, CA 94111

**Jayhawk Food Dealers,** P.O. Box 8067, Topeka, KS 66608

**Jewelers Security Alliance, U.S.,** Suite 1601, 45th Street, New York, NY 10017

**Missouri Grocers Association,** P.O. Box 10223, Springfield, MO 65808

**Missouri Retailers Association,** P.O. Box 1336, Jefferson City, MO 65102

**Montana Food Distributors,** P.O. Box 5775, Helena, MT 59604

**Montana Retail Association,** P.O. Box 440, Helena, MT 59601

**MS Association of Convenience Stores,** P.O. Box 991, Jackson, MS 39205

**NACS Scan,** 1605 King St., Alexandria, VA 22314–2792

**NARDA News,** 10 E. 22nd St., Lombard, IL 60148

**National Association of Certified Fraud Examiners,** 716 West Ave., Austin, TX 78701

**National Association of Chain Drugstores,** P.O. Box 1417–D49, Alexandria, VA 22313

**National Association of College Stores,** 528 E. Lorain St., Oberlin, OH 44074

**National Association of Convenience Stores,** 1605 King St., Alexandria, VA 22314–2792

**National Association of Music Merchants,** 5140 Avenda Encinas, Carlsbad, CA 92008

**National Association of Retail Dealers of America,** 10 E. 22nd St., Suite 310, Lombard, IL 60148

**National Association of Retail Druggists,** 205 Daingerfield Rd., Alexandria, VA 22314

**National Association of Specialty Food,** 215 Park Ave. S, Suite 1606, New York, NY 10003

**National Bicycle Dealers Association,** 129 Cabrillo Street, Suite 201, Costa Mesa, CA 92627

**National Confectioners Association,** 7900 West Park Dr., Suite A320, McLean, VA 22102

**National Fraternal Order Police,** 2100 Gardiner Ln., Louisville, KY 40205–2962

**National Grocers Association,** 1825 Samuel Morse Dr., Restononburg, VA 22090

**National Office Products Association,** 301 N. Fairfax St., Alexandria, VA 22314

**National Police Chief's Sheriff's Information Bureau,** P.O. Box 92007, Milwaukee, WI 53202

**National Retail Federation,** 100 W. 31st St., New York, NY 10001

**National Retail Hardware Association,** 770 N. High School Rd., Indianapolis, IN 46214

**National Sheriff's Association,** 1450 Duke St., Alexandria, VA 22314

**National Shoe Retailers Association,** 9861 Brokenland Pkwy, Columbia, MD 21046

**National Sporting Goods Association,** 1699 Wall St., Suite 700, Mt. Prospect, IL 60056–5780

**National Waterbed Retailers Association,** 36 South Street #1506, Chicago, IL 60603

**NBEA,** 194 Association Dr., Reston, VA 22091

**NCISS,** P.O. Box 2842, Washington, DC 20013

**Nebraska Retail Grocers,** 6509 Irvington Rd., Omaha, NE 68122

**Nevada Retail Association,** P.O. Box 722, Carson City, NV 89701

**New England Wholesale,** P.O. Box 374, 6 Beacon St., Danvers, MA 01923

**New Hampshire Retail Grocers,** 110 Stark St., Manchester, NH 03105

**New Jersey Food Council,** 30 W. Lafayette St., Trenton, NJ 08608

**New Jersey Retail Merchants,** 332 West State St., Trenton, NJ 08618

**New Mexico Food Dealers,** 4010 Carlisle Blvd, NE #A, Albuquerque, NM 87107

**New Mexico Retail Association,** 1229 Paseo de Peralta, Santa Fe, NM 87501

**New York State Food Merchants,** 111 Washington Ave., Albany, NY 12210

**News & Food Report,** 110 Stark St., Manchester, NH 03101

**NJRMA Retailer,** 332 W. State St., Trenton, NJ 08618

**NMA,** 2210 Arbor Blvd, Dayton, OH 45439

**North Carolina Food Dealers,** P.O. Box 6066, Charlotte, NC 28207

**North Carolina Retail Merchant,** P.O. Box 176001, Raleigh, NC 27619

**Police and Security Expo,** P.O. Box F, Hopewell, NJ 08525

**Retail Grocers Association,** 2809 W. 47th St., Shawnee Mission, KS 66205

**Retail Merchants of Hawaii,** 735 Bishop St., Honolulu, HI 96813

**Retail Merchants of Nebraska,** P.O. Box 94606, Lincoln, NE 68509

**Retail Merchants of New Hampshire,** 10 Ferry Street, Box 14, Concord, NH 03301

**Retailers Association of Massachusetts,** 294 Washington St., Room 440, Boston, MA 02108

**RGAF,** 105 Live Oak Garden, Suite 101, Casselberry, FL 32707

**Rhode Island Food Dealers,** 10 Orms St., Charles/Orms Bldg., Providence, RI 02904

**Rhode Island Retail,** 30 Exchange Terrace, Providence, RI 02903

**Risk and Insurance Management Society Inc.,** 205 E. 42nd St., New York, NY 10017

**Rocky Mountain Food Dealers,** 1015 Kipling St., Lakewood, CO 80215

**RSANC,** P.O. Box 2559, Dublin, CA 94568

**SAM,** 2331 Victor Parkway, Cincinnati, OH 45206

**Securex,** Seatro Management Services Pte. Ltd., 200 Jalan Sultan, 11–06 Textile Centre, Singapore 0719

**Securicom,** SEDEP, 8 rue de la Michodiere, 75002-Paris, France

**Security,** Jaarbeurs, P.O. Box 8500, 3500 RM. Utrecht, Netherlands

**SICUR,** Avenida de Portugal, s/n., 28011 Madrid, Spain

**Six S Society,** 5471 Lake Howell Rd., Suite 236, Winter Park, FL 32792

## LOSS CONTROL TRAINING

Training is one of the keys to success. This list includes many of the recognized training organizations available to your organization.

**Academy of Security Education and Trainers (ASET),** Route 2, Box 3644, Berryville, VA 22611

**American Society of Industrial Security (ASIS),** 1655 N. Ft. Myer Dr., Suite 1200, Arlington, VA 22209

**Anacapa Sciences, Inc.,** Drawer Q, Santa Barbara, CA 93102

**Cahners Publications,** 1350 E. Touhy Ave., Des Plaines, IL 60018

**International Foundation for Protection Officers,** 7327 Horne St., Mission, BC V2V–3Y5 Canada

**John E. Reid and Associates,** 200 S. Michigan Ave., Suite 900, Chicago, IL 60604

**Kobetz and Associates, Ltd.,** Route 2, Box 3645, Berryville, VA 22611

**LPSpecialists—Retail Security Training,** Loss Prevention Training Institute, 5471 Lake Howell Rd., Suite 236, Winter Park, FL 32792

**LSI,** P.O. Box 17286, Phoenix, AZ 85011–7286

**National Crime Prevention Training Institute,** University of Louisville, School of Justice Administration, Louisville, KY 40202

**Wicklander and Zulawski,** 1 Woodfield Lake, Suite 139, Schaumberg, IL 60173

## PROFESSIONAL DESIGNATIONS EARNED BY SECURITY PRACTITIONERS

Several organizations around the world provide voluntary certification programs to security practitioners. These designations denote a certain level of professional achievement and most of the major organizations are included in the following list.

**Certified Fraud Examiner (CFE),** National Association of Certified Fraud Examiners, 716 West Ave., Austin, TX 78701

**Certified Protection Officer (CPO),** International Foundation for Protection Officers, 7327 Horne St., Mission, BC V2V–3Y5 Canada

**Certified Protection Professional (CPP),** American Society of Industrial Security, 1655 N. Ft. Myers Dr., Suite 1200, Arlington, VA 22209

**Certified Security Trainer (CST),** Academy of Security Educators and Trainers, Route 2, Box 3645, Berryville, VA 22611

**Personal Protection Specialist (PPS),** Executive Protection Institute, Route 2, Box 3645, Berryville, VA 22611

**Retail Protection Specialist (RPS),** Loss Prevention Training Institute, 5471 Lake Howell Road, Suite 236, Winter Park, FL 32792

## REFERENCE BOOKS

There are many excellent reference books available to loss control practitioners. Good books are an indispensable tool for any competent security professional. Unfortunately, I couldn't list all of the exceptional titles currently in print, but, hopefully, you should find several books that suit your needs. To obtain a copy of a book, you may either purchase it directly from the publisher or go to a bookstore and order the desired title.

Barefoot, J. Kirk. *Undercover Investigation.* (Stoneham, Mass.: Butterworths, 1983).

Barnard, Robert L., *Intrusion Detection Systems.* (Stoneham, Mass.: Butterworths, 1988).

Brindy, J. *Shoplifting: A Manual for Store Detectives.* (Matteson, Ill.: Cavalier Press, n.d.).

Broder, James F. *Risk Analysis and the Security Survey.* (Stoneham, Mass.: Butterworths, 1984).

Carroll, John. *Computer Security, Second Edition.* (Stoneham, Mass.: Butterworths, 1987).

Cherry, Don. *Total Facility Control.* (Stoneham, Mass.: Butterworths, 1986).

Cleary, James Jr. *Prosecuting the Shoplifter: A Loss Prevention Strategy*. (Stoneham, Mass.: Butterworths, 1986).

D'Addario, Francis James. *Loss Prevention through Crime Analysis*. (Stoneham, Mass.: Butterworths, 1989).

Dimonenico, J. *Investigative Techniques for the Retail Security Investigator*. New York: Lebhar-Friedman).

Edwards, L.E. *Shoplifting and Shrinkage Protection for Stores*. (Springfield, Ill.: Charles C. Thomas, 1958).

Federal, R. Keegan, Jr., and Jennifer L. Fogelman. *Avoiding Liability in Retail Security: A Casebook*. (Atlanta, Ga.: Strafford Publications, 1986).

Fennelly, Lawrence J. *Handbook of Loss Prevention and Crime Prevention, Second Edition*. (Stoneham, Mass.: Butterworths, 1988).

Gallery, Shari M. *Security Training: Readings from Security Management Magazine*. (Stoneham, Mass.: Butterworths, 1990).

Inbau, Fred E., and Marvin E. Aspen. *Protective Security Law*. (Stoneham, Mass.: Butterworths, 1983).

Inbau, Fred E. *Criminal Interrogation and Confessions, Third Edition*. (Baltimore, Md.: Williams and Wilkins Publishers, 1985).

McGoey, Chris E. *Security Adequate or Not?* San Diego, Calif.: Aegis Publishers).

Purpura, Philip P. *Modern Security and Loss Prevention*. (Stoneham, Mass.: Butterworths, 1984).

Sennewald, Charles. *Effective Security Management, Second Edition*. (Stoneham, Mass.: Butterworths, 1985).

Sennewald, Charles. *The Process of Investigation*. (Stoneham, Mass.: Butterworths, 1981).

Sun Tzu. *The Art of War*. (New York: Oxford University Press, 1963).

Tyska, Louis A., and Lawrence J. Fennelly. *Controlling Cargo Theft: A Handbook of Transportation Security*. (Stoneham, Mass.: Butterworths, 1983).

United States Army. *FM 19–30 Physical Security*. U.S. Army Publications Center.

Walsh, Timothy J. and Richard J. Healy. *The Protection of Assets Manuals*. (Santa Monica, Calif.: The Merritt Company).

## LOSS CONTROL HARDWARE AND SERVICES DIRECTORIES

No buying decision is easy to make and with so many sources to choose from, it's even harder. This list should help you find the products and types of surveys that you need.

**Access Control Buyer's Guide,** 2655 Barfield Rd., Atlanta, GA 30328

**Academy of Security Educators and Trainers (ASET),** Route 2, Box 3644, Berryville, VA 22611

**American Society of Industrial Security (ASIS),** 1655 N. Ft. Myers Dr., Suite 1200, Arlington, VA 22209

**Butterworth Publishing,** 80 Montvale Ave., Stoneham, MA 02180

**Directory of Certified Fraud Examiners,** NACFE, 716 West Ave., Austin, TX 78701

**Directory of College and University Security Programs, LPS, Inc.,** 5471 Lake Howell Rd., Suite 236, Winter Park, Fl 32792

**Directory of Executive Recruiters (Security Personnel), LPS, Inc.** 5471 Lake Howell Rd., Suite 236, Winter Park, FL 32792

**Directory of Products and Services, Security Magazine,** 1350 E. Touhy Ave., Des Plaines, IL 60018

**Drug Testing Legal Manual,** Clark Boardman Company, Ltd., 375 Hudson St., New York, NY 10014

**Expert Witness Directory,** National Forensic Center, 17 Temple Terrace, Lawrenceville, NJ 08648

**Future Trends Report,** Security Magazine, 1350 E. Touhy Ave., Des Plaines, IL 60018

**International Association of Professional Security Consultants (IAPSC),** 835 Deltona Blvd., Suite 77, Deltona, FL 32725

**Jeffers Directory of Law Enforcement Officials,** Pace Publications, 443 Park Ave. South, New York, NY 10016

**Securitech,** Queensway House, 2 Queensway, Redhill, Surrey RH1 1QS, England

**Security Distributor and Marketing Magazine,** 1350 E. Touhy Ave., Des Plaines, IL 60018

**Security Industry Buyers Guide,** Bell Atlantic Company, 6701 Democracy Blvd., 9th Floor, Bethesda, MD 20817

**Security Letter Source Book,** Butterworth Publishers, 80 Montvale Ave., Stoneham, MA 02180

**Security Yearbook,** Queensway House, 2 Queensway, Redhill, Surrey RH1 1QS, England

**Seminars Directory,** Gale Research, Inc., Book Tower, Dept. 77748, Detroit, MI 48277–0748

**Technical Advisory Service for Attorneys,** 428 Pennsylvania Ave., Fort Washington, PA 19034

**Training and Development Organizations Directory,** Gale Research, Inc., Book Tower, Dept. 77748, Detroit, MI 48277–0748

**Who's Who in Security,** National Security Institute, Inc., 161 Worcester Rd., Framingham, MA 01701

**Who's Who in Speaking,** National Speakers Association, 3877 N. 7th St., #350, Phoenix, AZ 85014

# Appendix 13

# Model Civil Recovery Statute

(1) In addition to any criminal action, a person who commits an act for which he could be charged with the crime of theft, as defined in the state theft statute, shall be liable to the victim of the act for (a) the full retail price of the unrecovered property or the recovered property that is not in salable condition and (b) a civil remedy of not less than $150 and not more than $1000 for actual damages.

(2) If the person to whom a written demand is made complies with the written demand within 30 days after its receipt, that person shall incur no further civil liability to the merchant or business for that specific act of theft.

(3) A person who commits an act described in Section (1) and who fails to comply with a written demand within 30 days, shall be liable to the merchant or business for a civil penalty of $200 and reasonable court costs not exceeding $100, in addition to Subsections (a) and (b) of Section (1).

(4) An action under this section may be brought to small claims court. If the amount demanded exceeds the jurisdiction of the small claims court, the action may still be brought to the small claims court. However, the amount recovered shall not exceed the jurisdiction of the small claims court.

(5) A merchant or business may recover damages in an amount allowable under this section from the parent(s) or guardian(s) of a minor who lives with his parent(s) or guardian(s) and who commits an act described in Section (1).

# Appendix 14

# Model Retail Theft Statute

I. Theft by Shoplifting Defined
  A. A person commits the offense of theft by shoplifting if, with intent to appropriate merchandise without paying the merchant's stated price for the merchandise, such person, alone or in concert with another person knowingly
    1. Conceals the merchandise.
    2. Removes, takes possession of, or causes the removal of the merchandise.
    3. Alters, transfers, or removes any price marking, or any other marking that aids in determining the value affixed to the merchandise.
    4. Transfers the merchandise from one container to another.
    5. Causes the cash register or other sales-recording device to reflect less than the merchant's stated price for the merchandise.
  B. A person commits the offense of theft by shoplifting if, with intent to appropriate, such person, alone or in concert with another person, knowingly removes a shopping cart from the premises of the mercantile establishment.
II. Evidence and Presumptions
  A. Knowing concealment of merchandise shall create a rebuttable presumption that the person intended to appropriate the merchandise without paying the merchant's stated price for the merchandise.
  B. Evidence of stated price or ownership of merchandise may include, but is not limited to
    1. The actual merchandise or the container that held the merchandise alleged to have been shoplifted.
    2. The content of the price tag or marking from such merchandise.
    3. Properly identified photographs of such merchandise.
  C. Any merchant may testify at a trial as to the stated price or ownership of merchandise, as well as to other matters pertaining to the case.
III. Penalties
  A person convicted of theft by shoplifing shall be punished as follows:
  A. Upon a first theft-by-shoplifting conviction,
    1. When the merchant's stated price of the merchandise is less than or equal to $100, the defendant shall be fined not more than $250.
    2. When the merchant's stated price of the merchandise exceeds $100, the defendant shall be fined not less than $100 nor more than $500 and

such fine shall not be suspended or the defendant shall be punished by imprisonment not to exceed 1 year, or both.

B.  Upon a second theft-by-shoplifting conviction,

1.  When the merchant's stated price of the merchandise is less than or equal to $100, the defendant shall be fined not less than $100 nor more than $500 and such fine shall not be suspended, or the defendant shall be punished by imprisonment not to exceed 1 year, or both.

2.  When the merchant's stated price of the merchandise exceeds $100, the defendant shall be fined not less than $500 and shall be imprisoned for not less than 30 days and not to exceed 3 years. The first 30 days of such sentence shall not be suspended, probated, deferred, or withheld.

C.  Upon a third or subsequent theft-by-shoplifting conviction, regardless of the merchant's stated price of the merchandise, the defendant shall be fined not less than $500 nor more than $5000 and shall be imprisoned for 1–10 years. The first year of such sentence shall not be suspended, probated, deferred, or withheld.

D.  In determining the number of prior theft-by-shoplifting convictions for purposes of imposing punishment under this section, the court shall disregard all such convictions occurring more than 7 years prior to the theft-by-shoplifting offense in question.

IV.  Merchant's Immunity from Civil and Criminal Liability

A.  General Rule—A merchant who detains, questions, or causes the arrest of any person suspected of theft by shoplifting shall not be criminally or civilly liable for any legal action relating to such detention, questioning, or arrest if

1.  The merchant has reasonable grounds to suspect that the person has committed or is attempting to commit theft by shoplifting.

2.  The merchant acts in a reasonable manner under the circumstances.

3.  The merchant detains the suspected person for a reasonable period of time.

B.  Reasonable Grounds—Reasonable grounds to suspect that a person has committed or is attempting to commit theft by shoplifting may be based on, but is not limited to

1.  Personal observation, including observation via closed-circuit television or other visual device.

2.  Report of such personal observation from another merchant.

3.  Activation of an electronic or other type of mechanical device designed to detect shoplifting.

C.  Reasonable Manner—A merchant or peace officer who has reasonable grounds to believe that a person has committed or is attempting to commit the offense of theft by shoplifting, as defined in Section I of this act, may detain such person on or off the premises of the mercantile establishment if such detention is done for any or all of the following purposes:

1.  To question the person, investigate the surrounding circumstances, obtain a statement, or any combination thereof.

2.  To request and/or verify identification.

3.  To inform a peace officer of the detention of such person and/or surrender that person to the custody of a peace officer.

       4.   To inform a peace officer, the parent(s), and/or other private person(s) interested in the welfare of a minor, of the detention and to surrender the minor to the custody of such person(s).

       5.   To institute criminal proceedings against the person.

  D.  Reasonable Force—The merchant may use a reasonable amount of force necessary to protect himself, to prevent escape of the person detained, or to prevent the loss or destruction of property.

  E.  Reasonable Time—A reasonable period of time, for purposes of this section, shall be deemed to be a period of time long enough to accomplish the purpose set forth in this section and shall include any time spent awaiting the arrival of a law enforcement officer or the parent(s) or guardian(s) of a juvenile suspect, if the merchant has summoned such law enforcement officer, parent(s), or guardian(s).

  F.  Any detention as defined in this section shall not constitute an arrest.

V.    Arrest of Theft-by-Shoplifting Suspects

A law enforcement officer may arrest without warrant any person he has probable cause for believing has committed the offense of theft by shoplifting. "Probable cause," as used in this section, includes but shall not be limited to the statement of a merchant containing facts and circumstances demonstrating that he has reasonable grounds to suspect that a person has committed theft by shoplifting.

VI.   Definitions

  A.  *Conceal* means to hide, hold, or carry merchandise, so that, although there may be some notice of its presence, it is not visible through ordinary observation.

  B.  *Merchant* means an owner or operator of any mercantile establishment and includes the merchant's employees, security agents, or other agents.

  C.  *Mercantile establishment* means any place where merchandise is displayed, held, or offered for sale, either at retail or wholesale prices. Mercantile establishment includes adjoining parking lots or adjoining areas of common use with other establishments.

  D.  *Merchandise* means any goods, foodstuffs, wares, or personal property, or any part or portion thereof any type or description displayed, held, or offered for sale.

  E.  *Merchants stated price for the merchandise* means the price that the merchandise is offered for sale at the time and place of offense.

VII.  Effective Date

This act shall become effective 90 days after enactment.

VIII. Repealer

All laws and parts of laws in conflict with this act are hereby repealed.

# Index